Tourist Attractions

Tourist Attractions

*Performing Race and Masculinity
in Brazil's Sexual Economy*

GREGORY MITCHELL

The University of Chicago Press   Chicago and London

GREGORY C. MITCHELL is assistant professor in the women's, gender, and sexuality studies program and affiliate faculty in the Department of Anthropology and Sociology at Williams College.

The University of Chicago Press, Chicago 60637
The University of Chicago Press, Ltd., London
© 2016 by The University of Chicago
All rights reserved. Published 2015.
Printed in the United States of America
25 24 23 22 21 20 19 18 17 16   1 2 3 4 5

ISBN-13: 978-0-226-30907-1 (cloth)
ISBN-13: 978-0-226-30910-1 (paper)
ISBN-13: 978-0-226-30924-8 (e-book)
DOI: 10.7208/chicago/9780226309248.001.0001

Library of Congress Cataloging-in-Publication Data

Mitchell, Gregory (Gregory Carter), author.
  Tourist attractions : performing race and masculinity in Brazil's sexual economy / Gregory Mitchell.
    pages cm
  Includes bibliographical references and index.
  ISBN 978-0-226-30907-1 (cloth : alkaline paper) —
ISBN 978-0-226-30910-1 (paperback : alkaline paper) —
ISBN 978-0-226-30924-8 (ebook) 1. Male prostitutes—Brazil—
Social conditions. 2. Sex tourism—Social aspects—Brazil.
3. Prostitutes' customers—Brazil. 4. Male prostitution—Social
aspects—Brazil. I. Title.
  HQ119.4.B73M5B 2016
  306.74'3—dc23

                                        2015012860

For DKPI

Contents

Seeking to stand out from the crowd, the mostly hetero-sexually identified men selling sex to men in Rio de Ja-neiro's *saunas* (bathhouses) unwrap the bright-blue towels that distinguish them from clients and slowly massage their erect penises whenever they catch a client glancing their way, playing what they call *o jogo dos olhos* (the game of eyes). But on the *saunas'* "no-towel nights," dreaded by these *garotos de programa* (male sex workers; literally, "program boys") and loved by clients, the garotos become bashful and try not to let their coworkers see their bared backsides as they dance onstage and strut through a maze of bars, performance spaces, Jacuzzis, and steam rooms. There is a pecking order in the *sauna* that correlates with one's skill at performing masculinity, a performance that includes never indicating or admitting that your *cu* (ass) might be available. But the truth is that most desires in the *sauna* can be satisfied for the right price once the ga-roto takes the client upstairs, making this dance just one act in an elaborate staging of masculinity.

Celebrating gay pride at "ecoresorts" and venturing into the jungle on cruise ships, gay ecotourists, most of them white, visit the Amazon intent on exploring ecological diversity, but they are also interested in Brazil's famous racial diversity. In this nascent industry, a few intrepid ecotourists seek out indigenous sex workers in the trans-port hub of Manaus in order to have a more "authentic" Amazonian experience. Despite spending thousands of dollars to reach the remote jungle, many haggle with the men, coaxing them to lower their price from fifty dollars to thirty.

Taking its name from the Portuguese word for "whipping post," the Pelourinho district in Brazil's northeastern city of Salvador da Bahia was once a site for the public display and torture of enslaved and commodified African bodies. These days, commodified Afro-Brazilian bodies are still displayed on these very steps, but this is not slavery. Instead, these entrepreneurial garotos make a calculated decision to enter this economy. In addition to the local clientele, buyers now include many gay African American men. In this market, where many of the buyers are cultural-heritage tourists in search of Africa in the diaspora, it is the darkest-skinned men who fetch the highest prices.

Gay sex tourism is geographically widespread in Brazil, stretching from the impoverished Northeast even into the Amazon rain forest and down to the cosmopolitan Southeast. While academics, activists, and the government have paid markedly more attention in recent years to heterosexual prostitution and sex tourism in Brazil, they have almost completely overlooked gay sex tourism—a curious oversight given Rio's premier status in the gay travel industry. Young Brazilian men from a variety of economic backgrounds and racial groups derive income from formal and informal commercial sex transactions with other men, in which many of them putatively limit their sexual function to being *ativo* (i.e., penetrative) and identify as heterosexual, although identity categories can be slippery in the sexual economies of Brazil. The men are known as "garotos de programa" or, sometimes, as *michês* (hustlers). However, they tend to use the shorthand "garotos" or the English import *boy* to describe themselves and so I use these as well.[1] (Throughout this book, Portuguese terms will generally be italicized only at their first use in a chapter. To avoid confusion, however, I will always italicize terms that are the same as English words but carry a different valence or connotation, as in the case of *boy*, *sauna*, *normal*, etc. For a list of the most common Portuguese terms used in this book, see the glossary at the back.)

Gay sex tourists are similarly diverse: among their numbers can be counted men from a range of races, ages, political affiliations, and backgrounds. Likewise, the diversity in experiences and motivations among clients and sex workers is so great and the relationships between men from these groups are so varied that the terms "gay sex tourism" and "sex tourists" are themselves potential misnomers. Such loaded terms run the risk of merely being sex-negative straw men. Therefore, I use them only reluctantly and for practical, rather than moralizing, purposes here.

The terms "prostitute" and "sex worker" are also contentious, with the latter generally being the term preferred by advocates for sex worker rights and the former sometimes used pejoratively. In Brazil, however, activists tend to see "sex worker" as an unwanted foreign import and prefer to reclaim "prostitute" in daily advocacy work. Therefore, I tend to use "prostitute" unless I am referring to participants in a broader array of occupations in the industry that can be understood as sex work (e.g., escorting, stripping, working in pornographic films).

Unlike studies that focus on exploitation, drug use, or sexually transmitted infections, this book focuses on the personal experiences and identities of male sex workers in Brazil's sexual economy. To do otherwise sends the message that sex workers are valuable only as unfortunate souls in need of rescue or insofar as scholars can learn how sex workers may "harm" the public health of society. However, there is a genuine and ethically grounded *need* for ethnographic studies that take seriously intersections of sexuality, race, and economics as experienced in all facets of everyday life. Academics, students of sexual economies, and the general public know far less about sex workers as *people* than they do about sex workers as medical subjects or purported victims. Sensationalistic media outlets, antiprostitution activists, and public health organizations have largely been responsible for positioning sex workers in these terms, which is in and of itself a form of discursive harm against an already-marginalized population that perpetuates the idea that sex workers are most usefully seen as vectors of disease or people in need of liberation. The existing literature on sexual economies also focuses heavily on the supply side, neglecting clients out of practicality or personal interest or because of problems accessing a population that may be reluctant to participate in research. In this book, however, I am interested precisely in the interactions between foreign clients and sex workers because it's here that we see how the men from these different cultures and perspectives understand one another and their erotic relationships across the span of racial, cultural, and sexual difference.

Performative Labor and Racialized Masculinity

The men described in this book each understand race and sexuality differently, and yet these men must make sense of one another's subjectivity and try to understand *why* the other is there and what he wants to get out of this exchange. Failure to do so can diminish a garoto's career success or a client's pleasure, as *programas* (tricks, sessions with a client) can sometimes go awry when miscommunications occur or offense is given. People from different cultures think about, perceive, and navigate questions of desire differently. Racial categories in Brazil are different from those in the United States. So are sexual categories, although not always as much as foreigners imagine them to be.[2] Nonetheless, clients and sex workers in my research talk and think about race and sex in culturally inflected ways. This book is fundamentally about how these men move *across* different models of sexuality and race. Sometimes this means navigating different categories that may or may not translate neatly, such as racial categories like black, white, *moreno* (literally, "brown," an ambiguous category denoting mixed descent), or *pardo* (mixed race), as well as sexual categories such as straight, *normal* (heterosexual), and so forth.[3] Usually, though, it means trying to understand not only categories but also complex processes in which desire infuses these social constructs through which people organize so much of their lives—and that takes a lot of work and a lot of skill. I refer to this combination of particular performances and competencies as *performative labor.*

Far from being "easy money," as sometimes depicted in popular television shows and films, prostitution is hard work. Thanks largely to Marxist feminists and, later, sex-radical feminists in the 1980s who pushed back against antiprostitution radical feminists, terms like "sex work" and "sexual labor" have made their way into common parlance, emphasizing autonomy and the need to address exploitation through labor rights frameworks instead of criminalization. But these terms don't always capture the complexity and nuance of what goes into pulling off a programa, which is why throughout this book I also talk about sex work as performative labor.

A few scholars, mostly in studies of consumer society, have used the term "performative labor" in a more general sense. In his writings on the "Disneyization" of society, Alan Bryman defines "performative labour" as "the growing tendency for frontline service work to be viewed as a performance, especially one in which the deliberate display of a certain mood is seen as [essential]."[4] For Bryman, performative labor is meant to be "slightly broader" than and inclusive of "emotional labour."[5] Similarly, Bruce Pietrykowski says "performative labor entails the management and disciplining of the body and the emotions in the service of a customer or client."[6] These views of performance that divide the presentation of self into a front stage presented to customers and a more authentic backstage self are indebted to canonical work by the sociologist Erving Goffman.[7] However, to expand this notion into an ethnographic analysis of informal economies and daily life in a globalized world is challenging because all presentations of the self might be construed as performative and as situated within economic conditions. Goffmanesque views of performance don't fully account for the work of shifting across different cultural models and constructs of identity, and so I am limiting my theorizing of performative labor to the work of constructing, presenting, and maintaining facets of identity and of strategically (if unconsciously) shifting across complex models of identity.

All the cases I address in this book examine different instances of Brazilian sex workers and foreign clients refashioning themselves for one another within an economic setting. In each case study, I take up different racial categories and identity frameworks, different culturally specific sexual identity models and ways of describing sexuality, and different sexual economies with specific cultural and structural features. In all of them, clients and sex workers come together across different frameworks to collectively interpret and narrativize their relationship and its meanings. However, I also argue throughout this book that by studying these sexual economies in which garotos fashion racialized performances of masculinity at the behest of tourists, one can find moments of incoherence in identity models and contradictions in capitalist logics. Studying these contradictions in greater detail reveals how political and global economic forces in Brazil and the United States shape sexual identity and, therefore, how changes in capitalism are creating new wrinkles in sexual subjectivity.

The sex tourist industry in Brazil—like all tourism, really—is about pursuing opportunities to experience a culture and place sensually. Sex is just one sensual modality of many available options. The phrase "tourist attractions" in the title of this book refers to more than just the fact that the men in Brazil's sex trade are literal tourist attractions whose bodies and services foreigners come to experience. The sexual tourism I describe is about a particular constellation of attractions to difference. These kinds of tourist attractions are based on enactments of real and imagined differences, and this book, then, is about the contradictions that arise in the sexual economies populated by gay tourists: eroticizing an exotic Other who turns out to be remarkably (and sometimes disappointingly) similar to the tourist himself; pursuing racial and sexual community across vast differences only for the traveler to learn that he may not be part of the community he came to seek in quite the way he had hoped; wanting to experience a vanishing primitive environment only to have one's presence contribute to its destruction.

Pointing out the contradictions in sex tourists' relationship to an imagined exotic Other is not the same as criticizing or attacking these men as individuals. My interest is in how the structures of tourism and the ways that incentivized performances of identity function within Brazil's sexual economies perpetuate inequalities for some while also opening up opportunities for others. Despite the rhetoric of anti-prostitution feminists who insist that all prostitution is inherently exploitative and who portray tourists' actions, motives, and desires as immoral and racist, I found that tourists' approaches to their relationships with garotos were almost never malicious. Instead, their attitudes actually seemed rooted in an ostensibly utopic desire to understand their shared sexual experiences through a common essential experience and language of pleasure.

However, the fact of tourist desire for shared pleasure and the forging of authentic connections with garotos does not mean that these experiences were not racialized or that such desires can be understood outside long histories of race, capitalism, colonialism, and sexual subjugation. The stakes of these relationships with tourists, however short or long term they may be, remain very high for sex workers, who must earn their living by means of their ability to navigate and perform in the complicated affective terrain of desiring subjects.

In the language of the theater, "performance" is linked with "playing parts." It may seem trite, therefore, to talk of performance in the sex trades (though many sex workers I know are quick to boast about their Oscar-worthy performances for what they do on the job). But "performance" need not be synonymous with theatricality, artifice, or falsehood. Nor are these performances just for fun. One's life and livelihood can depend upon one's skill as a performer. Food, medicine, travel, immigration, class mobility, and family security may be on the line. For garotos who are poor, nonwhite, and/or on the sexual margins of society, there is a special need to demonstrate near-virtuoso levels of performative capacity. By focusing on the relationships between garotos and foreign clients, I try to show how garotos navigate the difficulties of performing racialized masculinity for a living in such a high-stakes environment. Understanding these performances helps us to better understand the political economy of sexuality, or how macroeconomic processes such as globalization, consumer growth, and economic development impact microeconomic exchanges of everyday life such as transactions between sex workers and clients. It also helps us to appreciate how the sexual exchanges between these garotos and their clients reflect broader social changes by revealing ongoing shifts in labor patterns, consumerism, family life, sexual identity, and other key concepts that are of interest to a broad range of scholars who study more traditional fields.

Gay (Money) Is Good

From the late 1990s onward, Brazil's reputation as a gay travel destination has grown. Rio de Janeiro's promotion firm, RioTur, reported in 2014 that a full 30 percent of tourist spending during *carnaval* (approximately 163 million out of USD 528 million total) came from gay tourists, and moreover, that foreign gay tourists spent twice as much as their heterosexual counterparts and 50 percent more than gay Brazilian tourists.[8] The sexual diversity coordinator of Rio de Janeiro's government reports that the city hosted 880,000 gay tourists in 2010.[9] Although this figure includes both foreign and domestic tourists, it still gives a general idea of the massive size of gay tourism and the government's perception of its importance to the industry. At the World Tourism Congress in 2009, the US gay television network Logo gave Rio its award for Best Global Destination. The city regularly appears in top-ten lists in gay travel magazines and in articles in gay publications like *Out* and *Instinct*. Paulo Senise, executive director of the Rio Convention and Visitors Bureau, declared, "The importance and growth of gay tourism in the world is indisputable. Rio has all the characteristics to be recognized as a gay friendly city," noting that "diversity makes a lot of money for the city, it creates jobs, it increases tax revenue and contributes to sharing out wealth."[10] RioTur boasts that "the city's best hotels and restaurants are gay friendly, and so are [its] top-notch bars."[11] The mayor's office is currently working with US agents to craft large-scale campaigns aimed at foreign gay tourists. Even mainstream corporations have noticed the trend. Delta and other airlines feature Rio as a "top destination" on the dedicated gay travel sections of their websites (the mere existence of which bespeaks the growing power of the gay travel industry).

These moves on the part of the Brazilian government and US travel industry professionals reify the notion of a "global gay consumer," a figure that has sparked the interest of scholars in humanities and social science fields who are critical of the growing privilege, exceptionalism, and nationalism accruing to a certain segment of mostly white, gay, upwardly mobile men (whose numbers include but are not limited to those gay tourists who purchase sex).[12] For ethnographers, the disjuncture between ideal types and living subjects can lead to difficulties in analysis. For example, in his study of male sex workers and gay sex tourists in the Dominican Republic, Mark Padilla says that he decided to privilege the voices of male sex workers over clients in order to shift academic focus away from the "symbolic being" known as the "global queer consumer."[13] Padilla's desire to center discussion on the comparatively disenfranchised male sex workers is astute and admirable. However, his concern points to a development in certain theoretical circles wherein the "global queer consumer" has become all too abstract, literary, disembodied, and unvoiced. The global gay consumer is an overly privileged but ultimately empty signifier onto which various anxieties about capitalism, racism, and nationalism may be projected, yet exactly who queer theorists are talking about remains unclear.

In this book I take the concerns of gay consumerism seriously, but I also employ an ethnographic approach to understanding who the actual consumers are and how these men see their own participation in late-capitalist economies. Ethnography has much to offer queer theory by allowing the examination of the ethnographic reality of people who live within and sometimes defy the bounds of rubrics like the "global queer consumer." So who are the gay leisure travelers composing the alternately coveted and discomforting gay consumer phalanx, and just how widespread is gay tourism in Brazil's sexual economy?

It's impossible to tell just how many tourists pay for sex directly or indirectly. Solely on the basis of the numbers reported to me by garotos (and accounting for the changing number of garotos and adjusting for the frequency of repeat customers), it's clear that thousands of gay foreigners purchase sex in *saunas* (bathhouses) offering brothel-style male prostitution each year.[14] This estimate doesn't take into account gay sex tourists who find sex workers online, in bars, or on the streets, which means the total number is actually much higher. Dozens of international and Brazilian gay travel agencies offer all-gay trips to Brazil (often including optional opportunities to visit *saunas*), and there is a growing cadre of independent operators (some of whom are occasional sex workers, many not) who rent themselves out as guides and interpreters to gay tourists wanting to purchase sex from garotos in *saunas* but who find the prospect socially or linguistically intimidating. Rio is the largest and most visible of Brazil's gay destinations and most of my data come from Rio, but as the vignettes that opened this book indicate, it is certainly not the only center for gay tourism in the country.

On its surface, organized leisure travel for gays and lesbians seems to be a new phenomenon. It's so ubiquitous now that it tends to make the news only when something goes "wrong" (e.g., when gay cruise ships are denied docking privileges or a tourist is gay-bashed).[15] Even Sandals Resorts, one of the world's largest and most visible all-inclusive resort chains, finally suspended its long-standing policy of refusing to allow same-sex couples on its premises in 2004.[16] It's not surprising that the first and most visible corporations to target gay markets were travel oriented, although this itself is a recent development. In fact, if one attempts to chart the origins of the corporatization of gay travel, one would only need to look back to 1993 to find the first major corporation hiring a liaison to the gay community. This important moment in mainstreaming came from American Airlines and was a major reversal for the company that had earlier that year sought to remove all blankets and pillows touched by gay travelers for fear of AIDS contamination.[17] Homophobia and fear of AIDS in the United States and elsewhere had prevented the mainstreaming of organized gay tourism in the 1980s despite the formation of the (now-expansive) International Gay and Lesbian Travel Association in 1983 and the publication of the first gay travel monthly, *Our World*, in 1989.

During the bleak apex of the AIDS crisis, gay men were not seen as trendsetters whose presence heralds the sudden popularity of a hot vacation spot. Rather, the travel industry treated them as diseased public relations liabilities. In light of this, it's important to remember that gay travel is not just a marker of consumerism but can also be a political act. Even today quite-progressive heterosexual people enjoy leisure travel in popular places such as Jamaica, Barbados, the Bahamas, Singapore, Egypt, and Dubai while not realizing that governments in these locations and so many others have laws against homosexuality, allow or encourage harsh sentences, or place restrictive policies on LGBT travelers.[18] Queer bodies moving in space are always political, and as conservative-government restrictions on gay travelers show, queer bodies are threatening to national interests and state-sanctioned visions of heteronormative culture. For example, authorities in Morocco and the Cayman Islands have denied gay cruise ships entry, and conservative political and religious leaders in Costa Rica have set up blockades to combat Costa Rica's emerging popularity with LGBT travelers. There are valid critiques of the cruise ship industry and consumerist models of gay travel as having the potential for neocolonialism and exploitation, but when groups take political, legal, or extrajudicial violent measures to dissuade gay tourists from coming, a common argument from

9

religious conservatives is that gay tourists are there to seduce the local men and/or pay them for sex. This line of reasoning illustrates the fears and assumptions about the overlap between gay tourism and gay sex tourism. But is this conflation mere homophobia? Or might it actually reveal something about the relationship of gay travel and sexual economies? What exactly does the gay commercial sex scene of Brazil look like, and how does the sexual economy relate to the gay tourist economy there more broadly?

Of Bingo and Brothels

It's a typical weekday night. I am heading into a *sauna* in Rio to watch the garotos engage in the intricate social choreography of the *sauna*, playing their aforementioned "game of eyes" with clients. Like most *saunas*, this one has several floors, which are necessary to accommodate everything this space offers. Approaching the *sauna* on the street, there is little signage to mark it as such. One needs to know where one is going and whether it is a *sauna* with garotos or one without garotos (i.e., a traditional gay bathhouse where clients have sex with each other). The real telltale sign of a *sauna* from outside is the overpowering smell of bleach and eucalyptus that wafts from the doors and floats down the street. Upon entering, I see a bored-looking man at a reception desk that is overflowing with credit-card-swiping machines. He types my first name into the computer and hands me a key attached to a wristband. On the way out, he'll check my band number and charge me about fifteen dollars for my entry fee and five dollars for a *caipirinha* (Brazil's national drink), but thanks to a special tonight I could have had my entry fee waived if I had rented a room and bought a *programa*. I look at the cashier's frame and face, slightly gone to seed but still handsome, and I ponder whether he is a former garoto, but I am off to my first stop: the locker room.

In an inversion of a lot of gay pornographic films and fantasies, at most *saunas* the locker room is just about the only nonsexual space. Most of the clients are local men, but tourists are scattered throughout the room, changing into white towels and flip-flops under the supervision of an attendant before heading to more exciting floors. The garotos have their own locker room, which may play heterosexual pornography so they can "recharge" their erections because they like to flash their wares for prospective clients. Sometimes they hang out and chat in there to get a break from clients or to exchange *fofocas* (bits of gossip). Because garotos may circulate among the half dozen or so *saunas* in Rio that employ rent boys as well as among the dozens of popular gay clubs, bars, and cruising spaces, there is an ever-shifting network of regular and intermittent workers who know each other from various venues. Likewise, clients may know each other from these venues.

Past the locker room areas are showers, a steam room, a dry *sauna*, and sometimes a small gym area with basic equipment. The heart of the *sauna* is the lounge, which has a restaurant/bar area and a stage for drag shows, stripping, go-go dancing, even standup comedy. It's a social space where regular local clients come to relax and hang out with friends, including favorite garotos, and they may not even purchase a *programa*. Livelier still are the rooms some *saunas* have for watching the evening telenovelas, where clients and garotos alike keep a running color commentary on the nation's favorite soap operas. Upstairs there are various *cabines* for rent. Some of these rooms have small bathrooms with showers; sometimes there is a TV, which is sometimes used to play heterosexual porn for garotos to watch during sex.

Around twenty garotos are moving through the space tonight, executing a kind of social choreography, adjusting their flirting, their demeanor, their comportment, and their habitus depending on the space and their perception of what clients want from them that night. They are mostly in their early twenties but range from the late teens to the midthirties. Except for a few noticeable teenaged twinks (i.e., young, slim, boyish guys), most are extremely muscular, and several have telltale patches of acne across the backs of their necks and shoulders from steroid use. Most of them are shaved clean of chest hair because they feel the smooth look accentuates their muscles. They're mostly whites and light-skinned morenos. There is only one dark-skinned man and he seems to be getting no attention tonight. They wrap and unwrap their towels, showing their dicks. Many of them are well endowed, but a few are enormous, and one of these guys cruises a slow circuit completely exposed, his shoulders thrown back, flexing his biceps with his arms at his sides, and walking, hard-on first, through the room, stopping by clients to see if they take an interest. One of the local clients pauses his conversation with another client, turns to the man, and squeezes the garoto's erect penis. He smiles and gives him a thumbs-up sign before casually turning away to resume his conversation.

Meanwhile, in the steam room, one of the garotos drops his towel completely and takes a quick and exaggeratedly luxurious shower in the corner of the steam room, running one hand through his shaggy hair and another down his torso to wash off his genitals before walking out nonchalantly. However, I notice that he pauses outside to see if a client will take the bait and follow him. One does.

Realizing how carefully all of this is staged was one of many surprising moments I would experience in *saunas*, which are at the center of much of the male prostitution in Rio de Janeiro. Another such moment came during my first week of research as I was walking up a staircase lined with garotos in blue towels, which are a different color so they won't be mistaken for clients. Such a mistake would be rare, as most clients are older and often not in the kind of top physical form that the garotos maintain, but on any given night there are almost always a few young, handsome, masculine clients whom other clients and garotos may regard with some confusion because "they shouldn't need to pay for it." A few of the stairwell garotos that night expose their dicks or stroke themselves. A couple of them smack my backside as I ascend the stairs, commenting on my *bunda* (ass) and making me blush. The staircase is steep and narrow, and I struggle to keep my towel on as they lean into me. I can see why some clients would be turned on by this. You're pushing through narrow, fleshy space, squeezing past a dozen straight, butch, naked men while they whisper dirty words in a foreign tongue and press themselves against you. It's the kind of scene played out in myriad porn films, which is not surprising, as many such films are shot in Brazil using garotos recruited from the *saunas*. So I *get* that this is supposed to be sexy—and on some level I am also registering the details, aware that the architecture is creating masculinity and queer space on this staircase that's acting as a gauntlet. So I also *get* that this is academically interesting. But I'm not turned on, sexually or intellectually, right then. I find it claustrophobic. Dizzying. I just want it to stop.

Suddenly, a *travesti* (loosely, a "transgendered" woman) appears at the top of the stairs and saves me. "It's Bingo, *bichas!*" she screams at all of us, stretching out the word: *bichaaaas* (pronounced "bee-shas," meaning "queers").

The world shifts.

The rent boys lose all interest in scoring a programa with me and begin murmuring the word, passing on the news like a game of telephone. *Bingo, Bingo, Bingo* . . . washing down the stairs and through the locker rooms. Their over-the-top hypermasculinity recedes into casual jocularity. There is a stampede up the stairs to the stage area, where a drag queen dressed like a cavewoman is gingerly spinning a Bingo ball-churner despite her long acrylic red nails. First, one of the rent boys, dressed like a caveman, does an awkward striptease for the clients, who hoot and holler, and then he does some go-go dancing, thumbs tucked into and tugging the sides of his little Speedo. At one point the "cavewoman" reaches for his ass, as if to spank it. "Oh, *bundinha* [cute little ass]!" she cries. The cavewoman has called this garoto's masculinity into question by directing her gaze—and that of the audience, including the other garotos—to his *bunda*, which isn't supposed to be on the menu. The dancer tries to turn his ass away from the audience, but it's too late. The other rent boys laugh and catcall. "*Viado* [faggot]!" one of them shouts teasingly, and they all laugh, apparently having forgotten the rows of "viado" clients sitting nearby.

The cavewoman starts calling the numbers and everyone forgets the *boy*'s ass as they study their game cards. The rent boys are so engrossed in this that the ones sitting at tables with the clients with whom they have just had sex (or soon will) forget to lavish any attention on their customers. Someone yells, "Bingo!" and his friends cheer gleefully as another garoto throws his card down, shouting, "*Porra* [fuck]!" The angry garoto's swearing raises tourist eyebrows. It's a disproportionate response to a mundane event, a bit like a tantrum. Later I meet this man, Donaldo, and learn that although he is still a teenager, he, like many of his coworkers, grew up very quickly after being raised in a tough home in a difficult neighborhood.[19] He's macho, quick to take offense, and has difficulty holding down a "regular job." He's ambivalent about his work in the *sauna*, but he's also loyal to his friends, protective of his family, and hardworking. The winner claims his prize from among the knickknacks—hair gel, combs, odd little baubles—and Donaldo scowls.

Despite Donaldo's petulance, everyone else seems to be having great fun. As a young graduate student first exploring my field sites, I wasn't sure what a male brothel was going to look like. I was surprised to discover so much community, playfulness, camaraderie, and unexpectedly campy fun in these bathhouses full of male prostitutes. I didn't expect there to be so much laughter. I marveled at the affection between these seemingly odd collections of mostly straight young rent boys alongside some gay ones, aging Brazilian gay clients, gringo tourists, a few travesti employees, and the drag queen performers. *Saunas* abound with performative possibility as the garotos navigate desire and attempt to stir up affective responses from possible clients, adjusting their performances of masculinity according to their reading of different clients and situations.

I don't want to romanticize all these spaces as some utopian queer imaginary, however. Even the best of *saunas* have racialized and masculinist pricing because this is a marketplace that rewards young, light-skinned, conventionally attractive butch men above others. I've collected complaints from garotos about working conditions, listened to them retell nasty comments from clients, and heard them articulate many times their desire to leave if they could just find a better job. I've been to a few grim, low-end *saunas* where the *cabines* are wooden stalls like barn stables, just large enough for a rubber mat to fit inside on the floor, with a roll of cheap toilet paper and a condom resting on a beam overhead under a naked, burnt-out bulb. There are even a few establishments where management violates Brazil's pimping laws and requires clients to pay the house rather than the garoto, so managers can take a cut from the garoto instead of making their profits from entry fees, concessions, and room rentals as allowed by law.

Brazilian locals make up the majority of the clientele and enjoy the *saunas* for socializing as much as for sex. For them, having a social space where commercial sex is available is not an especially exotic or remarkable feature of gay life. Over the years I learned how garotos came to experience these venues as well, yet I struggled to understand how an increasing number of tourists had come to these Brazilian spaces, how their different worldviews and experiences shaped the interactions they had in Brazil, and what motivated them more broadly.

The Paradox of Queer Desire

I never set out to study sex tourism per se. My research project began as a result of my desire to investigate the growing importance of consumerism in contemporary mainstream gay culture in the United States. I certainly didn't anticipate that I would find myself playing weekly rounds of Bingo with rent boys and drag queens or following a gay tour group on an expedition to the Amazon jungle, but I also didn't anticipate just how much consumer trending in the United States affects local sexual economies in far-flung places. Nor did I realize the degree to which "pink economies"—the market of goods and services for gay consumers—can influence the performances of race and gender in everyday life among the people who occupy geographic areas caught up in these global economic flows, something that Brazilian anthropologists such as Júlio Assis Simões have also observed.[20]

Within days of landing in the country, though, I realized that commercial sex in Brazil—be it gay or straight—is inseparable from the tourist industry as a whole. The sex trade was visible in both subtle and obvious forms on beaches and in grocery stores, bars, restaurants, and hotel lobbies. Because prostitution is not against the law in Brazil and cosmopolitan areas of Brazil are fairly gay-friendly, it was easy to meet gay tourists and garotos either together or separately. Within a week, I had the additional realization that a lot of the seemingly *non*-commercial hookups and relationships I was seeing between foreigners and locals included presents, shopping, cash given as a gift rather than payment, and access to fine dining and pricey venues. These Brazilian guys didn't always regard themselves as sex workers. Nonetheless, there was a sizable population of men with well-established patterns of sleeping with wealthier *gringos*. (In the Brazilian context, *gringo* is an emic term for any foreigner, including other Latinos,[21] and not necessarily a racialized epithet, although tourists often read it as connoting derision.)[22]

If such an enterprising young man might find just the right set of performative turns, the right words, looks, and actions, to "catch" his gringo, all manner of financial opportunities and sexual possibilities associated with the figure of the gringo could be unlocked. Gringo desires for their garotos are slippery, though. They generally fetishized the men's performances of machismo and were turned on by the fantasy of having sex with butch straight men, but they also wanted the garotos to experience pleasure and reciprocate desire. Such a shift on the part of the garoto, though, led to diminishing returns on the original fantasy of straight masculinity and often created a cycle in which the gringo became disenchanted with the garoto and would then need to pursue still another. Aware of this, garotos could use gringos' fantasies to their advantage by playing to this script, incorporating it into their seductions, and drawing out relationships with gringos in a careful dance of desire and shifting identity.

This seemingly contradictory structure of desire presents a paradox of queer desire that I encountered throughout my fieldwork in various forms. It was present not only in gringo-garoto relationships that evolved out of programas and interactions in the *saunas* but also in other ways. As I examine later, African American gay tourists pursuing traces of blackness in the diaspora similarly found their desire for authenticity thwarted as soon as they discovered that the garotos (and other Brazilians) did not always regard them as sharing in the same diasporic community they were seeking. And in the Amazon, tourists came in pursuit of a romantic vision of raw nature that their own presence immediately negated.

The paradox that all these gringos find themselves facing is queer in the sense that it is peculiar but also because it is fueled by and enmeshed in their sexual desire. My research shows empirically what the queer theorist Lauren Berlant compellingly demonstrated in her work on cruel optimism. "When we talk about an object of desire," she writes, "we are really talking about a cluster of promises we want some-one or something to make to us and make possible for us." She goes on to explain, "To phrase 'the object of desire' as a cluster of promises is to allow us to encounter what is incoherent or enigmatic in our attach-ments, not as confirmation of our irrationality, but as an explanation for our sense of *our endurance in the object*, insofar as proximity to the object means proximity to the cluster of things that the object prom-ises, some of which may be clear to us while others not so much. In other words, all attachments are optimistic."[23]

For Berlant and, indeed, for gringo-garoto relations, optimisms are cruel because regardless of the content of the attachments (in this case, the individual people), it is the continuity of the form (in this case, the fantasies clustering around masculinity) that provides the motiva-tion for continuing the attachment. "Cruel optimism is the condition of maintaining an attachment to a problematic object *in advance* of its loss."[24] In light of this, one can consider that although gringos may have utopian fantasies of their relationship to Brazil and particular Bra-zilians, operating in the queer paradox of desire means that they can never realize these fantasies, which are based on precisely the kinds of cruel optimism Berlant theorized. For gringos—always striving, never arriving—the paradox of queer desire is that their fantasy is agonistic. Even as the idealized future begins to arrive, it disintegrates and the cy-cle begins again. This complex interweaving of desires—carnal on the part of the tourist while practical for the garoto and often emotional for both—creates a diverse array of complicated relationships within Brazil's informal sexual economies. Sitting in the *saunas* of Rio watch-ing such relationships, conflicts, desires, and attachments unfold, I could not help but realize that my research project was going to get messy.

Methods and Ethical Concerns

Some ethnographers live among their sex worker interlocutors. Don Kulick, for example, lived in the same tenement building with the tra-vesti prostitutes whom he studied in Bahia.[25] The garotos whom I met usually do not live in the area where they work. Most of them are scat-tered among various far-off neighborhoods on the outskirts of their cities or sometimes in *favelas* (shantytowns). Even if it had been practical to live with them, my presence would have brought much unwanted attention to the men, the majority of whom are not "out" about their work to their families or communities. The garotos keep their lives so compartmentalized that even those with whom I was very close made sure to keep me away from their homes as a general rule. It would be too hard to explain my presence and could damage not only their reputation but those of their wives, children, and parents. Instead, I chose to live in the areas known for sex tourism where the men worked, primarily in Copacabana and Lapa in Rio and Porto da Barra in Bahia.

Over time, my own subjectivity proved important. When I entered known male prostitution areas, garotos would immediately solicit me as a client. My polite refusals and my explanation of my research project were usually met with incredulity at first. Sometimes we would make it halfway through the informed-consent process before a garoto would realize that I was serious. Word also traveled fast, and several times strangers approached me asking if I was the anthropologist they had heard about and if I was ready to write down their stories. Recording interviews, however, was a much more serious request and took considerable trust building and sometimes multiple interviews before it could occur. Consequently, I learned to take detailed notes and to capture quotations as accurately as possible during or immediately after interviews. Sometimes I was able to meet with the men again later to confirm the accuracy of my notes, which had the added advantage of producing further conversations as they provided clarification or caveats.

Several years into the project, grant money allowed me to hire a research assistant, a gay graduate student with experience in tourism, to help me conduct and transcribe interviews. Gustavo was an invaluable professional resource, but he also asked for a pseudonym and to have identifying details obscured for fear that being associated with this type of research would damage his academic career in Brazil. At his request, I've tried to minimize his appearances throughout the text except where he directly influenced events, but readers should know that he was invaluable to me during the last two years of the project, helping with transcriptions, interviews, and data management and analysis, keeping me safe, and steering me through no end of awkward moments while I lived as a gringo abroad.

Between 2006 and 2015, I made ten trips to Brazil, usually staying for several months each time, until I amassed around sixteen months of data. In the end, I conducted formal interviews with around forty gay tourists who purchased sex in Brazil. These interviews ranged from thirty minutes to three hours. Some of the men gave several interviews, and a few had ongoing communications with me via phone, email, and/or Skype. In many bars, *saunas*, and public venues I also had numerous informal (and sometimes extensive) interactions and conversations with men who purchased sex from either men or women. In Rio de Janeiro, around 70 percent of the tourist interviewees were white, with the remainder being African American, Asian American, and Latino. They ranged in age from late twenties to early seventies, with a median age in the early fifties. Those who lived in Brazil for a large portion of the year, who had properties or who had long-term boyfriends in Brazil, tended to be older.

Almost all the tourists had college degrees, with many of them holding graduate degrees. The few without substantial higher education tended to work in the travel industry (e.g., as flight attendants), thereby gaining access to travel opportunities. All these tourists were middle class or higher, and most of them complained about their middle-class salaries and the assumption that Brazilians made that they were rich, especially during the period of time when the real was overvalued and purchasing sex nearly doubled in price in real terms for them. (Throughout the book, I give numbers that approximate the exchange rate at the time of the interview and readers may notice considerable fluctuations.) Not all the men disclosed their salaries, but some of the older men were wealthy (with those on the upper end of the spectrum earning more than $200,000 a year) and could pay for luxury accommodations and expensive vacations with escorts and could afford to "keep" their boyfriends (i.e., pay their rent and expenses, provide gifts and allowances, etc.).

I conducted interviews of varying duration and formality with around fifty garotos. Sometimes, I got to know the garotos quite well and would see them day after day, spending long hours hanging out. Other guys I saw only once. In Rio and Manaus, these men came from lower-class backgrounds, but very few were destitute. In Bahia, many of the men selling sex on the streets and beaches were poor, and some had insecure and inconsistent housing. Men working in *saunas* usually attained middle-class incomes by Brazilian standards. During the years I was in the field, a garoto in a Rio *sauna* earned 100 reais (USD [2006–15] 35–60) for a forty-minute *programa* with a gringo (usually about 20 percent more than a local client would pay). Prices for street-based services were varied and context dependent but generally were lower. Many garotos also worked in escorting and sometimes pornography.

Although garotos made much less than women and travestis (who can make two to three times the amount of money for a programa in a comparably classed venue), the garotos could nonetheless earn enough to lift themselves out of poverty and soon attained consumer status with access to nightclubs, electronic goods, and fashionable clothes. Despite their new incomes, almost all the men reported spending all their money, and older garotos frequently regretted not saving when they were newer on the scene.

The garotos whom I interviewed had all been doing programas for a year or more, and the median was around six years of experience. They ranged in stated age from eighteen to thirty-five, with a median age of around twenty-four. Some had begun selling sex occasionally at age sixteen or seventeen—which is above the age of consent for non-commercial sex but technically illegal in terms of the age permitted for sex work—before working formally in *saunas*, porn, or escorting once they were eighteen. A handful of the men began selling sex as younger teenagers, but none reported considering themselves traumatized or exploited, instead arguing that their early forays into sex were a badge of honor and made them more virile and masculine.

Around 65 percent of the garotos interviewed identified as hetero-sexual and about 20 percent said they were bisexual. However, the men identifying as bisexual typically did not have noncommercial sex with men or express feeling attracted to men, so "bisexual" had a somewhat-different meaning than it might for people outside the commercial sex trades. The remainder identified as gay. The question of identity is dif-ficult because, as I document throughout this book, identifications are fluid, and some men identified differently depending on circumstance and whether they were discussing how they identified in their own mind versus how they identified to coworkers, clients, girlfriends, fam-ily members, or gringo boyfriends.

Generally speaking, a formal interview lasted about an hour. I fre-quently interviewed the same men several times, and I had many con-versations with garotos that lacked the structure of interviews but pro-vided important insights. Sometimes I did group interviews with two or three men because I found that when they engaged each other in dialogue and debate, they provided richer details and seemed to worry less about there being a "right way" to answer my questions. I also oc-casionally interviewed sex work industry managers such as *sauna* own-ers, gay travel agents/guides, or restaurateurs who owned venues ca-tering to sex tourists. I also had many interactions, mostly brief and informal, with heterosexual sex tourists and female sex workers, who are far more abundant in Brazil overall. In 2013 I also accompanied an anthropologist working for the Interdisciplinary Brazilian AIDS Association to a mid- to upper-tier heterosexual brothel to conduct formal interviews with female sex workers. And in 2014 I worked closely on a new project about prostitution and global sporting events with the Observatório da Prostituição, a research cluster of around a dozen independent researchers from around the world institutionalized at the Federal University of Rio de Janeiro (UFRJ). In that capacity, I participated in conducting surveys and doing interviews as well as site visits to heterosexual commercial sex sites, conducting participant observation in over a dozen heterosexual lower-, middle-, and upper-tier brothel venues and in red-light districts with street-based prostitutes in places like the area around Praça do Lido in Copacabana and Vila Mimosa, a poor slum consisting of dozens of commercial sex sites. I rarely quote from these heterosexual contacts, but they did provide additional context that inflected my other work.

I also had many interactions with Brazilian clients, who are more abundant by far than gay tourists. They provided rich contextualization that was helpful in making comparisons and understanding the similarities and differences between local and transnational commercial sex encounters, but they were not an overt focus of my research. Because I was specifically interested in US gay culture and how these men, ostensibly from my own community, interrelated and coconstructed narratives across cultures, I did not expand my data set to include Brazilian clients through formal interview procedures. Nonetheless, I wanted to gather background information in order to not overreach in my claims as I analyzed the data gathered from the United States. I also frequently asked garotos how they felt their own experiences differed depending on the nationality of the client (not only foreign versus domestic but various foreign nationalities as well).

Because I visited Brazil many times over the years, I was able to build some long-term relationships and to watch as men entered, left, and then returned to the industry, began and ended relationships with tourists, married girlfriends, had children, went to prison, or died. My many visits also helped me empathize with tourists, expats, snowbirds (those who traveled seasonally to Brazil), and those who struggled to maintain long-distance relationships with men who sell sex, with whom it can be difficult to stay in reliable contact.

Many of the garotos, especially the most impoverished, had never had an interaction with a gringo that didn't involve money. I tried to repay them for their help with my research indirectly: translating documents, writing letters or emails, passing along free condoms, and occasionally using my status as a gringo and academic to ward off police harassment when we were in public, which sometimes happened in Bahia, where tourist police units are on the lookout for *caçadores*, or "gringo-hunters," who solicit tourists for sex, cash, and meals. We generally passed the time in the outdoor restaurants, bars, and cafés where they cruised for tricks, and my grant money did allow me to share food and drinks with them, sometimes stretching our chats on for hours, as is the Brazilian way.

Money is another matter, as any ethnographer who has worked among the poor can likely attest. If an ethnographer assists someone in the field financially, it can create problems in the community. I didn't want to be seen as another form of client. But the garotos also lost money paying "exit fees" and bribes to *sauna* managers to meet me, as well as on transportation to and from the interview site, and they lost clients by not working. A few years into the project, I had grant money that allowed me a discretionary budget, and I could begin to give them money to offset these losses as needed (usually five to twenty-five dollars). While I was comfortable with this level and form of repayment, I had to draw the line at indemnifying them against the price of a lost *programa*; otherwise, I knew I would become a de facto client myself. Some of the men—usually the street-based and therefore most-impoverished men—turned down any money I offered on principle because they wanted me to know that their participation had nothing to do with financial gain. These men valued the opportunity to share their stories and even brought along friends in the industry to meet me.

I learned a hard lesson about "giving back" to the community early on in my fieldwork when I gave the equivalent of just over five dollars each to two garotos who worked the streets—Ronaldo and Inácio. I knew them pretty well, and I knew for a fact that they hadn't eaten all day, in part because they had gotten caught up in a long discussion with me about religion among garotos when they "should" have been working the tourists leaving the gay beach at sunset. Prime time for "hunting" (*caçando*) was vanishing and a storm was blowing in, sending sun-burnt tourists running for cover. Now they were going to be hungry *and* wet. I told them to use the five dollars for food, reminding Inácio to take his mother the rice she'd asked for so she didn't clobber him again. I thought nothing more about this until I later learned that once out of my sight, Ronaldo punched Inácio and stole his money, violating a strict no-stealing policy among the guys working in the area and breaking Inácio's much-prized Walkman cassette player in the process. This ruined their friendship, and Ronaldo had to go into hiding for several weeks to avoid retaliation and punishment.

As word spread of Ronaldo's betrayal, it became clear that I couldn't have any more contact with him—at least not for a while—or I would lose the trust of the whole group of garotos working in the neighborhood. What had seemed the obvious, right thing to do turned out badly for everyone concerned and left me feeling inept as a novice ethnographer. Rather than a problem with a single answer, giving back is an ongoing ethical process that requires continued reflection and case-by-case consideration.

For the garotos, I was a white gringo—but not a client, not a social worker, and not an evangelical Christian out to rescue them. My accented Portuguese and peculiar habit of combining formal grammar with slang acquired from hanging out with prostitutes also made me an anomaly and source of amusement to them. Stranger still, although I didn't want to "save" them from prostitution or take them to church, I also didn't want to have sex with them. I had many of the same forms of privilege as other gringos they had encountered and resembled these clients in many ways, but I was dedicated to learning about them and from them in ways that their clients were generally not. And I wanted to hear about aspects of their lives apart from sexual health or condom usage (for those who had met researchers, the only other kinds of questions they had heard). I tried to give back to them when I could and in ways that I felt appropriate, but I didn't shower them with expensive gifts or fine meals like a Papai Noel ("sugar daddy"; literally, "Father Christmas").

Tourists were another story. Some tourists were easy to recruit and eager to talk to me. Some men enjoyed that their sexual adventures were seen as worthy of writing down for posterity, and many were traveling alone and were happy to have someone to talk to. Many of the older men were surprised and excited that "gay research" could be undertaken in the academy now, and they wanted to participate out of political solidarity. Often, my interlocutors were tourists who were on their first trip to Brazil and had very little knowledge of the country. Their views often reflected entrenched stereotypes about the sexual culture of Brazil and the hypersexuality of people of color—views held not only by foreigners but also by some Brazilians themselves, as the Brazilian anthropologist Laura Moutinho has argued.[26]

There is a marked difference between relatively inexperienced tourists and highly experienced tourists. A loosely organized network of experienced men from the United States (along with a few Canadians and Western Europeans) who know one another from online forums and also occasionally in real life sometimes vacation together in Rio and go to *saunas* together. At times they pool their money to rent apartments or houses and throw parties, inviting garotos to come entertain and to be available for programas. These more experienced tourists and expats tend to be much more reflective about the industry and their participation in it. These men also have a deeper understanding of race, class, language, and sexuality in Brazil. It was only after several years that I began to build enough trust with members of this community that I was able to begin getting in-depth interviews and spending time with them. Much more will be said about these men in the chapters that follow, but my positionality as a researcher held very little sway with them. In fact, it actually made them quite skeptical at first, and probably rightly so given the depth and breadth of their knowledge of Brazil's sexual economies compared with mine. They were also much harder to recruit because they tended to be concerned with privacy and a desire to be represented fairly, having had some negative experiences with journalists' sensationalized accounts of "sex tourism." I am deeply indebted to them for overcoming their skepticism and opening up to me.

Elastic Definitions and the Accidental (Sex) Tourist

As I mentioned above, *sex work* necessarily includes a range of formal and informal economic transactions in which one person receives money, goods, or other forms of capital and in exchange provides sexual services. This is quite a slippery slope. On Copacabana Beach along a strip known as the *orla* (beachfront), there are a number of bars for heterosexual tourists. Some of the Brazilian women who frequent these bars do not always charge for sex when finding a gringo suitable for a longer pursuit, while in other areas such as Lapa there are women who adamantly do not identify as prostitutes but actively seek to date gringos for various financial benefits, earning the moniker "gringo-chasers." They hope to find a boyfriend who will take care of them financially and, sometimes, even help them emigrate. Anthropologists in Brazil have also observed that some women disidentify as "prostitutes," or *garotas de programa*, based on their motivations, separating themselves into those who sell sex for "moral" reasons such as providing for their children and "immoral" ones such as access to luxury goods.[27] Alternatively, there are women who charge men for sex only when they think the man is not a good prospect for a long-term relationship or immigration. These women may not necessarily consider themselves prostitutes. Gringos favoring these venues often deny being sex tourists or insist that they are not clients because they do not pay directly. I consider these informal exchanges to be a form of sex work and part of the broader sexual economy of Brazil, although I am hard-pressed to describe how the women are different from other familiar figures such as trophy wives. The danger of having a flexible definition is that one can fall prey to a reductionist Marxist interpretation that all marriage is prostitution or that all women are prostitutes. This is not my intent. Ever mindful of this trap, though, I beg the reader's indulgence and admit that, in recognition of the complexity of commercial sex, the key terms of "sex work" and "prostitution" will necessarily be elastic in this research.

On the other side of the exchange, one has the equally thorny problem of defining a "sex tourist." I interviewed a number of so-called sex-pats, who live in Brazil much of the year. At what point do they stop being tourists and become Brazilians, or at least some form of immigrant? (For many Brazilians, the answer to this is "never.") Is a college student studying abroad "allowed" to date only middle-class Brazilians, or would the class difference between that student and a lower-class Brazilian lover always render the relationship transactional? In Bahia, I found many American and European women surprising themselves by meeting a local man on the beach and having a whirlwind romance for the week, lavishing gifts on him.[28] Are they sex tourists? Does it matter if such a woman "happens" to do this on every trip? Is she any more or less a sex tourist if the local man has, without her knowledge—as is the case in my research—also done this with a different foreign woman or man every week for a year, making his income off of the gifts he gets from these people?

There is also the critical ethnographic question of the relationship between the academy itself and sexual economies. When I first began presenting my research at conferences and universities, I was initially taken aback by the number of gay male professors who approached me afterward and "came out" as clients of rent boys in Brazil or other countries. Once, on a job interview, several physical scientists confided that my work made them uncomfortable because it led them to realize that they counted a number of sex tourists among their closest friends and colleagues but had never thought to apply this label, finding it incongruous with their Ivy League image and status. Such examples show how the academy is at once part of the world even as it putatively rests above it, observing and studying. On a related note, many of my nonacademic sex tourist interlocutors regularly read academic books on homosexuality, and several made bibliographic recommendations to me or wanted to discuss works by noted scholars of Brazil such as Richard Parker and James Green.

Whether my tourist interlocutors are gay men who read academic books or are academics themselves, it's worth noting that the academy and the knowledge it circulates about other cultures and other forms of sexuality are implicated in the sexual economies I write about. Just as some antiprostitution feminist or evangelical Christian organizations point out that women who sell sex are "somebody's mother, sister, or daughter," I think it's equally important to remember that sex tourists are siblings, parents, sons, daughters, and—as I discovered—sometimes our colleagues and friends. Clients, like sex workers, are fully human despite certain antiprostitution feminist groups that label them predators. So what exactly are these individuals doing and what is this economy in which they participate?

I propose that to help clarify the situation and to understand how to position such disparate sexual experiences as packaged sex tourism in brothels, student study abroad romances occurring across extreme financial difference, and sex for travel or immigration opportunities, one consider sex tourism on a dual-axis scale (fig. 1). On the X axis are exchanges arranged according to how much planning, foresight, or intentionality went into them. Some men purchase packaged tours designed for sex tourists that facilitate or even include commercial sex. Others are surprised to discover how accessible and safe commercial sex in Brazil is and become clients on the spur of the moment. Some may be genuinely surprised when the young woman or man they have spent an evening eating, drinking, and having sex with asks them for money afterward. Such "accidental sex tourists" often have never met a sex worker in the United States and can be shocked precisely because "she didn't *look* like a prostitute" or because "he looked like he enjoyed it."[29] It's especially common for gay tourists who think they are cruising for sex in public areas such as certain parks—where poor and often-closeted married local men cruise—to find themselves asked for money afterward even though the local men may regularly cruise other Brazilians for noncommercial sex. The lower-class Brazilian men simply expect a donation when they hook up with a gringo. In this research, I include such men who pay someone with a cash "gift" and those who ask for such a gift under my elastic definitions of "accidental

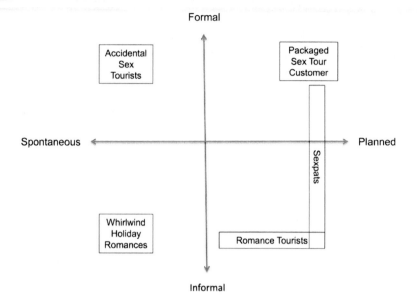

FIGURE 1   Structure and intention of sexual tourism

sex tourists" and "occasional sex workers" even though these terms are imprecise.

On the Y axis, one must consider how formalized the exchange is. Direct negotiations of specific fees for specific services (oral sex, anal sex, kissing, etc.) are at the top of the Y axis. Informal exchange (gifts, fancy meals, etc.) rests at the bottom of this axis.

Such ambiguities concerning sex, money, intentionality, and formality make it very difficult to study the question of sex tourism. It's even harder to study *gay* sex tourism because intentionality can be difficult to gauge. For some young men, selling sexual services isn't a very lucrative option, but it provides them with a more socially acceptable path for exploring same-sex erotic desire. That is, as long as money is changing hands, the guy has an excuse for his homosexual conduct. So if a young man does a programa or two while questioning his sexuality, is it useful to categorize him as a sex worker? There are also many young people who are questioning their sexuality and, as a result of this, are thrown out of their homes and families. These young people often turn to prostitution or transactional sex. Many men I met sell sex only to supplement their income when unexpected medical costs or special occasions like a loved one's birthday arise. Others work only during the high tourist season around *carnaval*, when they can make the most money. And some men I know form long-term relationships with gay tourists, introducing them to their families and sometimes even asking them to be their children's godparents (which carries special financial responsibilities). This kind of relationship, based on an open secret, creates a strikingly queer transnational family portrait. It also reminds us of another complexity: that of affective and emotional connections. In the work that follows, I untangle some of the complex threads of these and other relationships, but ultimately they resist firm categorization.

Structure of the Book

This book draws heavily from data collected in Rio de Janeiro, but in my last two chapters I focus specifically on the Amazon and Bahia respectively. In each of the three main sites, there is a distinct group of gay tourists whose participation in sexual economies reifies foreigners' conceptions of Brazilianness. Each site targets a different racial group (as defined by the tourists) and commissions a performance of a certain type of masculinity. Brazilians often describe their country as a racial democracy, emphasizing the historical importance and contributions of the three main racial groups—white, black, and Indian—to patrimony. Almost all government-sanctioned displays of nationalism— from public service announcements to the opening ceremonies of the World Cup—conspicuously include a member from each of these groups. This much-vaunted triumvirate is central to the racial mythology of Brazil. I likewise investigate the role of these racial figures in Brazil but seek to examine their symbolic and affective weight within the country's sexual economy so that the racialized performances of masculinity and productions of intimacy found therein may deepen understandings of gender in the political economy of Brazil.

In the next chapter, "Hustle and Flows," I develop my theory of performative labor as a way of understanding the work that goes on in sex industries, as well as in tourist economies in general, looking mainly at the lives of garotos in and out of Rio's *saunas*. I position sexual labor as performative, not only in the sense of requiring the labor of producing particular emotional states and/or affective responses, but because the sexual labor I discuss in this work requires the performance of race-based and class-based masculinities.

In chapter 2, "Typecasting," I focus on the role of race and the discourses and idioms that allow tourists to talk "around" race and reframe racialization. I then link garotos' responses and experiences of racialization to questions of exploitation and resistance while cautioning against academic tendencies to romanticize performances of resistance.

Chapter 3, "TurboConsumers™ in Paradise," is a case study drawing mainly on data from Rio de Janeiro and focusing on clients who fetishize Brazilianness and the garotos' heterosexual masculinity for its difference even while they ultimately try to convert the men to "egalitarian" sexual identity models or coax them into admitting they feel desire for the client so that the garotos can be rehabilitated into suitable boyfriends. These clients espouse the idea that gay travel is good for gays globally and that their participation in Brazil's sexual economy is beneficial for the garotos.

In Chapter 4, "Godfather Gringos," I continue to explore the idea of beneficence as I examine gay gringos who become the boyfriends of Brazilian rent boys. I argue that these men are forming transnational kinship systems that the state could never have anticipated but these kinds of families may not be as new or as foreign as they first seem.

In Chapter 5, "Ecosex," I examine how, in the Amazonian city of Manaus, ecotourists stop over on their way into the rain forest while businessmen come to oversee their company's interests in the country's only free-trade zone. While the ecosex economy there is nascent and nowhere near the size of sex tourism industries in Rio, the case reveals how the sexualization of indigeneity—through Las Vegas–style renditions of folk dances, tourist opportunities to pose for photographs with naked Indians, and reality TV's strangely homoerotic search for indigenous masculinity—allows ecotourists to construct false memories of their encounters as beneficial to local people and even as helping to save the rain forest.

In Chapter 6, "Sex Pilgrims," I turn my attention to Bahia. Here, African American gay men engage in diaspora or heritage tourism, visiting slave museums, attending Afro-Brazilian *candomblé* rituals, and watching displays of the Afro-Brazilian dance/martial art of *capoeira*. Sex with Afro-Brazilian garotos becomes just one more facet of a much larger experience, but I also examine the ways that Bahia stands in metonymically for Africa, how Africanness serves as the foundation for a certain type of valorized masculinity (revealing that colonial tropes of black masculinity are still at work), and how garotos feel about their role in this touristic search for Africa.

Throughout this book, I describe the packaging of desire for commercial ends. In each site, there is a distinct group of gay tourists whose participation in the sexual economies reifies foreigners' conceptions of Brazilianness. The performances of racialized masculinity that collectively compose the sexual economy of Brazil can create many pressures and challenges for the garotos, but these performances are important in an economy with ever-increasing diversification of sexual labor. The labor market in question is expanding both in high-end, formalized venues and also through informalization as occasional prostitution and quasi-commercial sex work become an everyday tactic for making ends meet. But this mode of commissioned performances is also familiar. In fact, the tourist industry has already commissioned performances of Brazilianness from everyone who works in or around the tourist industry and who has learned how to interact with foreigners, and in this book I ultimately press at the boundaries of sex work and sexual economies to argue that the production of intimacy and the maintenance of racialized desire are integral to tourist economies more broadly. In so doing, I position desire as a form of affect that must be understood as both transnational and culturally specific. Within this sexual economy, buyers and sellers must make desire in its myriad forms legible to one another through the performative register. Although these affective flows are complex and refractive, by examining them one can better understand how political and economic changes play out in embodied ways in the everyday lives of these men who construct, maintain, and perform racialized masculinity in order to make their living.

ONE

Hustle and Flows: Commissioned Masculinities and Performative Labor

From the beginning, I had become aware of overtures of defensive derision aimed by some scores [of clients] at those youngmen [*sic*] they picked up for the very masculinity they would later disparage—as if convinced, or need-fully proclaiming their conviction, that the more masculine the hustler, the more his masculinity is a subterfuge.   JOHN RECHY, *CITY OF NIGHT*

Repertoires of Masculinity

"My first time wasn't hard at all," Cavi explains, nibbling at a doughy ball of fried cod. He comes from a smaller city in the interior, and he's much more shy than Adilson, who talks and smokes constantly.[1] Cavi continues, "See, I got [*peguei*, "hooked up with"] a client who wasn't very old, so it was easy. He was thirty-five. Since I have to do this job, it's better when the ass is good-looking [*bonitinha*]."

Adilson interrupts him to explain. "We all say this: *se a bunda é bonitinha, novinha é uma coisa.*" Very roughly, this means that if the ass looks good, it's a much differ-ent matter. "Look, if *you* have a young woman and a very old woman, the young one will still be better. If a *gay* had to choose between these women, which would he choose?

It's the same for *heteros*. The *boys* [male sex workers] just don't want to talk about this."

Adilson admits that not everyone can stir up and maintain *tesão*—which is a particularly hard word to translate but roughly means "sexual desire." One can "give" tesão, so it also has the sense of making someone "horny," or sexually aroused. It can also be used to specifically separate out desire from other affective responses, as in "*É feio, mas me dá tesão*" (He's ugly, but he turns me on). So while tesão is frequently invoked throughout Brazil in daily speech, it has a special usefulness for many garotos when they talk about their work.[2] Some heterosexually identified garotos need to look at straight porn to feel tesão; others close their eyes and imagine the client is a woman. Many take knock-off versions of Viagra such as Pramil, which they say can cause terrible headaches, high blood pressure, irritability, and a throbbing penis. *Saunas* are filled with urban legends about *boys* who took too much Pramil only to have the heads of their penises explode or, as one young man excitedly told me about a *boy* he knew of, "a vein burst in the penis [so that] blood flowed like a waterfall until he died." Adilson, however, says Pramil "saved the *boys*" because Viagra was expensive and had to be broken into tiny pieces. But he never uses it, he insists. He can stir up tesão without it.

"If it's a young guy," Adilson explains, "he gives me tesão, but with an old flabby man [*velho todo caído*] . . . ooooh, that's more difficult." He makes a disgusted face.

Cavi nods enthusiastically in agreement. They're best friends. He looks up to Adilson and, I suspect, has a little bit of a crush on him. Later, Cavi will reveal that he once had sex with a client he liked for free, an admission that earned derision from Adilson. But for now, Adilson is holding court: "When the *boy* is there with an ass in front of him and a job to do, it's luckier to get a hot ass like Cavi did on his first time. Because, oh, my first time was horrible! I got this Danny DeVito type. He was American, really short and fat. Holy shit! [*Cruz credo!*] It was horrible, oh horrible, but I made a lot of money . . ." He trails off in raucous laughter that goes on so long that it becomes infectious and we laugh with him.

"So what did your mother say when you came home with all that money?" I asked, catching my breath.

"I tell my mother, my family, everything," Adilson said. "I have no secrets. . . . She understands, and accepts it now. It is better than if I became a thief. . . . She knows everything. She met my *gringo*. . . . My gringo even pays for her diabetes and came to see her in the hospital." Adilson talks about his gringo a lot, sometimes disparagingly or even homophobically and sometimes with affection. But he almost never uses the man's name. He is simply "my gringo" or "the gringo" and sometimes "the *bicha*" (the queer).

Cavi shakes his head. "Not me! My mother would die. I tell her I am a waiter. Other garotos, the beefy ones [*fortões*], they tell their mothers they are security guards. I hide the money, only give her what she needs to pay the bills. Sometimes, you have a lot of money, and she sees you with sneakers, maybe, but if she suspects she does not say anything. . . . Like in the beginning . . . you get a lot of money when you're new and you're fresh meat [*carne nova*], so then everything's coming up roses [*é flores*; literally, "it's flowers"]."

"Yes!" Adilson says, trampling over the end of Cavi's sentence. "I knew a *boy* who made 500 reais [USD (2009) 300] and spent it all on champagne! Champagne! He said tomorrow he would just make it all back again. He thinks every day is King's Day and forgets there are lean times, too [*vacas magras*, "skinny cows"]. One day you're a king, but the next you're a pauper. In six months, you're just like everybody else. . . . This is why you need to find a rich gringo, like me."

Cavi rolled his eyes. "So if you're sick, you're in bed, sick with the flu, are you going to start waiting for some client from the *sauna* to come there and give you medicine? They don't want to know about you. A gringo wants you when you're a nice, hot, young *boy*. When you're sick? When you get old and you're not pretty anymore? 'Fuck you!' [*Foda-se!*] That's what he's going to say to you."

Adilson is uncharacteristically quiet for a moment. He seems to be pondering this, possibly having a moment of doubt about his own gringo. Several years later, his gringo did leave him, in fact, and Adilson was sadder and wiser the last time I saw him, but neither of us could know that then as he sat there contemplating Cavi's admonition over his cigarettes and bar snacks.

"So what *does* a gringo want?" I ask. "Everyone in the *sauna* I see is young and handsome, but some guys make much more. Is it just the size of their dicks or how many *programas* [sessions with a client] they can do?"

Adilson is happy to change the subject. "No, look, when you're well-endowed [*bem dotado*], when you have a big penis [*pênis bem grande*], it's more difficult for you to get it erect [*ereto*] and keep it hard when you put it in [*botar ele duro*]. Yours is normal, right?" he asks Cavi.

"Yeah," Cavi confirms simply.

"So in your case, it's not as difficult to maintain [an erection]."

Cavi concedes, nodding, and decides to go along with Adilson's theory of biology.

Adilson continues his lecture: "Look, some customers want a big penis, but Cavi makes as much money, and his penis is normal. . . . But customers in the *sauna* want affection, and he is very good at that. But they also want *homens* ["men," meaning straight men]. The *boy* should have the *postura* [manner] of an *homem*, and we do have *gayzinhos* [little gays] now who work as *boys* sometimes, but like it or not, when a gay *boy* takes a step, he looks like a model on a catwalk." Adilson shakes his head in disgust at this image. "The *hetero* is different from the bicha, the postura is different, everything is different. Clients want a manly guy, but many need a lot of *carinho* [affection], too. So it's difficult. . . . But then there are some [clients] who call for a lot of *pegada* [swagger, a forceful and macho approach]. And they are like women, they go crazy for pegada, . . . and a *boy* needs to learn how to do all these things if he is going to keep working and be successful."

Adilson and Cavi's conversation encapsulates many pressing aspects of my research. Questions of desire loom large: How does one find tesão? How can it be maintained? Can you trick yourself into feeling it? How do garotos feel emotionally about clients and long-term "boyfriends"? How do they make sense of their own sexuality? The passage also demonstrates how much performance is happening here: the performance that goes into creating a long-term double life to lie about to one's family; the performances that go into navigating the relationship with one's gringo; the performances of masculinity and pegada that go into "catching" clients in a *sauna*, as well as sexual performance (maintaining erections) and the caresses, kisses, and words that make up the realm of carinho.

Beyond the large amount of physical and emotional labor going into these performances, a lot of the work also deals with hard-to-translate feelings and intangibles like tesão, posturas, pegada, and carinho. These are good examples of culturally specific *affects*, and this chapter is devoted to understanding what these affects are as well as how affect and labor shape the performance of masculinity among garotos both historically and in the present day. However, it's also important to understand how performative labor shapes tourist-based economies on the whole and why the garotos choose to continue engaging in performative labor rather than the other kinds of jobs available to them.

In theorizing sex work as performative labor, I'm strategically (even if only partially) disentangling it from affective labor, a mode of analysis focused on the work of provoking feelings that emerge prior to an individual's consciousness. Sex work certainly includes affective labor in that the garotos' performances are intended to elicit affects in clients such as desire, attraction, and even love. Moreover, affective labor and performative labor clearly overlap inasmuch as performances of masculinity are part of the process of stirring up affect and both are important for garotos, but there are moments where the analytic of the performative is better for ethnographers who want to address particular relational questions of identity.

I describe the work of prostitutes as *performative* because their success or failure depends on constructing certain styles of gender that are often rooted in neocolonial variations of archetypes such as the lusty *mulata*, the Latin *macho*, the hypersexual masculine black buck (and the dangerous thug from the *favela*, or slum, its contemporary corollary), the suave Latin lover, and so on. Calling masculinity *performative* doesn't necessarily mean that the men are consciously constructing their masculinity, or that they are inventing characters for themselves to play as if in the theater, although both of these maneuvers are actually quite common. Instead, as Judith Butler has famously said, "Gender is the repeated stylization of the body, a set of repeated acts within a highly rigid regulatory frame that congeal over time to produce the appearance of substance, of a natural sort of being." In Butlerian terms, the garotos' masculinity is real only to the extent that it is performed, and their performance is always a reiteration of dominant conventions available in a society's repertoire of masculinities, but there is no real, authentic, or original version of such a masculinity. Moreover, as Butler notes, "the appearance of substance is precisely that, a constructed identity, a performative accomplishment which the mundane social audience, including the actors themselves, come to believe and to perform in the mode of belief."[3]

When I first began doing ethnographic work in *saunas*, the particular shape of masculinity there surprised me precisely because it was so over-the-top that it came close to parody and therefore always seemed to call its own authenticity into question. The men were so muscular, so quick to assert their heterosexuality and status as dominant tops, and so deliberately and stereotypically butch in their gestures and walk that it reminded me of drag king shows. Researchers and clients alike have often remarked that masculinity is to the garoto what femininity is to *travesti* sex workers.[4] The essential (and even stereotypical) features of the gender being performed are rendered so completely that they become exaggerations and collapse away from the perfection of the ur-form by virtue of their proximity to it. Whereas travesti sex workers inject silicone to enhance their backsides and breasts into an almost inhumanly perfect shape and size so they can be "better than women," garotos adopt a hypermacho walk, demeanor, and body.

For example, Pacu was a twenty-six-year-old light-skinned garoto who worked in a *sauna* in Rio. Pacu, whose telltale nickname refers to a species of fish that has a peculiar underbite and is related to the piranha, had such bulging neck and shoulder muscles that he seemed to have difficulty turning his head from side to side. He kept his torso waxed to make sure every rippling abdominal muscle was visible from a maximum distance, but because of the thick, coarse hair on his arms and legs, he seemed to have been naturally hairy otherwise. Although studious in the maintenance of his persona as a "total top" and prolific in his frequent use of mildly homophobic epithets lobbed at clients, staff, and fellow garotos alike, he was more fastidious in his grooming than nearly any garoto I met. He kept his hair perfectly coifed and liberally gelled, ran to the locker room to pluck any stray chest hair that he discovered he had missed, and enjoyed frequent pedicures to stave off damage from the famously grimy and broken cobblestoned streets of Rio that are so at odds with the Brazilian love of flip-flops. Beyond merely being metrosexual or attentive to grooming practices, Pacu tried to embody masculinity, yet his need to conspicuously showcase that masculinity resulted in practices that were not stereotypically masculine.

Pacu's *bofedade* (butchness) was so artificial that he complained that whenever he went to other businesses near the *sauna*, he stood out among the other working-class men, whose masculinity seemed natural and effortless next to Pacu's. The shopkeepers would treat Pacu rudely or give him poor service "because they see my body and they know I'm a *boy* and they think that this makes me low class." Alternatively, he worried that they "might treat me badly because they think I'm a bicha because I do this work. But they don't know I'm a real man [*homem*] so I would never give my ass." He constantly compared himself to other garotos in the *sauna* as well, worrying that someone else was bigger, tougher, more masculine, or more attractive. Just as the clients find themselves in a paradox of queer desire, so too did Pacu find that the cruel optimism of masculinity meant that the more he strived to attain the ultimate bofedade, the more it slipped away because it just isn't manly to worry so much about manliness. Still, Pacu never wanted for clients, who found in him a macho and avowedly straight guy with rough and not even conventionally attractive features, someone who overcompensated for his insecurities with homophobia but who kept himself in flawless physical condition.

For garotos, though, the performative labor that goes into producing a macho persona with a lot of pegada, or swagger, is something that must become naturalized if they are to succeed in this career. For example, for Renato and Washington, two cousins who were both *carioca* garotos (*carioca* refers to a person from Rio de Janeiro) in their early twenties, life in the *sauna* was largely about figuring out how to attract clients. Sitting beside the beach late one night in Copacabana, Renato, who had been selling sex since he was fifteen, explained how he moved through the *sauna* and how walking was important. "In the *sauna*, I'm always walking from one side to the other casually, but also moving a lot so that I can always be looking to see if a tourist is watching me a lot—especially tourists, because they pay more than Brazilians." As many of the garotos would later explain to me, walking was important because it separated real men from any gayzinhos who might be trying to work in the *sauna*. Gayzinhos might work out and even have a lot of muscle, but their feminine walks—as Adilson was fond of asserting— always betrayed them as gay and, therefore, less desirable.

Washington nodded in agreement. Washington had first penetrated a *bicha* in his favela neighborhood for money at the age of twelve, later entering the sex trade full time when Renato brought him to the *sauna* two years ago. "[Unlike tourists,] more Brazilians are married gays, closeted, who have to go to the *sauna*. So I try to call the tourists to me first . . . with a look, or a nod, or a gesture. Each person has his own method, but mine works for me. I exchange glances and now it is like a ritual, to tell you the truth; . . . it's totally normal now." Washington, I notice, has stunning green eyes, lightly tanned skin, naturally toned muscles, and a perpetual puppy dog look that is only slightly diminished by the fact his eyes are often bloodshot from his marijuana smoking. He fits into the smooth, boyish "twink" type much more so than he does a "macho daddy." His particular method of "calling" tourists to him was probably well chosen and no doubt helped him to become successful enough that the stream of steady clients could make work in the *sauna* become regular.

Commissioned Performances and Racialization

Gender performativity refers to the conscious and unconscious aspects of an individual's self-presentation, and so encompasses the entire process of the garotos' gender performance, including tactics like walking the floors and all the less conscious cultural markers of masculinity, such as internalizing and emulating the kind of macho pegada one sees in telenovelas. These presentations are all part of gender *performances*, but to call them "performative" means they are aspects of a greater *performativity*, or phenomenological structure, that includes all the contexts, circumstances, and conditions that make these performances. Thus, "performative" is a much more theoretically rich analytic than simply talking about one particular "performance," which can be a simplistic mode of analysis that quickly stretches the usefulness of the concept.

Deborah Cameron and Don Kulick make a parallel distinction with two terms that are also related to performance and performativity and that help to illuminate this definition: "identity" versus "identification." They write, "Identification is a psychoanalytic concept concerned with the operations through which a subject is constituted. Identifications are processes through which individuals assimilate an aspect or property of an other, and are, in that process, transformed." They go on to clarify, "A crucial difference between 'identity' and 'identification' is that identifications are not entirely conscious. On the contrary, identifications are structured just as much by rejections, refusals, and disavowals as they are by affirmations."[5]

For Cameron and Kulick, identifications are not harmonious. A person's identity can be disrupted by processes of identification of which he or she isn't even conscious. Just as Cameron and Kulick distinguish between identity and identification, one can also distinguish between the social construct "race" and processes of "racialization," bearing in mind that "racialization" accounts for the complicated and sometimes-contradictory processes of a subjectivity that is always in the process of coming into being within a particular cultural matrix. It's for this reason that throughout this book I refer to "racialized" masculinities of the garotos rather than "raced masculinities," which would imply a static and unified subject. For tourists, garotos' "exotic" Latin character is part of their allure, and this is built into popular discourses about the hypersexuality of men of color and the perception of Brazilian sexual excesses that circulates in the media through endless depictions of bacchanalian carnival celebrations and Brazil's prolific porn industry.

It's necessary to understand the performativity of garoto masculinity as far more than the simple imitation of stereotypes by garotos; rather, it should be seen as a process of performing certain gender and sexual identifications that are also racialized. This understanding allows us to see how garoto performances of masculinity are not at all "natural." Rather, garotos' performances of racialized masculinity are actually shaped by gay clients' eroticization of straight men and macho masculinity. This is an example of a *commissioned performance* of masculinity in which economic incentivization structures and guides the contours of idealized gender presentations available in a given culture's repertoire of masculinity. The end result is that the garotos' masculinity consists of a lot of macho straight men trying to perform a version of straight masculinity constructed and desired by gay men.

The *performativity* of gender and race includes all these processes of identification and racialization, as well as how race and gender are intricately bound together—an intersection especially visible in sexual economies. It's also useful to consider a subject's gender performativity as more than just one gender performance that exists in a given social context and instead as a series of possible performances. Diana Taylor conceives of the "repertoire" as enacting "embodied memory: performances, gestures, orality, movement, dance, singing—in short, all those acts usually thought of as ephemeral, nonreproducible knowledge."[6] That is, the repertoire consists of the phenomenological attributes of a particular subject as stored in the body as opposed to text, or what she calls the "archive." The garotos have a *repertoire of masculinities,* and their performativity includes this entire repertoire of fully and semideveloped racialized characters with different *nomes de guerra* ("street names"; literally, "names of war"), favorite stories and their many variations, and particular embodiments and ways of being and moving in the world depending upon the specific clients and sexual environments they are in. As in Adilson's advice at the beginning of this chapter in which he described affecting a butch postura, performing competently and succeeding in the industry means cultivating a repertoire of masculinity and drawing from it effectively, whether consciously or not.

Male sex workers have a distinct and highly visible repertoire of masculinities from which to draw. They can be very muscular or lean and toned, but bofedade, or butchness, is paramount in all of them. The *sauna boy* is clean-cut, well-groomed, and affable. He may alternate between his use of pegada (swagger) and carinho (affection), but he is ultimately service oriented and wants to please his clients. *Michês* (hustlers) working on the streets have to be tough. They can be exploited by clients or police. They may also deal drugs or engage in petty theft, and they may have violent run-ins with each other. But their tough persona and lack of emotional availability is also part of their allure. And under the right circumstances they can become a rescue project for a client. Consequently, some enterprising michês have performed their own reformation multiple times and extracted money and benefits from multiple patrons. The repertoire breaks down along racial lines, with lighter-skinned *boys* more likely to become projects for a client's rehabilitation efforts, a phenomenon the sociologist Kerwin Kaye has also observed in the United States.[7] In respect to such Pygmalion-like scenarios in which a client introduces a garoto to a better life, furthers his education, and provides travel opportunities and new cultural experiences, darker-skinned garotos were more likely to be stigmatized and perceived as too dangerous to take on as pet projects.

I am not the first to allude to the performative nature of prostitution in Brazil. Public health scholars Rubens de Camargo Ferreira Adorno and Geraldo Pereira da Silva Junior describe competence at "performance" as central to the success of michês in the state of São Paulo. These competencies include coded forms of walking, speaking, gesticulating, and dressing in order to be legible to clients, and they note that the men sort themselves into both social hierarchies and territories on the basis of performative competence, so that lower-performing men are relegated to darker parts of the street.[8]

In a chapter entitled "A prostituição como espetáculo" (Prostitution as spectacle), Margareth Rago describes the presence of prostitutes in public as "a fixture, but less an empirical figure, endowed with flesh and blood, than as an identity to be established in terms of enunciation." She likens the prostitute to a *fantasma* (ghost) that "erupt[s] from the depths of the unknown feminine body as a possible danger that could inhabit the sexuality of all women."[9] Rago's analysis is in keeping with Taylor's definition of "repertoire." The prostitute fantasma is part of a repertoire of femininity available to all Brazilian women, and it is precisely through her apparition, her newfound widespread iterability, her haunting of polite society, that she becomes a threat to gendered social relations. However, I argue that the male prostitute represents another kind of performative danger: the homoerotic potential of even putatively macho males. Just as Rago argues that the figure of the prostitute is a version of performative femininity that any woman might access within herself, the hustler as a figure contains within himself a great and threatening potentiality—a dangerous thread in the repertoire of masculinity that can likewise inhabit the sexuality of all men.

In contemporary Brazilian sociology, Lucia Rabello de Castro has examined consumer culture as a mode of performance among the country's poor, urban youth to analyze the types of gendered roles available. Some girls transform into the figure of the *crente* to gain legitimacy, respect, and the ability to move unhindered through public spaces. The crente is a born-again evangelical Christian with a recognizable and conservative manner of dress and bodily comportment. Other youth perform identities through performative consumerism, seeing it as a "mode of inclusion" in society, achieving "short-term gains that narrow down prospective visions of the self." That is, in the absence of substantive and promising educational and work-related opportunities, the country's urban poor turn to other forms of expression (e.g., consumerism, *baile funk* music) to force their participation upon society. De Castro argues that they don't always do this in the creative or subversive ways that these forms allow, but rather, they may present themselves in a "depleted" form and take up "consumer values and ideology in a monolithic way faced with the dearth of other narratives and discourses that can mediate the impact of consumerism." For example, they buy fashionable clothes they cannot afford in order to hide their poverty, move unpoliced through public space, and distance themselves from their nonconsuming peers and family members. "Accordingly, ideals and moral expectations based on values such as self-renouncement, collective realizations above individual ones, compassion and solidarity seem to go in the counter-current of the established consumerist *modus vivendi.*"[10]

The garotos from Rio I know are mostly from very poor neighborhoods in the Zona Norte area of Rio, but some also come from the favelas. Very few have bank accounts, and as Adilson and Cavi alluded to above, garotos often spend their newfound cash on alcohol, drugs, expensive clothes, and electronics. Like de Castro's interlocutors, the garotos I know think that dressing in knockoff designer clothes or carrying expensive cell phones will earn them acceptance and respect. Yet the garotos are dismayed when they are treated badly by local businesses and are denied service, stigmatized, and derided as troublemakers— which is especially vexing because so many entered prostitution precisely because they did *not* want to become thieves, drug dealers, or gang members. The elitist adage goes: *dinheiro não compra classe* (money doesn't buy class). And in the case of garotos, they feel this acutely. The men find they still lack the proper bodily comportment, dialect, diction, and knowledge of current discourse necessary for "respectable" forms of masculinity. Stigma persists. This embodied part of the repertoire of masculinity that requires so much cultural capital is incomplete. In their own experience of queer paradox, the very performances of hypermasculinity that call tourists and other clients to them repel society's more respectable members.

The Evolution of Hustler Masculinity

Hypermasculine garotos working the beaches, *saunas*, and streets are an essential part of gay tourism's investments, but they are also a relatively new figure in the sexual landscape of Brazil. James Green has documented the rise of *putos* (male prostitutes) in mid-nineteenth-century Brazil, but these were often effeminate men, sometimes wearing articles of women's clothing, and served as passive partners for masculine men.[11] By the late nineteenth century, the figure of the *fanchano*—a masculine and penetrative man whose primary interest is the effeminate male—emerged as a distinct type known within the homosexual underworld.[12] It's at this time that the medical establishment began to divide men who have sex with men into those who were *ativo* (active), *passivo* (passive), or *misto* (mixed, here meaning versatile). Most ativos were soldiers, businessmen, and artists, while prostitutes were passivo and apparently charged less than women did, which medical researchers assumed to be their allure. Thus, the ativo was merely desperate and poor, not actually desirous and not properly homosexual.

By the mid-twentieth century there were middle- or upper-class *tias* (aunties; effeminate older gay men) as well as bofes, or masculine men who sometimes made themselves sexually available to tias and other bichas (homosexuals). The bofe is the clearest direct antecedent to the contemporary garoto, a lineage that stretches from the predictatorship years through the entirety of the military regime (1964–85) and through the economic tumult of the 1990s and then the booming "age of the BRICs"[13] in the 2000s. In those early days, some tias were wealthy enough to support bofes as kept men. The bofes of that time didn't self-identify as michês or garotos, but some were certainly engaged in a form of sexual labor. It's difficult to say whether and how kept bofes experienced desire, pleasure, or love with the tias who kept them long term or with lower-class bichas, who might have kept them for shorter periods. Certainly, there are gay Brazilians who regard bofes today simply as butch, closeted gay men who had the luxury of passing and who denied their true selves by pursuing relationships with or marrying women. But this allegation ignores the complexity and fluidity of sexual identity and sidesteps uncomfortable questions about relationships between sex and economic security. Not surprisingly, this is the same allegation that many gay tourists make about michês and garotos today: that they are merely butch gay men who are in denial and sell sex in order to rationalize their same-sex desires.

41

As Brazilian gay subculture continued to grow in the late 1960s and early 1970s, it did so despite the country's military dictatorship. By the early 1970s, michês flooded downtown areas in both Rio de Janeiro and São Paulo,[14] receiving press coverage largely focused on the possibility of murder and theft at the hands of michês, a trend that continues in media coverage of both michês and travesti sex workers.

The few scholars who have studied male hustlers have made frequent references to hustling's performative dimensions, and my own work expands on this theme. From 1982 to 1985, Néstor Perlongher—a poet and radical activist who fled Argentina's much bloodier military dictatorship—conducted field research among michês in São Paulo in preparation for his master's thesis in anthropology at Brazil's prestigious university UNICAMP. The thesis eventually became the only book-length study of hustling, titled O negócio do michê (The business of the hustler).[15] Perlongher was an intriguing character best remembered for his provocative and surreal poetry, which grew increasingly mystical after he moved to the Amazon and began taking the powerful hallucinogen ayahuasca with devotees of the drug cult Santo Daime before dying of AIDS in 1991. Perlongher considered both condoms and Anglo-style gay identity to be an apparatus of the state intended to control and discipline desire and the body, and he was sexually and intellectually enamored of the michês he studied, whose behavior pushed the boundaries of sexual identity.[16]

While Perlongher's work provides a baseline understanding of michetagem in the early 1980s, he also expanded the boundaries of ethnography in several ways. His surreal poetry was another form of ethnographic epistemology, and it is likely that the bodies of his interlocutors were as well. No stranger to theories of performance, Perlongher was a disciple of Antonin Artaud's Theatre of Cruelty, and as such he perceived humiliation and suffering as having divine qualities and as sources of revelation. While his methods were unconventional, he wrote performatively, echoing his much-beloved Deleuze as he drifted with his readers "around the streets—and [moved] down—in terms of income, class, legal position, and physically onto the street, down into nightclub basements or public toilets—into the city."[17]

For Perlongher, michês are nomads, circulating along customary paths from point to point, client to client, always reaching a point in order to leave it behind rather than to dwell. It is in the state of cruising—when betwixt and between points—that he feels the michê is best understood. This instability allows the michê to remain a mercurial and romantic figure for Perlongher, and so it is difficult to say how the famed poet-anthropologist would have theorized the great migration of michês indoors, where they have become increasingly static and nonnomadic.

Shortly after Perlongher published his work on michês in São Paulo, another, more practical project emerged. In the late 1980s and 1990s, as Brazil succumbed to astronomical inflation rates that crippled the country, Projeto Pegação, a small group of five men led by a young social worker named Paulo Longo, began doing outreach work with street michês. Longo reports that his group was almost solely responsible for introducing and normalizing condom use among michês, who quickly adapted to them.[18] Projeto Pegação worked exclusively with men on the street, although in the late 1990s gay tourism in Rio became increasingly focused on indoor *sauna* prostitution, which was far safer for all parties, more convenient, and generally free from police harassment. Whereas Perlongher conceived of michês as continually remaking their own meaning, Longo knew that AIDS was drastically reconfiguring all aspects of the michês' lives and worlds.[19]

By 2000, prostitutes were increasingly moving indoors and catering to a growing number of gay tourists, who mingled among the majority local clientele. As gay tourism became a recognizable and sought-after niche industry on a global scale, gay tourists in Brazil came to be seen as the most lucrative clients. Those tourists willing to pay for sexual services directly tend to prefer the relative safety and the relaxed social environment of *saunas*.

Having experienced rampant inflation, Brazil has always been a nation of consumers rather than savers, but the Brazilian consumer class is spending as never before.[20] When I speak to michês and garotos now, even the poorest describe what they'd like to purchase next. They imagine themselves in various scenarios as wealthy playboys, as kept men traveling the world, or as fine upstanding men reinserted into their own families and communities as honorable businessmen. One street hustler in Bahia, Carlinhos, desperately wanted to start a kiosk from which he would sell magazines, but he could never manage to save the money. "First I will begin to sell fruit. . . . I'll get out of this life, and someday in the future I will sell magazines. I'll go home and take my mother away from my stepfather and buy her a big house that makes her friends jealous. . . . I'll buy myself a car and I'll take girls to the clubs and get them nice things. . . . But right now I need to do this [sell sex]."

As Carlinhos's aspirations show, the upside to this turn toward conspicuous consumerism and performative spending is a renewed sense that there *is* a hopeful future, or even that there is to be a future at all. This is an interesting development because research among michês in Rio de Janeiro carried out in the early 1990s by social workers from Projeto Pegação revealed a consistent hopelessness, an apathy toward sexual and personal health and hygiene, and a belief that their lives would be violently foreshortened by forces far beyond their control, including death at the hands of parents or police or through starvation. Such hopelessness was so pervasive that the government officially recommended de-emphasizing the lethality of AIDS in outreach work. Ana Filgueiras, director of the Brazilian Center for the Defense of the Rights of Children and Adolescents, explained: "Equating AIDS and death can blunt a campaign's effectiveness. If you say 'AIDS kills,' [they say] 'it's just another thing to kill us. The police kill us, too.' Killing is not serious to them. But if you tell them AIDS makes you very thin and weak, that's something they are afraid of."[21]

While doing archival work, I found original records, including handwritten notes and selected quotations, from dozens of interviews with michês conducted by Projeto Pegação's small staff in the early 1990s. Their interviewees consistently expressed an intention to leave prostitution soon (*mudar de vida em breve*) but also seemed disillusioned about the future. During his third meeting with one michê who worked in Via Ápia, a dangerous area where police and gangs tormented both clients and michês, one social worker wrote that the young man was "feeling the weight of his years" (*sentindo o peso dos anos*) in prostitution because of the "police pressure" (*pressão policial*) he experienced.

Police "pressure" may be an understatement. A short distance from the Via Ápia is Candelária Church, where in 1993, around the time these archived interviews were being done, a death squad of off-duty police and others opened fire on approximately one hundred street children, some of whom were involved in prostitution, who were sleeping on the church's steps. Such death squads were aimed at social cleansing, and in this instance the squad killed eight youths between eleven and twenty years of age in one of Brazil's most infamous historical events. In light of the crippling poverty and harsh living conditions, it is no wonder that the michês at this time described their futures in bleak terms. Rather than envisioning upward mobility, one michê who was interviewed said that his "dream" was to return home to the shacks of his impoverished favela, but he was "afraid of the bandits there" (*medo dos bandidos da favela*).

However, my own subjects are not so pessimistic about the future, instead talking at length about their plans and dreams, imagining elaborate scenarios of luxury, migration, and performative excess. Whether they are garotos de programa working indoors or lower-end and functionally homeless michês working beaches and streets, these men are accessing a middle-class consumerist Brazilian dream in order to imagine their futures, even while remaining marginalized within their communities. Carlinhos imagined himself performing a restored masculinity in which he could rescue his mother, carrying her off to a life of luxury. This form of masculinity was, in his mind, more honorable than the depleted hustler masculinity that he practiced as he worked the streets trying to find clients.

This turn to a hopeful imaginary is not the same as actual upward mobility, of course. Consumerist dreamscapes remain a poor substitute for actual social change, but they do signal a noteworthy shift in the men's affect and relationship to society that is both owed to and circumvented by neoliberalism and the increasing global gay tourist trade even as good jobs are increasingly hard to find for many sex workers amid rising costs of living. That is, late capitalism has taught them to dream in new ways, but at the same time it prevents those dreams from coming true.

Performing Identity across Difference

Perlongher's and Projeto Pegação's work had also coincided with significant advances in gay rights. In the early 1980s the dictatorship loosened its grip and Brazil saw the emergence of many civil rights organizations that emulated those in the United States, including feminist, black power, and gay rights movements.[22] This is also why the term *gay* entered the Portuguese language, where it has essentially the same meaning as in English. The gay rights movement has been largely class based, however, and sexual subjectivities continue to reflect differences in class. Because performative labor requires navigating issues of sexual scrutability and intelligibility across these identity models, it's important to understand the complexity of the models in question.

Poor and rural areas often feature the so-called "Latin model" of homosexuality. In this formation, one's sexual identity is determined by one's active/passive role rather than the gender of one's object choice. So a *normal* (slang, "straight") man can penetrate a gay man or a woman and still be *normal*. In a groundbreaking ethnographic study of same-sex interactions in a nightclub in the low-income periphery of Rio, Leandro de Oliveira describes in great detail the particular rules that make it socially acceptable for young heterosexual men to go to a bar frequented by cross-dressing gays, *bicha-boys* (effeminate gays), travestis, and masculine gay men and the circumstances under which they can engage in certain sex acts with each of these groups. *Normal* men aged eighteen to twenty-five can go to such spaces, but only late at night after drinking and partying. In addition to being drunk, they have the excuse of entering the gay venue because there is free entertainment in the form of heterosexual pornography playing on televisions, and because they will receive free drinks from other clientele and free admission for being real homens (straight men). They may have sex with the most feminine customers such as travestis and effeminate bichas, only resorting to sex with more masculine gays at the end of the night as a last resort or for a bit of money, which inoculates them against stigma. This system in which the homem-bicha is the idealized pairing is consistent with the Latin model.

The effeminate gays and travestis police one another and heap shame and physical abuse on any of their own kind who has sex with a gay man instead of one of these "real men." In Oliveira's study, his interlocutors not only follow the Latin model but militantly, rigidly, and evangelically enforce it as house policy.[23] Performative labor requires enacting masculinity across these different models, strategically shifting between them, and working to render one's self legible to another as a potential sexual partner but also defining the roles and expectations of that sexual encounter.

In more cosmopolitan areas and among more educated classes, it's common to find the so-called "egalitarian model" that's prominent in Europe and North America, in which gay men seek out other gay men for sex and relationships, and both are considered gay regardless of their status as top, bottom, or versatile. Middle- and upper-class gays well versed in the politics and discourses of the gay rights movement in Brazil may deride poor people such as the patrons in Oliveira's study as unenlightened and backward. Yet it would be wrong to assume that the Latin model is simply fading away as people become increasingly exposed to "the West" and "evolve" out of the traditional sexual modes of congress, although that was frequently the thinking of my tourist interlocutors. Multiple forms of same-sex desire and identity exist in Brazil, and men who have sex with men often slide between them. Even in Oliveira's nightclub, the numerous rules and exceptions illustrate that the model is far more complicated than generally realized, making the Latin model more interesting and revealing as an imagined sexual phenomenon than as an actual ontology.

It's also worth noting that the egalitarian model is quickly becoming the norm in Brazil even in poor areas and, in truth, has long existed in Brazil despite North American academics' tendency to foist the label of "Latin homosexuality" onto Brazilians as a way of marking them "non-Western," as Sérgio Carrara and Júlio Assis Simões have forcefully pointed out.[24] The overall trend in Brazil toward adopting cultural signifiers of gay identity as well as the egalitarian, or gay-gay, model (as opposed to the Latin, or homem-bicha, model) is also due at least somewhat to the large number of gay characters on evening telenovelas (which are a national obsession for men and women alike) and movies. The performances on-screen shape actual performances in the everyday realm. Consequently, even in areas where "Latin homosexuality" may exist, Brazilians are keenly aware of the egalitarian model, actively participate in and construct it, and sometimes challenge it, and the two models function simultaneously, often overlapping as men move between them either unconsciously or strategically. The notion of Latin homosexuality also influences heterosexual models and modes of sexual conduct, as Kulick has noted in the case of soccer superstar Ronaldo, "the Phenomenon," who was caught up in a scandal after purchasing sex from three travestis—a case that caused a national conversation about shifting models of Brazilian *heterosexuality*.[25]

Street and beach garotos in Bahia in my study did adhere to Latin homosexuality very strongly, in part because it enables them to make a living without questioning their sexual identity. Garotos in Rio, who make significantly more money than the street hustlers in Bahia and often come from poverty but not total destitution, varied in this regard. Some espoused traditional Latin homosexuality, insisting that any garoto who bottoms is a fag, regardless of whether he did it for money or whether he had noncommercial male sexual partners. They tended to be more open-minded about oral sex, and many describe themselves as *ativo liberal* (liberal tops), meaning that they will perform oral sex but not be *passivo*. Because it could be seen as more intimate and personal than fucking, kissing was sometimes seen as being even more threatening to masculinity.

Those garotos who had been in the life for a few years were more nuanced about sexual identity, however. Many stated that garotos who bottomed were, indeed, gay, no matter how such men self-identified; that exclusive ativos were perfectly *hetero* (heterosexual); but that those who both topped and bottomed (sometimes called *completo*, "complete") were *bi* (bisexual, pronounced "bee"). In this case, *bi* had less to do with whether the man felt desire or chose to have noncommercial sex with other men and was simply an appropriation of the term "bi" into the Latin model. So a garoto with an American boyfriend who would both *comer* ("fuck"; literally, "eat") and would occasionally *dar* ("be fucked"; literally, "give") with his tourist boyfriend and other occasional clients might identify as *bi* even if he was not sexually attracted to both men and women. Still others, mainly those masculine men who bottomed fairly regularly, insisted that no matter how much a garoto bottomed, if they were not attracted to clients, then they were *hetero* or *normal* because they were merely working. These class-inflected models of Latin homosexuality and gay identity come into conflict with one another most obviously in male prostitution precisely because this is one of the few times that middle-class gay-identified Brazilian men interact intimately and at length with lower-class men.

Commissioned Performances

The gay client's fascination with masculine "straight" men is common to both local Brazilian clients and tourists. The heterosexual garotos' performances of masculinity are their attempts to enact the gay fantasy of the macho straight man, which makes the question of "authenticity" important for thinking through the success or failure of their performative labor. Paradoxically, many garotos were highly conscious of their own tactics for constructing hypermasculinity, but they were also essentialists who believed that not everyone could achieve successful performances of masculinity. Adilson explained, "When I was working in the *sauna* as a supervisor, there was a group of garotos de programa who were acting like gay boys [*gayzinhos*], you know? Talking a lot, lots of little gossip [*fofoquinha*]. I went and said, 'Get to work! Break it up! Stop with the faggot stuff [*viadagem*] in this club! Clients come here looking for *men* [*homens*]!' What the fuck?!"

Adilson's anger at the memory was palpable. "Otherwise the *sauna* loses, you know? A client once came to me and said, 'I came looking for men, but there's only faggots [*viados*]!' And then I was ashamed [*E aí a minha cara foi aonde*; literally, "And then my face went to the floor"]. I couldn't respond—because he was right. You can't have that. Everyone loses."

In Adilson's description of his policing of the gayzinhos' poor performances of masculinity in the *sauna*, he highlights the fact that mistakes in performances of masculinity harm the team. This line of reasoning is quite similar to what the sociologist Erving Goffman maintained about presentations of the self in everyday life in his seminal work on dramaturgical sociology in the 1950s. Even though the men are competitors, they must also work together to keep certain "strategic secrets" from tourists, such as the lower pricing available to locals. But the garotos also perform for one another, keeping what Goffman calls "dark secrets" that could damage their impression management, such as the fact that they might bottom. When they are in the garoto locker room, they practice idealization, exaggerating their earnings or their number of girlfriends, in order to prove their sexual stamina, masculinity, and sexual prowess. In so doing, they dominate one another by proxy, finding a pecking order by the sexual subordination of one another by imposing and policing heteronormative frameworks as a defense against the queer positions they occupy.

The rigid policing of garoto masculinity makes performing appropriately an imperative, as Adilson's shaming of the gay garotos shows. Jon McKenzie's *Perform or Else: From Discipline to Performance* begins with the titular demand—lifted from the cover of *Forbes* magazine—and emphasizes that under the rubric of "organizational performance," small cadres of powerful people sometimes have the authority to demand performance.[26] In *Performing Consumers*, Maurya Wickstrom similarly identifies the seductive powers of "magical capitalism" through which corporations like Disney and the American Girl Doll teach consumers, young and old alike, to engage in mimetic performances.[27] For garotos, larger economic factors such as media (telenovelas, pornography), economic shifts, and tourism markets shape their performances of masculinity, but their performative labor is fundamentally interpersonal, and the masculinity in question is what I refer to as a *commissioned performance* incentivized by these political economic considerations.

Those with economic privilege have long commissioned performances and art, including plays, paintings, music, and buildings. When the Brazilian government chased out the residents of Bahia's historic center to rehab it into a pristine and utterly transformed UNESCO World Heritage Site that stripped away its essence along with most of the grit, they demanded that local women selling traditional food purchase traditional "mammy" costumes to lend atmosphere to the touristy area.[28] This was a commissioned performance of race and gender in which the women had to render their specific cultural and gendered figure of the *baiana* (female Bahian) intelligible for tourists in a way that was both exotic and welcoming, strange and familiar. When the Jamaican government began running hospitality training camps to ensure that all locals who interact with tourists knew how to present themselves as smiling, happy, and grateful hosts, this was a commissioned performance.[29] What goes on in a *sauna* or in red-light districts is similar, even if the patron participating in the economic commissioning is the tourist. A comparatively wealthy foreigner pays for particular performances of gender, race, and sexuality. These commissions also include the performance of specific sexual acts. Performers who can play the necessary type, who dress the part, and who demonstrate intimacy do well. As for those who don't perform . . . they fail and they suffer for it.

Authenticity and the Question of Desire

The sociologist Elizabeth Bernstein theorizes commercial sexual exchange as "bounded authenticity," in which sex workers attempt to "manufacture authenticity" and to "simulate—or even produce—genuine desire, pleasure, and erotic interest for their clients," which can be either "surface acting" or "authentic (if fleeting) libidinal and emotional ties with clients."[30] She draws on Dean MacCannell's influential theory of tourism that postulates that tourists bogged down under the artificiality of modern life choose to travel in search of "authenticity" (i.e., "authentic" local cuisine, down-home charm, interactions with local residents, etc.). It makes tourists feel special to know that they have had an experience that is in some way unique, and tourists enjoy feeling as if they have surpassed their role as tourists and made a genuine connection.[31] Katherine Frank's ethnography of strip clubs reaches similar conclusions about the motivations of strip club regulars' pursuit of authentic (if unrealistic) connections with women.[32] Bernstein contends that many sex workers try to genuinely produce pleasure and desire for clients.[33]

Bernstein's theory holds up if one considers the full range of sex work. At the low end of the prostitution hierarchy is the abject stereotype of the "crack whore," of whom little emotional labor is expected and to whom little money is paid. At the other extreme is the high-priced call girl or "kept woman" who serves clients who want "the girlfriend experience." The degree of emotional labor expected and the amount of authenticity generated correlate to payment amount, indicating that emotional labor requires a certain skill set that is then added to other sexual skills and attributes.

The question of tesão raised in the beginning of the chapter illustrates Bernstein's theory. Men must whip up tesão for a client, but the garotos also think about tesão (and their work) as being more than just emotional. Consider the following conversation between two garotos and myself in Bahia about tesão and the Latin model:

João: I am a person who traveled. For me, this belief that any man who is passivo in a programa is a fag [viado] is a prejudice found in the people of the north and northeast [historically poor regions of Brazil]. Because there's this difference in the south and center of the country compared to the northeast and the north, . . . because people there think differently, they know more about the world. People here [in the northeast], they are more misinformed. Down south [in Rio and São Paulo] it's better.

David: Sure, what people here do not understand is this: one situation is you have tesão for another guy, you take pleasure in it. It's another thing if you are a hetero and you do it for money, not for pleasure. But, for example, I can still do a programa with Gregório [the author] because he's good, you are a nice guy, so I'm not going to accept your money because I would be *with* you [i.e., like a boyfriend]—you understand? But I'm still straight [homem]. That's in one's head, see? Each person knows himself, it's not for another to give [trails off].

Gregory: Wait, wait. So you can have tesão for a man and be *hetero*?

David, *thinking a moment*: No. For me, a gay is one who has tesão for another man. If you have tesão for another man, then you are gay.

João: Walking on the street and seeing a man and having tesão, sure. But if you have tesão while fucking [comendo] another man, you aren't gay.

David: But you're talking about the tesão of a hard dick, right [pinto duro, né?]? I would not have tesão for a guy. The dick is different; it stays hard because it is a sexual organ that has to do with touch.

João: But that's tesão. It's still tesão. Do you keep your dick hard with men?

David: Sure.

João, *to me*: That's it! Then he felt tesão. There are many guys who say they do not feel tesão with men, but his dick is hard, you know? That's tesão.

David: But I imagine it's a woman. The penis may rise just as much during relations with a man as with a woman because if a man puts his mouth and the woman puts her mouth, the mouth is going to give the same sensation.

João: But what is tesão? What is tesão, David? You're with a woman, going to a party. Then you don't end up hooking up with her [não estava nem afim de pegar ela], but without a woman you have tesão and so you could hook up with a bicha instead. You still have tesão.

David: Okay. Sure.

João: He felt tesão! He has tesão with men when fucking [*comendo*]!

David: Okay, yes, fine, but I'm only talking about this here with you, because it's between these four walls [*entre quatro paredes*], understand?

In this conversation, the men reach the limits of emotional labor. They know that tesão is important to the exchange, but they are thinking beyond bounded authenticity and are now theorizing an affect for themselves: imagining how the affective energy diverts, when and where in the body it forms, whether it changes its nature once diverted. In his seminal work on sexuality in Brazil, Richard Parker analyzes the importance of tesão: "The notion of tesão breaks down the boundaries that have been built up around the erotic in the world of normal daily life, as sexual meaning becomes both a metaphor and a model for all forms of experience. It is through this notion of tesão, more than any other single construct, that desire invests itself in the excitement of the body."[34]

Parker goes on to note that tesão is felt throughout the entire body but also pools and focuses at sexual organs and erotic regions and includes not only the desires but the physical responses of erections, hardening nipples, the swelling of the clitoris, the moistening of the vagina. Parker's analysis proves apt when considering how João and David describe tesão transforming, moving, but also pooling in the "hard dick." Parker's work also illustrates that tesão, as a culturally specific affect, refers to both the preconscious bodily response and the whole, generalized feeling of desire and excitement throughout the body and mind, collapsing that Cartesian distinction. For David and João, tesão is pulling at their bodies in specific ways, and they are able to redirect the flow of the affect as necessary along different lines of desire, channeling it away from the failed pursuit of a woman and toward a bicha, for example.

Parker doesn't use the language of affect per se but rather builds on John Gagnon and William Simon's idea of "conflicting and contrasting sexual scripts" to analyze the "cultural frames of reference through which sexual meanings are organized" in Brazil that are evident in the "complex stories that Brazilians tell about their formation as a people," including stories about race, "tropical" sensuality, and the "complex cultural elaborations around *carnaval* as an expression of a unique and particular way of approaching the regulation and transgression of sexual desires and practices."[35] Parker in turn shaped the work of Brazilian social scientists interested in the performance of sexuality, such as Vera Paiva's explorations of feminine and masculine sexual scripts to examine power between partners and untangle issues of structure and agency.[36] Positioning my own analysis within this lineage, I read David and João's conversation as illustrating that affect theory must account for cultural specificity, and that ethnographic analysis is a useful heuristic method through which scholars can place such affects within the sexual universe that men like David and João create through what Parker would term "their own performances of interactive or interpersonal scripts as well as their intra-psychic elaboration of desire," noting that this elaboration is "part and parcel of their unique constructions of the self."[37]

In her work on queer phenomenology and affect, Sara Ahmed builds on Althusser's idea of interpellation—or the calling of a subject into existence by hailing them as a particular identity and encouraging them in all sorts of subtle ways to accept the roles they are assigned such that they feel that those roles are natural to them. Ahmed takes up this idea of interpellation in a way that is of special interest to David and João's conversation. For her, complex sets of ideologies and desires summon us along particular lines of direction. One powerful set of such lines that propel our bodies through space in particular directions and that call our subjectivity into existence is the set of lines constituting heteronormativity. Ahmed's lines are performative because they usher us along them over and over again every day without us even noticing, demanding the kind of repeated stylization of the body that Judith Butler figures as central to gender performativity.[38] However, bodies that deviate from the lines will find themselves looking askew at the world, from queer angles that most normatively behaving people do not see.[39]

João and David, for example, propel their bodies and all those attendant desires along heteronormative lines toward women, as when João asks David to imagine that he is at a party pursuing a woman. His desires extend, reaching toward her. But he fails to "hook up with" her, and so instead—as João points out—he may respond to a man, such as a client who hails or solicits him, and then his body and desires are oriented differently, leaving him in a queer position from which he may see the world askew and notice new and different complexities and possibilities. David can now hook up with a bicha instead. As João and David ponder these complexities, they use their unique positionality to debate what new perspectives they have on the affect they call tesão. In so doing, they take up concepts from queer theory but retheorize them using their everyday lived experiences.

Affective Labor, Emotional Labor, Performative Labor

David and João's struggle to produce tesão as part of their commercial sexual encounters is an example of *affective labor*. *Affect* is a much more theoretically rich concept than *emotion*, but it is notoriously hard to define. Many people encounter the term in the context of psychology, where researchers speak of people who have a "flat" or "inappropriate" affect. In this case, "affect" simply means an "outward display of emotion." Among critical theorists, however, "affect" means something very different: or rather, several very different things. It is one of those terms, like "queer," that loses its impact if it is too well defined, and so theorists deploy it somewhat loosely, making it difficult to grasp.

Patricia Clough treats affects as "pre-individual bodily forces, linked to autonomic responses, which augment or diminish a body's capacity to act or engage with others."[40] Thus, affects flow through and all around us, inciting still other affects to flow in a maelstrom of affects. Deborah Gould's take is a bit simpler: "nonconscious and unnamed, but nevertheless registered, experiences of bodily energy and intensity that arise in response to stimuli impinging on the body."[41] Examples of such forces and registered experiences include actions like blushing, crying, cursing reflexively, laughing, or even having an orgasm. The forces can also be feelings, both positive (pride, love, hope, wonder) and negative (shame, disgust, embarrassment). For Gould, the language of emotions puts words to affects but doesn't really represent them because affects are unstructured, noncoherent, and nonlinguistic, whereas emotions are expressions structured by culture.[42] Most significantly, affects do not come from conscious thought but instead originate in the realm of the preconscious. This is similar to what laypersons sometimes speak of vaguely as "instincts," "intuitions," or "unconscious" feelings.

In the context of prostitution, Melissa Ditmore argues that the work of Arlie Hochschild and Wendy Chapkis, both of whom theorize "emotional labor," does not delve "deeply into the components of labor that create value."[43] Instead, emotional labor, for Hochschild and Chapkis, is mainly about managing one's own emotions to produce certain emotional states. According to Ditmore, the complicated refractive process of producing affect in another and then being influenced by it in turn is what really has the potential to heighten the value of the commercial sex encounter. "The world's oldest profession," she quips, "is also the world's oldest form of affective labor."[44]

When I refer to sex work as a form of *affective labor*, I do so because

I want to highlight its relationship to a particular affect and the need sex workers have to stir up certain aspects in clients such as tesão. But it's often useful to think of these same exchanges as *performative labor.* The two have a great deal of overlap, but the frame of performative labor shifts focus away from intangible and often invisible affects that trouble the mind-body distinction and exist sometimes on the surface, sometimes below, sometimes ricocheting around the room. Performative labor calls attention to the very visible products of labor: the masculinity that is embodied, commodified, and consumed. Affect is part of this exchange, but affect across cultures is difficult to analyze. How does João's own growing feeling of tesão—which he understands in such a specific way and which is likely not even a familiar concept to a gringo client—stir up desire and attraction on the part of the client? The work of affectively bridging these cultural divides requires careful adjustments in the body—cruising on the beach, the game of eyes, feigned indifference, a flexed muscle, a careful jutting of the hip to accent the *bunda* (ass), finding just the right amount of macho pegada for the particular client—that are the performative aspects of masculinity that enable the affect to flow. In this way, performative and affective labor are intertwined.

While the garoto produces affects within himself in constructing performances for consumption, he "whips up" affects within the client.[45] That is, his performance arouses various desires on the part of the potential client. A client in a *sauna* feels drawn to one particular garoto over another and then makes a conscious decision to attempt to negotiate a suitable price for those sexual services the garoto is willing to offer. During sex, the garoto will whip up still more affects in the client, including, for example, orgasm, gratification, shame, pleasure, power, or subjugation.

If affects are preconscious or even preindividual, they can be challenging to accurately analyze in specific ethnographic cases. I can make very few claims about David's and João's preconscious minds. But I *can* observe their interactions, which is why I prefer to talk about performance even as affect simmers below the surface of these interactions and sometimes bubbles up into the observable realm. Cultural geographer Nigel Thrift says of the methodologies of affect studies, "it is extremely important to note that none of these approaches could be described as based on a notion of human individuals coming together in community. Rather . . . each cleaves to an 'inhuman' or 'transhuman' framework in which individuals are generally understood as effects of the events to which their body parts (broadly understood) respond."[46] That is, for affect studies scholars, the human is often secondary and illusory. People—in this case, sex workers—become bodies that are merely the effects of affect. Therefore, theorizing sex work as performative labor rather than only affective labor offers a subtle, but rehumanizing shift that emphasizes an agentive framework that better captures the ethnographic reality of sexual economies.

By thinking about sex work as one possible, if prominent, mode of performative labor, the specific contours of gender performances come into relief, allowing observers to see the constructed and often-problematic nature of these performances and the performative contexts in which they are situated. One can see the contradictions and the lingering effects of colonialism, or the gaps and fissures wrought by economic inequality, but also see the nuanced ways in which individuals perform and enact difference to sometimes-subversive effect.

Performative labor is precarious. Because it is *so* immaterial, so hard to quantify, to discipline, to control, or to precisely monetize, it is difficult to protect. Debates about sex work frequently collapse into a radical feminist position that characterizes prostitution as inherently degrading and exploitative versus a pro-sex feminist position emphasizing individual agency and control over one's body and its labor. The latter works from a labor rights perspective to think about the exploitation that can exist in commercial sex trades. I follow this latter line of advocacy but refocus academic and activist attentions on the performative labor of prostitution because doing so unearths more of the social structures through which a subject forms.

One can also see in examining performative labor the tensions between how one sees and constructs one's own self and how one can be reconstructed within the worldview of another—a disjuncture that is jarringly apparent in transnational tourist contexts. This focus on the work of performing across difference within sexual economies lays bare the myriad social constructs—gender, race, sexuality, class—that forcibly mold individuals, sometimes in otherwise-imperceptible ways, sometimes in starkly painful ones.

TWO

Typecasting: Racialized Masculinity and the Romance of Resistance

The task that awaits all of us, then, is to speak desire plainly, to pay attention to what we think when we fuck. . . . We must not only think as we fuck but also pay close attention to all the implications, good and bad, of those sometimes startling thoughts.

ROBERT REID-PHARR, *BLACK GAY MAN*

Sitting with Lutero at a restaurant buffet, I listened as he described his recent difficulties finding someone who would rent an apartment to him. "I'm *negro* [black]," he explained. "And there is so much prejudice. And I have the look of a *boy* [male sex worker] so I have these muscles and I am very big. In the *sauna*, that makes some of the people come over to me. . . . Outside the *sauna*, in Rio, that scares them away."

Lutero was one of very few dark-skinned *negros* to work in his particular *sauna*. Unlike clients in Bahia who choose Bahia specifically for its prevalence of dark-skinned men, clients in Rio tended to prefer white garotos and *morenos*, or men of mixed or ambiguous race whose skin tone falls into a wide spectrum of brown. Thus, Lutero found his race to be a challenge in attracting some clients no matter how he tried to fashion his self-presentation through demeanor or speech, but he also knew that those who did seek him out were generally doing so because of a racial fetish.

Suddenly a middle-aged Brazilian man appeared and took a seat nearby. Lutero became very agitated at the sight of him. "Turn off the recorder. Turn it off!" he hissed at me. "I have to tell you about that man. You can write it, but I can't put this on there."

After I obliged, he leaned in and whispered. "Okay, look. A lot of clients treat *garotos* like objects. You know that, right? Okay, so that guy, one time when we went upstairs [to do a *programa*] . . ."

Lutero slowly extended his arm outward and held his fingers in front of my face. "This man, he put his hand in his own ass [*cu*] and then gave it to me to smell. He put it under my nose like this and told me to sniff it. Oh, man, I hated him for that. It was disgusting. Smelling his shit."

Lutero paused, and the silence stretched on. I was not sure what to say as I watched him seething over the memory. The important fact was that the client, by asking Lutero to smell his fingers in this way, had rendered him abject. Julia Kristeva argues that the abject is threatening precisely because it troubles the distinction between a subject and an object.[1]

While clients may treat garotos "like objects"—to use Lutero's own words—this particular client had done something even more offensive. Psychoanalytic and queer theorists consider abjection the result of a person's psychosexual development, stemming from a time when we separate self and other, humans and beasts. As Mary Douglas notes in *Purity and Danger*, the parts of the body associated with waste are the most reviled.[2] It is a primal distinction that renders the abject—in this case the smell of the client's rectum transported on his fingers—capable of disturbing identity and order. Yet the queer theorist Leo Bersani famously celebrated the rectum as fundamental to queer desire, noting that "it may, finally, be in the gay man's rectum that he demolishes his own perhaps otherwise uncontrollable identification with a murderous judgment against him. . . . Gay men's 'obsession' with sex, far from being denied, should be celebrated."[3]

Bersani's explanation does, in fact, explain why the gay client might express his anal eroticism in this way. Perhaps in his version of the story, the client was just enjoying and sharing his own ass. Yet in Lutero's mind, the client does not merely want Lutero to finger or penetrate or otherwise engage the client's *cu*. He wants Lutero to inhale. Little abject particles going in his nose. Penetrating the straight male's body. The client expects the prostitute to take the abject into his own body, to embrace not only his own abjection but with it, following Bersani, his death.

Lutero stared at the client, watching the man shovel forkfuls of food into his mouth noisily. Many garotos had stories about the occasional client making what the garotos felt were odd requests such as peeing on the client or penetrating the client with particular objects. But Lutero had not consented to participating in the client's fetish. For this client, Lutero is not only abject, not only shit-worthy because he is a prostitute; Lutero is also *negro*.

In Brazil—as in many places marred by legacies of slavery, colonialism, and racial subjugation—black bodies have long been associated with the abject, as whites considered their bodies dirty and unclean. Even Néstor Perlongher, the Argentine expat anthropologist and poet who first lived among and wrote about the dark-skinned *michês* (street hustlers) of São Paulo, built the erotic-abject dyad into his research and intimate encounters. Perlongher was known for his love of dark-skinned young men, once having sex with as many as eleven in a day. One of his friends, the noted Brazilian author João Trevisan, explained, "A youth Néstor once took to one of the cheapest hotels mugged him. . . . Such a situation filled him with fear—but also with delight, for the bodies he desired in his fantasies were black. Precisely because they are associated with the most sordid poverty, Brazilian blacks have always been a component of sadism in white fantasy."[4] The erotic divinity of humiliation is a continual theme in Perlongher's poetry as well, and he was fascinated by spaces of carnal inversions of order (high-low, dark-light, rich-poor), which meant that he found Brazil highly congenial, because such temporary inversions are a key feature of Brazilian culture.[5]

Lutero performs black masculinity well enough to be successful and to attract clients, but he is also trapped by that racialized masculinity and unable to muster the affects associated with Brazilian whiteness. Although born poor, he left the *favela* behind and lives in Copacabana now. He dresses well. He works out for hours every day. He masks his lower-class accent. He wears cologne. But he does not speak, dress, or comport himself convincingly. He tries too hard and applies his efforts to the wrong details. He hasn't mastered the performative repertoire of upward mobility, and if anything, his attempts to do so make him even more of a target for derision. The *sauna* is a space where middle-class Brazilian men and *gringos* alike find socialization and intimacy across class and often across racial boundaries with poor men like Lutero.

In Rio, the poor and the middle class rub against one another in various ways. For example, there is a tradition of live-in servants (*empregadas*, usually nonwhite women from poor communities) that creates close and complicated intimacies. The close proximity of favelas on the mountainsides directly abutting rich neighborhoods creates a peculiar blend of hypersegregation, but also intimate friction. But few spaces sexualize this class tension as directly as the city's bathhouses and brothels. The *sauna* can be a space in which the bourgeois gay plays out racial and class conflicts—conflicts that are always undergirded with sexual tension, but in the *sauna* that sexual subtext oozes to the surface of the relationship, congealing like a film.

As we exit the restaurant, Lutero pauses at the client's table. I wait to see what he is going to do. Instead of acting violently or rudely, Lutero leans over slightly to catch the man's eye. He flashes him a huge smile and gives him a thumbs-up sign, a common gesture of friendship in Brazil. "Hey! How's it going?" he asks cheerfully.

The client looks up, surprised, and waves Lutero away as if he does not know him. The waiters look over apprehensively at this large black man bothering their customer, but they are slow to act. Instead, the hostess opens the door for us. We exit and stand a moment on the street as Lutero peers back inside the restaurant, looking both scornful and wounded.

Eating the Other?

Because Brazilians have their own complicated system of racial categorization, it can be difficult to analyze the role of interracial desire in clients' relations with sex workers, particularly foreign clients, who bring their own complicated understandings about race. Yet I find it is worth investigating the question of race in Brazil's sexual economy precisely because it is a subject that both garotos and clients had a lot of difficulty discussing. In fact, their comments on whether and how the desire of gringos for Brazilian garotos was racialized at all were so inconsistent that the subject could prove controversial. Social scientists understand race to be both a social construct and a lived reality that can bring with it privileges and oppressions, yet how these constructs come to be eroticized within a tourist economy is nebulous. Some feminist scholars and activists who oppose all prostitution have singled out sexual tourism as especially pernicious because, as feminist activist Lin Chew says, she believed it to be inherently "imperialism, sexism, and racism rolled into one," which inevitably results in "total exploitation of womankind—sexual, economic, and cultural."[6] Despite such concerns, it's unclear whether racialized desire and/or racial fetishization are necessarily indicative of de facto oppression or exploitation in sexual tourism when considered from the perspective of sex workers. Therefore, in this chapter I take up two central and somewhat-related themes: what role does racial fetishization play in structuring the buying and selling of sex in Brazil's gay tourist economy, and how are inequalities and power imbalances experienced?

In an effort to bring theories of affect to bear on questions of racial identification, José Muñoz takes up the question of why the identity of Latina/o, which is less coherent than identities predicated on the state like Chicano or Nuyorican, fails "to index, with any regularity, the central identity tropes that lead to our understandings of group identities." For Muñoz, the Latina/o subject cannot perform the racialized normativity that is required to access the majoritarian white sphere, and he notes that performances take place on an affective register. In Lutero's case, he is a black Latino man who tries hard to perform the affects found in the majoritarian public sphere. He has changed his dress, his speech, and the jewelry he wears and even musters the performative competence to offer a cheerful greeting to the client he despises. But despite his desire to perform the tropes of Brazilian middle-class white society, he remains marked by his race. As Muñoz explains, "Normativity is accessed in the majoritarian public sphere through the affective performance of ethnic and racial normativity. . . . Acting white has everything to do with the performance of a particular affect, the specific performance of which grounds the subject performing white affect in a normative life-world. Latinas and Latinos, and other people of color, are unable to achieve this affective performativity on a regular basis."[7]

My theory of performative labor in Brazil's sexual economy is indebted to Muñoz's understanding of identity as a set of performative competencies that require the manipulation of affect. Muñoz is also clear that performativity must always be understood as racialized because failures to perform competently and to manage affect appropriately are at the core of racialization. The Latina who laughs too loudly, enjoys too much, and indulges, who appears over the top, becomes racialized as Latina through that very excess and the failure to perform whiteness, making "Latino-as-excess" ontologically fundamental and rendering majoritarian whiteness by comparison affectively "flat and impoverished."[8] Nominally white subjects with too much affect similarly fall into the category of "ethnic whites," such as stereotypical "guidos" and "gypsies," who may be the focus of reality television shows precisely because they fail to perform normative whiteness.

Garotos similarly must perform to excess if they are to be successful. In their case, it is an excessive form of masculinity, although they must perform for mostly local clients in the *sauna* while also being able to adjust when interacting with a gringo, which is a shift that often requires appeals to Brazilianness and its associations with sensuality, sexual excess, machismo, and romanticism. As the largest country and largest economy in Latin America as well as a non-Hispanic country that is overtly nationalistic, Brazil is prone to asserting its exceptional status. Brazilians are quick to point out that they are not Hispanic, and Brazilian migrants whom I've interviewed in the United States are often frustrated at the lack of knowledge US citizens have about race and ethnicity, especially when it comes to understanding that Hispanic and Latino are ethnic categories that are understood in racialized terms but are not races, per se, and one can be black and Latino just as one can identify as both white and Latino. Many Brazilians identify as white and, moreover, are shocked to come to the United States and be put in the same ethnic category as, say, Mexicans and Puerto Ricans. So when tourists from the United States arrive in Brazil packing their own ideas and politics of identity, racial discourses can become contentious.

Hector, a light-skinned, second-generation man of Mexican descent in his twenties who had graduated from an Ivy League university, told me how he became livid with a Brazilian garoto named Gilberto who referred to Hector as white. "I was like, that is not cool. I'm not fucking white, because I do not have those privileges. Oh, I had to school him!"

"About what?" I asked.

"About the realities of being a person of color today," he said angrily.

Hector's real experiences of oppression (and the tensions of becoming privileged through an elite education despite his nonelite background) were carried with him to Brazil, and so he could not see that in Brazil he was perceived and treated as *branco* (white) because his fair skin and facial features made him phenotypically white by Brazilian standards. Moreover, he felt the need to "school" Gilberto, who identified as branco. Hector wanted Gilberto to know that they were the same, but that sameness was *not* rooted in shared whiteness. Hector was Latino and a "person of color." Hector explained his own identification in terms of privilege to the garoto, eventually telling Gilberto that the garoto, too, was a person of color. This made little sense to Gilberto, who experienced his own life in Rio as a white majoritarian racial subject, although not a very economically privileged one. Gilberto's misreading of Hector's own racial identification resulted in a failed performance but one that illuminates the complexity of interacting across different conceptions of privilege, race, and desire.

Because race looms so large in international sex tourism, racial fetishization was a touchy subject for my tourist interlocutors, even though they included large numbers of African American men in Bahia, as well as several Asian men and Latino men in Rio. Most clients immediately relegated race to the nonconscious component of their desire, speaking instead about "types" of guys to which they felt drawn. They invoked the conservative notion of being blind to color, or they preferred to think of race in positive terms of finding oneself simply unconsciously attracted to a type instead of viewing their choices as actively rejecting or disqualifying any particular racial category of person. Finding oneself drawn to a person of a particular type is a good example of an affective response, but this does not mean that types are not deeply—if unconsciously—racialized.

One man, an Asian American named Martin, had thought about race deeply and addressed it quite candidly as we sat in Ipanema having lunch one day. "My friend, he's so terrible, he jokes about the Afro-Brazilian [sex] workers. His joke is [that] at the end of the night, just go up to one of the Afro-Brazilian guys and offer them fifty [reais, then around thirty dollars] because it's not like they've worked at all anyway. And he's joking, but I think it pretty much sums it up."

"But isn't there a fetishization there, too?" I asked, thinking of garotos like Lutero and of some of the clients I knew who preferred dark-skinned men as a matter of course.

"You do have some of the white Americans who really gravitate to Afro-Brazilians specifically. As for me, I've always been more into the moreno types [brown, mixed race]. I've always had a thing for Latino guys, and so morenos are more what I go for. As for the lighter-skinned guys and the darker-skinned guys, when I was in São Paulo [recently], I did six programas—I did two morenos, two white guys, and two black guys. . . . I like all types, but more likely than not I gravitate to morenos; they catch my eye first. As far as white guys and black guys, I'm maybe a little pickier, but with morenos I maybe give more slack about other aspects of their appearance not being completely my type."

While some clients would tell me that they "don't see race" or are "color-blind," Martin admits that he does see it. "Moreno" is also a general category (literally just meaning "brown") and can cover a large spectrum, including light-skinned people with dark hair and also people of mixed race. So for Martin to talk about being drawn to moreno types, he is essentially excluding only the whitest and blackest of garotos. And while he sampled the racial diversity of garotos in São Paulo, he also was sensitive to accusations of racism.

"I remember one time at [a *sauna*] this Afro-Brazilian guy came up to me and introduced himself and I told him I didn't want a programa, and he asked me, 'Why? Don't you like black guys?' and I said, "No, I do, but right now I'm not interested.' . . . But I know foreigners who will [telephone in order to] ask if there are light-skinned guys working at a *sauna* before they go."

"Because they won't waste their time going if lighter guys aren't working?" I ask, and he nods.

"But me, I like a little bit of everything," Martin says.

My own observations bear out Martin's comment about black sex workers in Rio not getting as much work and existing in much smaller numbers, whereas in Bahia it was morenos who complained that they were often not dark enough to suit the tastes of African American gay tourists. Martin's framing of "having a thing for" certain types while not necessarily avoiding others is best analyzed on the level of affect. He's not consciously deciding to whom he wants to be attracted. He "goes for" and "gravitates" toward certain "types" that "catch his eye." The garotos stir up affects in him, and some of that has to do with their race and presumably Martin's own racial subjectivity as Asian American and experiences in a racialized world, but some of the attraction was also, as Cavi and Adilson articulated earlier, more about *postura* (posture, manner) and *pegada* (swagger), or their self-presentation. For Martin, racialized masculinity also had to do overtly with sexual orientation.

"I have to admit I'm into the whole straight aspect," he said, leaning back and looking at me intently. "For me, I'm turned on by the whole macho culture thing. Not just Brazil, but other Latin countries. And even in the Philippines or like Korea, sometimes the guys are pretty macho, and I just kind of like the swagger. . . . I like variety, though, sometimes I'm in the mood for guys to be more affectionate, and sometimes I want them to be more thuggish. But a lot of the tourists, they're just looking to get laid. Seriously."

Martin's regular trips to Brazil were specifically for purchasing sex. He planned them far in advance, and he explicitly mapped out his plans to have as much sex as possible with as many men as possible because he did not often have sex in the United States. He sought racial variety but had a definite preference for morenos while also associating that type with "swagger," or what the garotos talked about as pegada. In this case, one can see that the garoto's performative work of manufacturing pegada, a culturally specific affective form, stirs up an affective response of attraction in Martin, who interpreted this performance as moreno swagger. The performance of masculinity was successful but relied on marshaling affects that were also unconsciously racialized.

Similarly, Glenn, another longtime tourist who came to Brazil annually, explained his interpretation of "type." "Everyone has their type. When you go anywhere. The darker-skinned guys there [in Brazil] have more European looks than [African Americans do] in the US. I've met some very good-looking *pretos* or *negros*—I don't know which [of those terms] to use because I want to be politically correct."

"*Negros*," I advise gingerly. *Preto* (black) is used for objects, and applying the term to human beings is insensitive.

Glenn pushed on. "In the end, I prefer the 'frat boy next door.' And so I'm not really interested in color so much as look." Like Glenn, who found dark-skinned Brazilian morenos and *negros* to have "more European" features and to therefore be more in keeping with his "type," many tourists told me they found dark-skinned black men attractive only if they did not have, in the words of one of them, "negroid features." That is, garotos could be very dark-skinned and still "catch" a programa, as long as they had what tourists perceived to be a "more European" bone structure.

Wayne, who lived in Brazil about half the year and knew the country and culture well, was utterly matter-of-fact as he laid out his views on the subject of attraction to certain "types" of men. "I like them butch and furry. Five o'clock shadow, hair on the chest . . . and I like them light-skinned. I don't like dark-skinned. *Cariocas* [residents of Rio], or guys from Bahia, or Paraíba, or the *nordestinos* [northeasterners]—I don't like that look; it's not what I like unless there's something special about the facial appearance . . . but mainly it's all about the attitude. Not only when you sit down at the table with them, but how they talk and how they act. Some have this standoffish attitude." He glowered at the thought of such *boys*. "They get very *alto nariz* [nose up in the air] like they're above this, but they need the money . . ."

Here Wayne highlights the exacting nature of the commissioned performance. Garoto masculinity must be properly racialized but also decidedly "butch," and the body must be maintained in a typically masculine manner by having a hairy chest and scruffy face. Moreover, the garoto must not act "above" the gringo or seem like he does not enjoy the programa. He must be able to sit at the table with Wayne and comport himself properly.

Wayne continued, "There was this most beautiful guy at [another *sauna*], and I feel like the dirty old guy when I say this, but the guy's name was Johnny, and he would not do a programa for under eighty reais." Eighty reais (then about fifty dollars) would be a good price compared to the hundred dollars most tourists are charged, but Wayne was an experienced client, spoke Portuguese, lived as an expat much of the year, and knew how to avoid being overcharged. "And he was so beautiful, but he was not white. He was dark. Johnny's skin was just smooth and he was always in the shower [showing off], the kind of guy [who disappears from the *sauna*] after a few days because someone snatches him off the market. . . . More than being light-skinned or medium, there's something about them that's incredible. It's like *Gypsy*: you gotta get a gimmick," he said, quoting the signature song from the old Broadway musical before explaining, "You need something special about you."

Here again one finds the language of the ineffable. Clients and garotos operate at the edges of scrutability, which is why the idea of affects—which are always in the process of bubbling up into iterability—are so apparent in these sexual exchanges.

Wayne decided to provide an example of someone with that "something special." "I knew this guy . . . and he had been a paratrooper, and he had that very kind of erect—and I don't mean his penis, but of course that was as well—but very erect, official, educated, practiced military bearing. And he was incredible in the sack; he was *completo* [sexually versatile], or I guess it was *ativo liberal* [a liberal top]. And he wasn't the prettiest or the youngest or the most muscular; . . . he was just butch and would kiss and suck and fuck . . . but he wasn't light-skinned and it doesn't matter. You see how someone is downstairs [in the *sauna*] and how they act and you can translate their behavior, their attitude, into what they're going to be like upstairs in a *cabine* [room for sex]. And that's much more important than race."

What I find compelling about Wayne, Martin, and other men's statements is that race is not invisible within the garotos' repertoires of masculinity, but that it is one aspect that shapes the garotos' larger performances. That is, the most important performance is not race but masculinity even though the tourists' stories also show that the gender presentation is always and already shot through with racial identifications, and these racial significations cannot be severed from gender presentation and its reception.

In her oft-cited essay "Eating the Other," bell hooks describes overhearing white Yale undergraduates setting out on a contest to seduce women of various races. She writes that for these white men, "fucking was a way to confront the Other as well as a way to make themselves over, to leave behind white 'innocence' and enter the world of 'experience,'" as they assumed that nonwhite people were "more worldly, sensual and sexual because they were different."[9] In this statement hooks has astutely described the reason for many progressives' scorn for foreign sex tourists who pursue sexual pleasure in the Global South. For hooks, white men "get a bit of the Other" as a "transcendent ritual," but one that is shaped by legacies of "imperialism, colonization, and racist domination."[10] These legacies are inescapable. Indeed, by the end of the piece, it isn't entirely clear whether white people and nonwhite people can ever have sex at all without being under the shadow of racist domination. Nor is it clear what an ethical sexual encounter would look like between them if it were possible. Indeed, this is rather beside the point of her analysis because she is primarily concerned with how the erotic structures racial encounters in society at a more systematic level. hooks's critique notwithstanding, I think it is important to give further consideration to the question of power imbalances in gringo-garoto relationships if one is to understand what the stakes are in the ethics of sexual tourism.

When considering how race functions in Brazilian contexts and how tourists navigate those discourses in their pursuit of sexual pleasure, it's useful to look at how black feminists have thought about interracial desire. Patricia Hill Collins, for example, writes that black women "pursuing White men" isn't necessarily a good solution for finding a suitable partner because these women's interracial relationships carry a heavy symbolic value.[11] She quotes Jill Nelson, who is disdainful of the claim of people who practice interracial dating that they did not make a conscious choice but simply fell in love. "They conveniently cloak themselves in an adolescent notion of love as a state independent of history, politics, and cultural conditioning that we inadvertently and unintentionally 'fall' into, like a sinkhole."[12] Nelson is not wrong that love is culturally constructed, as anthropologists, such as Donna Goldstein and Linda-Anne Rebhun, studying love in Brazil have described.[13] Racial processes, histories, and disavowals, both conscious and unconscious, inform all desire, and there is a political and affective economy of sex that implicates racialized desire in uncomfortable questions of inequality. However, when analyzing the experiences and actions of garotos whom I met, it also became clear that there is a danger to feminist and queer approaches that cast professional intellectuals in the role of restricting the sexuality of other people, foreclosing (sometimes with eager and righteous indignation) the sexual choices and erotic possibilities of others.

The Other Bites Back

Discussing racialized desire with the garotos was often one of the most difficult parts of any interview. Brazilians tend to find discussion of race impolite and referring to someone's race or asking about their racial identification can be seen as offensive. There is a common refrain among Brazilians that there is no racism in Brazil and that Brazil is "a racial democracy." This belief was brought about in part because after slavery ended the white government was concerned with the "problem" of having too many blacks in the general population and therefore decided to whiten the population by encouraging interracial coupling. This racial policy in Brazil, which had been the world's largest importer of African slaves, was markedly different from that of the United States, where officials took up the cause of antimiscegenation. Although different from that of the United States, this Brazilian approach was nonetheless similarly rooted in the racist beliefs and values of whites.

Garotos know that sexual economies are not color-blind, however. And so while they felt conflicted about the role of race in their performances of masculinity and their ability to "catch" clients, they also acknowledged that they had to figure out how to play with racialized desire when dealing with gringos. With local clients, they felt this was less of an issue because they assumed Brazilians to be more color-blind than gringos, either because the garotos had internalized the idea that Brazil is a racial democracy or because they knew they weren't read as racially and sexually exotic by local clients in the same manner that they were by gringos. In this way, garotos tended to focus not so much on the race of clients as they did on the clients' status as foreigners or locals. Moreover, when interacting with both gringos and Brazilian clients, garotos tended to view class as the paramount axis of difference but did not necessarily talk about this difference as one that had much of anything to do with power in the relationship.

Gringos came to *saunas* in Rio looking for what they felt were exotic and macho Latin men. However, garotos frequently presented this desire in terms of nationality rather than race, remarking that they were excellent lovers, skilled at seduction, or exceptionally attractive to gringos because they were Brazilian (not because they were moreno or *pardo* [mixed race] or some other particular racial category) and that these qualities are all naturally Brazilian ones, thereby deploying popular stereotypes for their own gain.

Another reason garotos disliked talking about racial fetishization was that they felt that being fetishized might be interpreted as exploitation or as their lack of agency. Thus, it was often easier to talk about questions of power and exploitation than to overtly discuss race and racialized inequalities in the sexual economy. Fetishized people are acted upon; they are objects—not subjects—in such a construction. Tellingly, one garoto in Bahia reclaimed agency in the fetishization process by explaining to me when I asked if the gringo clients preferred him because of his color, "No. I *make* them choose me because of my color."

Power is not unidirectional and agency is too complicated to be rendered in Manichean terms, yet race imbues the performances of masculinity I have described, raising the stakes for success or failure and highlighting questions of exploitation and of resistance. This false dichotomy of exploitation/empowerment has surfaced in debates about sex work throughout feminism's history, and so it's important to examine how my theorizing of sex work as performative labor speaks to the issue of resistance and how, when viewed through the lens of performative labor, garotos' performances of masculinity challenge such simplistic dichotomies.

Garotos have a host of tactics for enacting resistance through performance against potential class-based and race-based power imbalances, and it's worth considering these in a variety of contexts even (and perhaps especially) where race is *not* overtly invoked and to examine these tactics in both garoto-gringo and garoto-Brazilian configurations. Despite media stories and popular stereotypes of dangerous street hustlers, garotos rarely robbed, drugged, or harmed clients. They did confess, however, to scamming them for money, seducing them, preying on their loneliness, and exploiting it.

Martin, the middle-class Asian American who had earlier described his penchant for macho moreno Latino men who had a lot of "swagger," also told me a compelling story one day about how he had been susceptible to a garoto's performance and then, wounded by the experience, hardened his approach to them. "My good friend and I took one of the *garotos* we met shopping at Rio Sul [a mall]. I bought him some clothes; my friend filled his car with gas; we took him out to lunch at Porcão." Porcão is a famous restaurant in the *rodizio* style, an all-you-can-eat meat extravaganza. It's expensive and a favorite of both tourists and upper-middle-class Brazilians who live in the more posh parts of the city's southern zone. Martin was speaking quickly but quietly as he continued.

"We went to the movies. I remember it was *Freddy versus Jason*, because he wanted to see that," he said, laughing and rolling his eyes. "So we sat through it. And then we took him to a nice dinner and back to the hotel. He and I had oral at the *sauna* before, but we had never actually had sex up to that point, and then it had evolved into a friendship kind of thing. He dropped me off at the hotel, and he would do this thing where he would wink and smile, make me swoon a bit, kind of. And we were standing there and he tells me he had guard duty [at his other job as a security guard] tomorrow, and then he asks me: 'Can I have 200 reais [USD (2009) 120] for the time I spent with you tonight?' And I was just stunned. I was hurt, actually."

Martin took a deep breath and sighed, fidgeting with his empty glass for a moment. "I just couldn't believe that everything my friend and I had done for him that day, after all the money we spent on him, that he still wanted to be *paid for his time*." He pressed on, more quickly, resolved. "It was at that point that it kind of clicked for me that you're really not here for love or whatever; you're here to have a good time. And I just said okay, and I gave him the money. And he could tell I was disappointed. I'm not good at hiding at my emotions. When I'm upset or sad, it shows."

He sighed again, pausing and collecting himself. I was considering interrupting when he finished. "And so the day after next he showed up and told me he was going to take me home to Niterói to show me around and whatnot, and that kind of made up for it, I guess. But still, I had realized that they're doing this for money, and they are going to try to get all the money from you they can."

The question of who is able to control the affective quality of a relationship and set its parameters is important because it speaks to issues of agency. In this example, the comparatively wealthy tourist demonstrates that he is vulnerable, and the garoto, without malice, learns he has the ability to inflict pain on another. Power is multidirectional. But kindness is multidirectional, too. And so is performative labor. As the power dynamic begins to shift, Martin finds himself trying to anticipate what kind of client the garoto wants him to be. Just as tourists have their own fantasies based on common tropes and even outright stereotypes such as suave Latin lovers and thuggish machos, Martin attempts to don the mantle of a common garoto fantasy: the sugar daddy, or Papai Noel. He endures what he sees as the younger man's lowbrow taste in horror movies in an effort to woo him. He takes him shopping at Rio Sul and to Porcão for dinner.

Even as Martin performed his own masculinity, it was imbued with distinctions of class and nationality. But his performance may have succeeded too well, making sure the garoto saw him even more thoroughly as a rich gringo to take advantage of. Only when his façade crumbled and revealed his more personal emotional investments did the garoto have a sympathetic and perhaps guilty response, which prompted him to show the man around his home neighborhood. What Martin seems not to have fully registered was that for the garoto to take him to Niterói, to reveal to him a bit more about his own personal life, was hugely significant for a sex worker. This rare and touching gesture came too late, as Martin was already feeling disillusioned. It was a tragic series of performances from both client and garoto that failed precisely because neither understood the cultural significance of the other's actions and did not know how to interpret the gestures.

The second theme that needs concretization is the issue of desire from the garotos' point of view. Near a famous cruising ground in São Paulo's Ibirapuera Park, I ventured into a parking lot where michês stood around smoking, looking tough, and trying to score programas from the Brazilian motorists who drove around them, circling the hustlers before making a selection. Sitting at a little table alongside this scene, however, was a white Brazilian client in his sixties who had his arms wrapped around a slim, slightly effeminate young man in his late teens who read as *moreno claro*, or a light-skinned moreno. We struck up a conversation and the client, whose name was Franz, was very interested in my then-nascent project.

"I am not young," Franz said in impeccable English with a twinkling eye. "But my tastes never matured with me, you see. When I was the age of Kaique here, I could have any man I wanted. But now I do not want other men like me, and the boys like Kaique do not want me."

Kaique deduced that we were speaking about him and gave me a sour look. He tightened his grip on Franz and gave him a kiss. Franz asked in Portuguese, almost in a "baby talk" tone of voice, "And Kaique, does Kaique want me?" To this Kaique made a little biting motion, nipping the air as if trying to gobble Franz up.

"Kaique, do you work in the park?" I asked, wanting to draw him into the conversation, but he still looked at me suspiciously, as if I was there to lure away Franz.

"No," he said. "Not here. Over there." He gestured to the thick wooded area where men cruised for sex, and where I had just stumbled across a group oral scene in the trees. It was a sort of classic cruising ground, similar to those in New York or San Francisco before policing efforts and fears of HIV diminished their role in gay culture.

"Working?" I asked, confused. Kaique then explained that he went there to have sex with men for free because you could find straight men and closeted, masculine guys there after work. "But then I found Franz." Eventually, it emerged that Franz was a Papai Noel more than an outright client and that he was "keeping" Kaique by giving him a monthly allowance. They liked to go to *saunas* and parks, sometimes to have sex with others, but also because no one in the park was going to judge them, unlike at gay bars, where each man had to endure knowing, pitying, or derisive looks. Franz excused himself at one point to urinate, leaving Kaique alone with me. I apologized for thinking he was a michê, but he responded that his relationship with Franz was very much commercial.

"[Franz] knows I would leave if there was no monthly salary for me, but he also knows I am having fun."

"You enjoy it?" I asked.

"I love the sex. It's so much fun," he said, wide-eyed with excitement. He looked so boyish in that moment that I wondered if he was actually younger than the eighteen years he claimed. It seemed possible, if not likely.

"With him specifically?" I asked, trying not to sound incredulous.

"Oh yes!" Kaique gushed. "He is old, but he is strong. And he wants sex all the time and so do I. And he's macho, which is the most important thing for me. Well, that and money, but only because I like nice things."

Kaique provided me with my first lesson in the field about the difficulties of trying to break sex work down into discrete types of work. He also challenged my biases and assumptions that sex workers cannot experience desire for clients, even ones who are not considered attractive within society's narrow parameters. Kaique illustrated Elizabeth Bernstein's notion of "bounded authenticity," producing a genuine emotional reaction in himself but also speaking much the same way that clients did about having a "type" that stirred up attraction for them.[14] Franz's performance of masculinity was more important than his aging physical body.

Years later, Martin, the tourist quoted above who had become disillusioned by his failed attempt to take a garoto on a date, offered his own equally telling example of the complicated forms desire can take between a garoto and a client. "This garoto I knew [from around the *sauna*] for a couple years and done programas with [a few times], he had a baby girl with his wife. He was really interesting sexually, though, because for one thing, he was tremendously huge 'down there,' and he was really aggressive in bed," Martin said, dropping air quotes with his fingers and glancing downward coyly.

"I'm usually in the bottom role, but we had had sex and we had stopped and I was like 'Oh, good!' Because it kind of hurt so I was ready to go downstairs and pay him, and then he took out *another* condom and unwrapped it, and I was like 'Oh no, here we go again.' But then he put it on me, actually, and *he* got on *me* and I was stunned by that. I was trying to reconcile that, you know that someone you perceive as straight and you know him for two years, and then on our third or fourth programa he goes and does that. He just got on for like a minute, and he immediately came."

I must have looked surprised or confused. Martin took on an explanatory tone. "He just did it to get off, to release. Didn't say a word to me. I was stunned, because I don't usually take that role; I don't *ask* for that role. But I couldn't ask him about it because it's such a macho culture, and I didn't want to question his masculinity in any way. But it was weird. It makes you wonder more about how the men here perceive themselves sexually."

In Martin's story, the garoto's unexpected desire to be penetrated hints at the impossibility of defining sexual identity or orientation through any one specific act. Earlier, Martin articulated his desire for straight, macho men. This garoto fulfilled that role, and Martin pointed to the man's wife and children as evidence of his heterosexuality. Being fucked by a macho straight man was Martin's fantasy, and the garoto performed that role well, and yet Martin was delighted at the sudden reversal in which this straight man wanted to be penetrated by him. Far from causing the performance of masculinity to fail, the unexpected contradiction and the collapsing of identity models proved exhilarating for Martin and evidently for the garoto as well.

This scene also shows how complicated desire is. It is somewhat unusual for a garoto to ejaculate without negotiating this in advance, as they sometimes charge extra to do this. However, at the end of the night, many garotos will orgasm with a final client because they have been aroused for several hours and want release. The garoto in this story, though, didn't just ejaculate for free. Nor did he penetrate himself with a finger or otherwise provide himself with anal stimulation to aid in his release (as many heterosexual men do). He bottomed for Martin, apparently out of his own desire, and thereby disrupted the past two years of repeated, congealed performances of masculinity that he had engaged in for Martin. To Martin's surprise, both desire and power flow in a myriad of directions and in complicated ways in the *sauna*.

Performative Labor and the Romance of Resistance

"Exploitation" is a loaded term because it often relies on a narrow view of poverty and either assumes a total absence of choices or projects an air of enlightenment onto someone who opts to sell sex instead of engaging in some other low-wage profession available to them. Martin had already indicated that he'd thought about the question of power in his relationships with the dozens of garotos he had paid for sex over the years, so I pushed him on this point.

"They are often in the position of power," he said. "As soon as they spot you as a foreigner, you're at their mercy. They have these expectations of what you're able to pay. And I think as far as this word 'exploitation' goes, I think maybe we exploit each other. We take advantage of our ability to have sex cheaply, and they take advantage of the traveler's naïveté. And they charm us, and take us in."

"But there's something neocolonial about all of this, isn't there?" I asked, which was a position I was genuinely struggling with in the field as I worked through the ambivalence I sometimes felt toward the phenomena I was observing.

"As far as if this is neocolonial, my feeling is that my family is from the Philippines. And I don't go there for sex. That's just not my scene. But I know towns, places where you can go up to any guy on the street, literally any guy, and offer money for sex, and 90 percent of the time they'll say yes, because they need the money to survive. There's grinding poverty, there's not many jobs, . . . unlike here, in the Philippines they're not buying sneakers with the money. They're buying rice to feed themselves and their families. People will say that it's the government's responsibility to take care of them. And maybe it is, sure, but in the meantime what are they going to do? What's the reality while they wait years or generations for something to change?"

"And that's different than here," I say.

"It's a very different sort of thing than here," he agrees, looking somber. "Here, in the *sauna* scene anyway, they are not starving. They are making good money, and they don't talk about hating it. They could get other jobs that might not pay as well, but they do have options. They say they have a lot of fun working in the *saunas*; it's not seen by them as a bad job. None of them over the years have ever said to me that they hate what they do. I don't honestly believe that this situation is exploitative of their situation the way it is in many other places—certainly not in the *saunas* at any rate. And there's the question of how you actually treat someone who is providing a service for you, who is doing a job where you are the customer."

Although Martin made the case for Brazilian exceptionalism, he also drew on a labor rights framework in invoking accountability and appropriate client treatment toward sex workers. I couldn't help but recall Lutero and the white Brazilian client who had degraded him by asking him to smell his fingers, remembering Lutero's hurt at being treated "like an object," but also how he forced himself to greet the man cheerfully.

"If you treat them nicely, they respond to that," Martin said. "A lot of people don't treat them nicely, don't act respectfully. I ask them about themselves, about their kids or girlfriends or whatever. In macho cultures, respect can be an especially big thing. . . . And so I always want to be good to them, too. You want to treat everybody well in this situation because it can be weird, right? It can be awkward for them, or for you, and the whole thing is better for everyone when everyone just respects each other. . . . You have to respect the locals; you have to respect the host country. I don't think we're taking advantage of anyone, and it's not a very big imbalance of power, to be honest with you."

I was struck by Martin's conscientiousness about his own performance of gringo masculinity. In Martin's interviews, he describes himself as showing deference and respect and highlights the importance of humanizing the garotos by asking them about themselves and their families. He links this to appealing to their machismo, which he considers to be important in Latin culture. He is consciously trying to make himself, his motives, and his desires legible across a cultural divide. He understands that it is necessary to manage relations with garotos by demonstrating an understanding of the cultural norms that structure the masculinity he finds so appealing. Through his own performative labor, he is able to mitigate possible imbalances in the relationship, at least in his view.

Curious about these assertions, a few weeks later I asked a garoto I knew named Julio whether he felt prostitution had a lot of exploitation in it. Julio responded with a grim look and said, "I'm not going to lie to you. There are some good people in this business, but most *boys* are bad. We have to love people and not things, but nowadays I, too, love more things than people. It's getting harder to put your heart out there [*coração na frente*] . . . for most clients; I feel sorry for them; . . . they come here lonely and then we exploit them. But nothing is free; you have to pay. And so a *boy* takes everything from them he can."

When I clarified that I had actually meant to ask whether *boys* were exploited by the system, by clients, by *sauna* owners or others in the industry, he simply laughed and reiterated his point that while working in a *sauna* is "not a party," the only exploitation he can recall is what he inflicts on his clients, which he says is starting to weigh on his conscience.

Colleagues and students often ask me why the garotos continue to sell sex when the life can be difficult, when they say they want to exit, and then when they make enough to get out they find themselves staying in it. Antonio's response was typical when he said, "This is the best job I could find. I make a lot of money and I don't work at all, you know. I make a lot and do almost nothing. . . . The first time I had a client, I almost threw up in his mouth when I kissed him . . . so yes, in the beginning it was difficult. It was work, but now it's all good. . . . I want to save money and quit someday, to open a business for [selling] livestock feed, I think. But not now. For now, I'm happy."

Not everyone was happy, though. Adilson was adamant about wishing his life had turned out differently. "I regret having been introduced to the *sauna*. I never studied. I was always in the *piranhagem* [being promiscuous], women, *zueira* [having fun], friends, you know?" But then Adilson exhaled a drag on his cigarette, remarking, "But those friends are the ones who took me to work as a *boy*. I regret it a lot. This is no way to live . . . but I stay because the money is very good."

The garotos' emphasis on consumerism reveals another important facet of performative labor. Their virtuosity at constructing masculinity brings them the spending power they need to reinvent themselves yet again, escaping class-based and race-based stigma this time by performing a *playboy* masculinity. In Brazil, the English import *playboy* is a somewhat-derogatory term for a (usually white or light-skinned) bourgeois guy who has money to throw around, impressing women with gifts and making men jealous with his conspicuous consumption. Lower-class men from backgrounds like the garotos may refer derisively to *playboyzinhos* (little playboys) when they want to insult someone's street cred or masculinity, but the garotos also move into the role quickly themselves when given a chance. Their successful performances in the *saunas* and streets allow them to expand their repertoire of available masculinity, this time into the realm of the bourgeois as part of their aspirational climb into the middle classes. Men working in the *saunas* really can climb across classes, but their performance of the bourgeois precedes any actual shift in class.

Many garotos held other jobs before coming to work in Brazil's sexual economy and/or held down other jobs between stints of sex work. Gonçalo, for example, learned he could arrange to make a little money (*arrumava um dinheirinho*) from the big queens (*viadão*) in his favela when he was a "little brat" (*desde molequinho*), selling sex in his early teens. When we met, he often worked as a carpenter, but money in the *sauna* was faster. "Everyone says it's easy money," he warns me. "But it's not. Fast yes. Easy no. . . . There are some *boys* in the *sauna* that are nice guys [*maneiros*], but there are some that are snobbish [*marrentos*]. . . . I prefer not to make friends with anyone. . . . This year I stopped working almost the whole year. I work for a short time, get some money, and stop. But then something always goes wrong. My woman just had a baby, so the money goes. I want to be out wandering, being a vagabond [*vagabundo*], but we need money so I go back to the *sauna*."

Here Gonçalo struggles to perform respectable masculinity—someone who can not only father children but also provide for his family—and so even though he wants to experience the *playboy* lifestyle, he returns to the *sauna*, using his ability to perform one kind of homonormative masculinity for gay clients in order to enable him to perform a heteronormative masculinity for his family. These two types of masculinity can threaten one another, too, and so it was hazardous for Gonçalo to let these worlds collide. "Someone showed my mom a [gay] porno I made last year. She said I must be a *bicha* [fag] to do this, but now she knows better and she does not criticize me. But she does not support me, either, and I live with [Lino] here."

Lino chimes in. "[The sex] *is* difficult. I close my eyes, try not to think about what I am going to do. I think to myself, *I want to have this money*. Then images enter my mind and I close my eyes. Images of women. Images from movies, whatever. And of the money. What I'll do [with it.] Creating fantasies in my head and forget what's right there, you know [*esquece que é aquilo, tá ligado*]?"

Lino's comments make explicit the connection between the two performances of masculinity. He pictures a movie or pornographic mental images that he fantasizes he is engaging with so as not to think about the male client he is actually with. And to keep himself focused, he has the mantra that he tells himself: *I want to have this money*. He focuses on the money, fantasizing about cash to keep himself stimulated during the programa.

It is only by picturing the cash and envisioning himself spending it that he is able to stir up *tesão*, the desire necessary to sustain an erection. Money itself becomes the erotic object, and it is his ability to imagine himself spending and consuming material things that makes affect materialize in his body, blood pulsing its way to his genitals, making possible the embodied and commissioned performance of masculinity necessary for the client. In this moment when his performative labor is so visible, he is able to penetrate the client, but this is only possible for him through the consumerist dreamscape.

Meanwhile, Washington, he of the puppy dog eyes bloodshot from smoking weed whom I quoted in the last chapter, says he works periodically as an office boy, doing odd jobs and errands. As I mentioned earlier, he had first had sex for money in the favela when he was twelve; his partner was a *"viado"* whom Washington reckoned was in his twenties. This neighborhood man offered him the equivalent of seventy dollars (a huge sum in that community), leaving his keys hidden for Washington at the corner of his house so the boy could let himself in and not arouse suspicion by being seen in public with the effeminate man. Washington crept to the house as planned, used the key to let himself in, and, finding the viado there, fucked him. "I felt no shame or guilt. I had money for the first time in my life."

Washington's story is in keeping with other anthropologists' research on sexual economies in Brazil. For example, the *travestis* of Salvador with whom Kulick lived often talked about being initiated sexually at young ages but not finding these experiences to be traumatic per se.[15] On the contrary, they described finding the material benefits empowering. Although Washington now worked sometimes as an office boy, he said he could make "more money in a day [in the *sauna*] than I do in a month as an office boy." He continued to work in the office once in a while though because it was "respectable work," and so it allowed him to feel that he had a legitimate vocation. He sold sex two to three days a week, on average, and did two or three programas a day. "Some days are difficult, like today, with no one. But I get a hundred [reais] at least for a programa. . . . Later, I began to do both active and passive."

Renato laughs. He is versatile now, too. "At first it was really difficult to face this part of work, of being passive, because it hurt! But not now because my asshole doesn't tighten any more." Washington giggles at his cousin's bluntness, looking around in embarrassment to see if anyone overheard. Renato continues, "I would never do it for pleasure, but some clients want *ativos* and some *passivos* so I have more clients this way." Washington agrees. "It's not for pleasure, no. Clients want you to enjoy it. I never enjoy it at all, but if the client asks you to enjoy it, then you have to pretend. . . . Tourists want things to be more calm, they want more affection [*carinho*], act as if they are getting to know a person. . . . They are totally different from Brazilians because the Brazilian is more aggressive." He mimes a Brazilian pounding fast and hard. "[The Brazilian client] knows he is paying and so it's different between [a Brazilian] and us [garotos]."

Here the two men illustrate two other important aspects to their performances of masculinity. They must pretend to feel pleasure for clients, creating "bounded authenticity" within the sexual economy. They also point to what they see as a difference between gringo clients and Brazilians, which is that Brazilians are less likely to project a romantic cast to the relationship. In this way, it is the local client who is more likely to use the garoto roughly or to be too aggressive. This potential for gringo vulnerability (as in Martin's case) is one that for both garotos and foreign clients meant that power and agency in the exchange were tied to a more complicated set of questions about power that are not captured by my initial and simplistic question to Martin about whether sex tourism is "neocolonial."

The other jobs available to the men are usually low-paying, low-status forms of manual labor. They require hard work and long hours that are often inflexible. Commercial sex trades allow great flexibility and fast access to cash, but the most lucrative programas are with over-paying tourists, and these require performances of enjoyment, affection, and desire as well as masculine, heterosexual comportment. This contradiction is key to understanding the nature of the performative labor of masculinity in the *sauna*. The garotos must perform a realistic awakening of desire and pleasure that contradicts their sexual identity and hypermasculine façade even though they may be fantasizing about women or indulging in the erotic pull of consumerism by envisioning spending the money.

The garotos may not be exploited in the conventional clichéd sense: there is no pimp forcing them to sell sex, they are not starving or addicted to hard drugs, and they have the same options available to them that peers in their home neighborhoods do. They are not coerced. In fact, they think of themselves as the ones doing the exploiting, illustrating how complex the question of oppression is in this corner of the commercial sex trades. The political scientist and anthropologist James C. Scott sees resistance as somewhat different from an oppressed person's turning the tables on his oppressor. In *Domination and the*

Arts of Resistance, Scott claims that marginalized people rely on "hidden transcripts" to resist hegemonic power. For example, when factory supervisors impose Taylorized regimes on the bodies of workers to increase productivity and extract profits, factory workers might not overthrow the foremen and seize the means of production (i.e., the factory), but they do discourage each other from becoming a "rate buster"—from exceeding norms and expectations.[16] Likewise, garotos police one another to prevent anyone from underselling or undercutting prices. While outwardly accepting that they are there to serve clients regardless of how they feel about those men, their private conversations reveal elements of resistance to the idea that they are subservient.

So how do garotos talk among themselves? When they talk about clients, they don't like to discuss what transpires in the cabine, as it could damage their masculine reputation. Garotos usually don't "burn" (*queimar*) clients behind their backs unnecessarily, but they'll denounce customers who are "too chatty" (*lero lero*) and don't want to close the deal. They warn one another if a client that night is an "addict" (*viciado*), meaning that "he goes *boy* to *boy* grabbing your dick [*piru*], your ass, wants to kiss you, but then he says he needs to think about it and goes to another until we spread the word to each other and no one talks to him." *Viciados* may be described privately with profane expressions like *chato pra caralho* (boring as fuck).

Lastly, they dislike what they call *camelos* (camels). Adilson explained, "When a client comes to drink and doesn't go with any of us, we call him a 'camel,' because he doesn't make any noise, he doesn't fight, he never does anything. He stands still, drinking, and walks around, that's all. He comes, drinks a drink, goes there, look, look, wants to play, maybe chat, but leaves without going up for a programa." Adilson laughs suddenly, remembering something. "You, actually," he says, pointing at me. "We thought you were a camelo at first!" I laugh, too, realizing suddenly that this was a perfectly natural way to interpret my behavior as an ethnographer within their worldview.

Michel de Certeau, frames resistance as "tactics," or activities that are hidden under a veneer of conformity.[17] People use tactics to push back against "strategies" deployed by institutions such as the police, various state apparatuses, the church, and so on. Strategies are static and cannot be adapted easily because they are so heavily institutionalized, and also because they manifest materially in the form of large structures such as corporate headquarters, military compounds, prison complexes, and the like. Tactics are flexible, fragmented, spontaneous, and without an organized center. Users deploy tactics out of necessity to subvert and sidestep (rather than overthrow) powerful strategies that oppress them. Tactics can be as banal as stealing office supplies or—in the case of sex work—upselling or maybe taking an extra bill from a client's wallet when he's not looking.

Tactics also include matters of sexual performance, and the garotos incorporate tactics into their work. If a client is new to the scene, they'll tell him a programa is thirty minutes if it's really forty. They want clients to orgasm quickly (*acabem logo*) so they can leave for the night or go find another programa. If the client is going to take the whole forty minutes, then they want to proportion the time to their advantage, reducing the amount of time they have to spend in undesirable activities such as being penetrated or kissing on the mouth. Thus, one of Julio's first tricks was learning to suck nipples or nibble the neck, which—even if the client wasn't particularly turned on by it—kept him from having to kiss on the mouth or perform oral sex, and so he did this for as long as the client allowed. Fingering the man is another delaying tactic to cut down on the amount of time penetrating him. They make fists on the base of the tourist's penis to prevent themselves from having to "deep-throat" them. They tell clients they have a cold to avoid kissing, and some accuse the client of having bad breath from alcohol, cigarettes, or halitosis in order to embarrass him into not kissing with an open mouth.

One problem with Scott's and de Certeau's conceptions of hidden transcripts and tactics is that it is very difficult to tell what is actually subversive, what is a redeployment of oppression upon someone even lower down the hierarchy, and what is merely "making do." The above modifications of sex acts are hardly going to bring about revolution. So if substantive change never happens, these examples of microresistance aren't very useful models. Scott disagrees with this critique, noting that to insist on a distinction between "real" and "unreal" resistance "fundamentally misconstrues the very basis of the economic and political struggle conducted daily by subordinate classes."[18] But under Scott's definition, nearly everything could be read as resistance.

In his analysis of travesti prostitutes' resistance to those who would dominate them, Kulick likewise singles out Scott for his idea that subordinate groups use hidden transcripts to imagine a "world upside down." "Transgendered prostitutes among whom I work resist dominant depictions of them and their lives, but not by countering those portrayals with alternative, oppositional, offstage-generated 'hidden' ones of their own design," he writes. "Instead, they oppose and resist hegemonic notions of gender and sexuality that degrade them by drawing on precisely those notions, and using them to their own advantage with members of the dominant group."[19] According to Kulick, the travestis *dar um escândalo* (give a scandal) to heterosexual male clients, causing embarrassment by drawing attention to the client or attempting to shame him into giving more money and sometimes by hurling homophobic epithets at him or calling his masculinity into question. Such *escândalos* have no place in Scott's theorization of resistance.

While I appreciate that resistance need not be revolutionary, I can't help but notice that if a sex worker succeeds in, say, selling *programas* to tourists for more than the price he usually charges locals, this tactic is simply absorbed into the sexual market. Eventually, prices adjust in order to mitigate anticipated losses. Many tourists tell me they refuse to tip because they assume they are paying more than the going rate as gringos anyway, or they drive extra hard bargains (squabbling over every dollar) so as not to overpay.

There is a long history of ethnographic literature on poor people "making do." Nancy Scheper-Hughes has described such "tactics for survival" in the case of impoverished Brazilian women "relying on their wits, playing the odds, and engaging in the occasional *malandragem* of deceit and white lies, gossip and rumor, feigned loyalty, theft and trickery. But can we speak of resistance, defiance, opposition— themes that are so privileged in critical circles today?"[20] She notes that her own interlocutors don't "fool themselves" as academics do and actually joke about a time when "the revolution" will come, when things will be different.

Such holes in theories of resistance illustrate the tendency of some academics to romanticize resistance. Lila Abu-Lughod criticizes anthropologists and sociologists for this inclination to locate resistors (particularly in unlikely places) and to "restore to our respect such previously devalued or neglected forms of resistance" as foot-dragging, gossip, and rumors. Instead, she asks us to accept that (in an inversion of Foucault's axiom) "where there is resistance, there is power" in order to examine power materially rather than through abstraction.[21]

My own approach lies somewhere between Scheper-Hughes's pessimism and Scott's optimism, and while I concur with Abu-Lughod, my task is not to understand how garotos resist the structures of state power but rather to follow her model and adapt it to examine how particular racialized and gendered tropes alter garotos' relationships within commercial contexts. The garotos' efforts to master different valences of performativity in order to lift themselves up economically and expand the repertoire of racialized masculinity available to them are ambivalent and complex. In taking them up as objects of analysis, I wish not to romanticize them but to demonstrate the power that performative labor has for thinking about how affects move across difference. Precisely because sexual economies are so often built on ideas of racial difference and the transactions on this plane frequently occur across class divisions, it's all the more important to acknowledge that sometimes this performative labor really does subvert hegemonic paradigms.

An example by way of conclusion: when a garoto works as an escort outside the *sauna*, he often plays the role of a tour guide, taking a gringo to the Christ Statue or Sugarloaf Mountain, which is ironic, as many of the garotos have never been to these places because they are expensive, and so they may make poor tour guides. But I've also witnessed garotos who offer up different narratives. Miguel, a New Yorker of Puerto Rican descent who was very fit and perhaps forty years old, hired Aurélio, a quick-witted young man in his early twenties with light skin and dark hair, to be his guide/escort. This date resulted in not so much a conventional tour as a history of Brazil as seen from below.

Upon heading to Rio's central district, instead of telling Miguel about colonial Brazil and church architecture, Aurélio taught him about massacres of street children at Candelária Church by police, describing the lives of the urban poor from his home community, and lectured him on why Brazilians ought to be allowed to vote in presidential elections in the United States, noting that they were impacted at least as much by US policies as Miguel was. He explained that voting is mandatory in Brazil and was horrified that Miguel did not bother to vote. Aurélio told Miguel about Sandro Rosa do Nascimento, a street kid who was orphaned after watching his mother murdered in a favela and who survived Candelária only to die in 2000 after he hijacked a bus and took hostages. He told gringo clients about how the state had failed to take care of the Candelária children despite their attempts to placate the shocked and outraged public into thinking they really took the massacre seriously and wanted to take better care of street children going forward. But nowadays, he pointed out, there is a *sauna* a block from the site of the church massacre, where young men like himself work to provide for themselves because the state still isn't doing it, social programs from the Workers Party be damned.

As I sat in Ipanema at a café outside Miguel's luxury hotel, watching Miguel sullenly sip coffee and Aurélio happily smoking and chatting away, I asked Miguel if he was as irritated with the "tour" he received as he seemed. "It wasn't really what I was expecting. It wasn't what I had asked him to tell me about."

"Poverty?" I asked.

Aurélio gave a little wink, clearly enjoying needling Miguel. "He doesn't like being reminded about poor people."

Miguel was terse. "It's fine you did that," he said to Aurélio, "but it wasn't very fun."

Miguel seemed uncomfortable thinking about all this inequality and his own privilege, perhaps especially because it was being pointed out by a sex worker. The relationship was also notable for the fact that Miguel was Latino, and Aurélio, though white by most Brazilians' standards and fairly well educated, was substantially less wealthy than his gringo client. I wondered whether it would have changed the situation if it had been an official tour guide who had educated Miguel, or whether Miguel's discomfort was because Aurélio had not performed the role expected of a male escort, as if somehow his presence served as a constant reminder of the disparity between the two men.

Aurélio, though, was a very successful escort and he knew when he had pushed far enough. He put a hand on Miguel's arm and bent forward across the table so he could force eye contact with Miguel. He smiled at him and gave a squeeze, grinning wordlessly for a minute until Miguel finally stopped pouting and smiled back, giving in to Aurélio's charms.

Then, with Miguel ensorcelled once again and back just where he wanted him, Aurélio landed one last little jab at his gringo. "But you did learn something, yes?"

THREE

TurboConsumers™ in Paradise: Sexual Tourism and Civil Rights

The national bourgeoisie organizes . . . pleasure resorts to meet the wishes of the Western bourgeoisie. Such activity is given the name of tourism. . . . The beaches of Rio, . . . the half-breed thirteen-year-olds, [in] the ports of . . . Copacabana—all these are the stigma of this depravation of the national middle class. Because it is bereft of ideas . . . the national middle class will have nothing better to do than . . . set up its country as the brothel of Europe. **FRANTZ FANON, *THE WRETCHED OF THE EARTH***

Robert, a North American manager in his fifties, sits in a Copacabana *boteco* (informal eatery) looking nervous.[1] Wesley, the gay porn star he has hired as an escort, is late. Robert has booked two first-class plane tickets to Spain, where they will begin a Mediterranean cruise. He has flown to Brazil to pick up Wesley because the last time he booked an expensive vacation for a Brazilian escort, that other escort never showed up and Robert was profoundly disappointed.

"What happens if he doesn't turn up?" I ask.

"I guess I'll just go by myself," he says nonchalantly, but when Wesley arrives a few minutes later, Robert's face lights up and he leaps to his feet in the middle of our interview.

Wesley is a fairly big-name porn star in gay adult films. His movies regularly play in gay bars in the United States and he has fan sites devoted to him. Robert found his movies on a porn site and contacted the webmaster to see if he would forward an email to the young man. Within days, Robert had a response, and the two men were arranging to meet. Fast-forward six months or so, and here they sat at the boteco with me on the eve of their departure. But as we chatted, it became clear that Wesley didn't understand how a cruise worked. Robert speaks no Portuguese and Wesley's English isn't good. Gustavo (my research assistant) and I muddle our way through some translations and suddenly find ourselves in the middle of some much-needed clarifications between Robert and Wesley. "We get off the boat?" Wesley asks.

Yes, Robert explained. They would be going to many countries. First, to a friend's wedding in Spain, then to Italy.

"We can see the pope?" Wesley asks, his big brown eyes widening in excitement.

Robert laughs, "I don't want to see the pope!" But before Wesley can look disappointed, Robert concedes, "but we can go to the Vatican, yes." Then, in his endearingly curmudgeonly way he warns him, "But it is overrated."

Wesley is all optimism, though. "I would love to see it," he gushes. As I start to ask him about his religious background, thinking that his desire to see the pope might be related to his Brazilian Catholicism, he barrels on, proving me wrong. "Ever since that movie with Tom Hanks, *Angels and Demons*, . . . I want to see the Vatican."

I laugh at myself for jumping to conclusions, but Wesley is now thinking through the rest of the itinerary and realizing that they won't just be sailing past these countries but actually getting to disembark. "And we are going to Egypt?" he asks, his voice faint with growing disbelief at his good fortune.

"Yes, you'll see the Pyramids. And you can ride a camel!" Wesley's eyes light up like a child's on Christmas morning. His week just got a lot more exciting.

But then they discuss rules for the trip. Robert says that Wesley can have sex with other men on the cruise, but it is clear from the pained expression on his face when he says this that he wants Wesley all to himself.

"No! No, of course, I don't want to do this," Wesley assures him. It seems a bit of a sore spot and I wonder how they will feel when they are on the cruise, surrounded by thousands of mostly heterosexual people who will see this aging wealthy white man and his twenty-something Brazilian porn star companion and almost certainly find it noteworthy.

As the afternoon wears on, we turn away from the cruise and discuss

Wesley's experiences with *programas*. "I enjoy doing porn very much. But I hate programas with clients." He describes riding the bus home from programas and just sitting there, leaning against the windows crying as strangers stared at him. "I just don't like the way it makes me feel." Sometimes the clients are especially unattractive or they say mean, disrespectful things to him about being a sex worker. He prefers porn because he enjoys his colleagues and is better able to dictate his working conditions and sexual partners. He finds them attractive and enjoys the sex, he says. He doesn't want to be in prostitution, he says, and feels depressed about the stigma.

"Did you cry after our first date?" Robert asks, alarmed. It doesn't seem as though they've ever really talked about Wesley's feelings about his work.

Wesley assures him no with a quick shake of his head but isn't enthusiastic enough, and Robert looks a bit wounded.

To go on this trip, Wesley has to leave his two children with their mother. Unlike most of the *garotos de programa* in my research, who identify as heterosexual, Wesley now identifies as gay. But he was married and had children before he began doing programas and making porn. Robert seems less enthusiastic about the idea of Wesley's children and struggles to remember their ages or many of their details, although it's clear they've talked about this before.

A few weeks later, Wesley is home and I see pictures of the vacation. There he is: Wesley the gay porn star at the Vatican; Wesley standing in front of the Great Pyramid; Wesley posing in his Speedo on the cruise deck, taut abs glistening in the Mediterranean sun; Wesley laughing and smiling with his *gringo* boyfriend, traveling first class around the world, and having the trip of a lifetime.

Mission Impossible

This chapter examines gay sex tourists' motivations, rationalizations, and explanations for their activities in Brazil as well as how they make sense of their relationships with garotos. It questions the ways in which tourists position gay tourism and purchasing programas as a benefit to local men and a means of uplifting the community economically. It also explores the contradictions inherent in these encounters that make the missionizing activities of identity politics problematic. Robert enjoyed the fact that Wesley identified as gay and enjoyed sex with (some) men. However, as past chapters have shown, many gringo tourists fetishize the masculine heterosexual garotos even though they also want these men to experience pleasure in the encounter. That is, even though the gay tourists are drawn to the garotos for the men's virtuoso performances of heterosexual Latin machismo, they persist in their beliefs that the men are really gay or bisexual "deep down" and simply in denial or closeted.

In addition to tourists' performance of gay rights rhetoric that reifies gay identity politics as a model for global export, garotos perform racialized masculinity for tourists, moving across and through different models of sexual identification. In a paradox of queer desire, many tourists want to awaken same-sex desires in the garotos and to encourage the men to accept these desires (as Wesley had). However, if such desires actually congeal into a gay (or bisexual) identity framework, the very performance of heterosexual masculinity that was the source of attraction would be negated.[2]

If my chief aim as an ethnographer were to demonstrate that sex tourists (gay or straight) from North America and Europe are racist or that sex tourism is inherently exploitative, it would have taken me only a few weeks of research to gather up damning but selective quotations from *saunas*, bars, and online forums. A quick visit to sites like the World Sex Archive will quickly confirm any stereotypes about predatory foreigners looking for LBFMs, or Little Brown Fucking Machines, as the heterosexual sex tourist saying goes. But to paint this picture would require too narrow a mind and too broad a brush.

Unfortunately, that's generally as far as journalistic and popular depictions of sex tourism get. It's easy to cherry-pick the worst examples from Internet comment sections and the like. Media images stick with the tawdry surface elements and ignore the fact that people who purchase sexual services are not inherently bad people and that male sex workers, while sometimes living a tough life, are neither dangerous criminals nor wounded souls in need of rescue. The commercial sex scene in Brazil is not an industry of scrappy heroes trapped in a noble struggle against predatory villains. The sexual economy of Brazil is a complex one in which actors on both the supply and the demand side of transactions have differing needs, experiences, and hopes. My goal is not to incite sympathy for the sex tourist but rather to demonstrate the variety of motivations, kinds of relationships, and approaches to race and power that exist in the gay tourist and commercial sexual economies while also exploring the paradoxical elements of the desires that flow through these economic landscapes.

This isn't to say that the sexual economy that I study is without problematic elements. On the contrary, gay civil rights rhetoric permeates the rationales of tourists as they describe the benefits that their travel brings to gay people everywhere and to the men from whom they purchase sex. The tourists' fetishization of Brazilian masculinity and the so-called "Latin model" of homosexuality ultimately eradicate the very subject that gay tourists fantasize about liberating. Even as the garotos perform masculinity across these models of sexual identity, tourists' contradictory desires hasten a collapsing of the identity models and confound the masculinity being performed. Therefore, my critique is aimed not at gay sex tourists per se but at a particular logic that relies on the worst elements of essentialist identity politics.

I also need to be clear that many of the fantasies in question are not unique to tourists. The local Brazilian clients who identify as gay are attracted to the same tropes in the garotos' performances of masculinity: they may fantasize about heterosexual men or even desire the transgression of sexual identity models. I focus on tourists' experiences because the Brazilian government itself and many companies are invested in selling Brazil to foreign audiences, including specifically to gay tourists. To do this, they market sexuality across the semiotic gap of cultural difference by emphasizing both the exotic and the erotic to tourists. Unsurprisingly, tourists then exoticize their experience and contribute to the racialization of the affective exchange they have with garotos, which makes it worthwhile to understand the touristic dimensions of the sexual encounter on their own terms.

In order to understand this sexual economy, it's useful to delve into how tourists who are attached to the idea of "Latin homosexuality" and an exotic, erotic Brazilian *macho* are now binding this discourse to their own rhetoric of purchasing power, consumerism, and foreign exceptionalism.

A few of the tourists fetishized wielding economic advantage over straight-identified macho men, presuming every vendor, waiter, and passerby was sexually available for the right price.[3] Most tourists, however, were well-intentioned men who were passionate about Brazilian culture and treated their sex worker companions respectfully. Not a few fell in love with garotos whom they met in the *saunas*, attempted to "rescue" them from prostitution, and paid for their education, housing, or family expenses. As in the case of Robert and his lavish displays toward Wesley, these romantically minded tourists commonly took the garotos on shopping sprees, dined out with them at nice restaurants, gave them access to trendy clubs, and took them on vacation in South America and Europe or helped arrange visas to travel to the United

States. Garotos who can perform authentic attachment for clients find their performative virtuosity well rewarded.

Although the gay tourists I met still enjoyed their travels, they often complained that global gay travel itself is under attack (especially in Latin America and the Caribbean), citing religious hostility by evangelical Christian leaders, protests against gay tour groups, instances of gay bashings of tourists, port closures to gay cruise ships, bans effected against gay couples by hotel owners, and draconian local sodomy laws.[4] For example, Mark, who was an educational administrator in his late thirties, complained about the dangers of traveling while gay. "Straight people don't understand this. There will be a conference in Jamaica or something and I can't go because I'll get killed. If you read the gay blogs, like if you read *Towleroad* or *Queerty* or whatever, you will see shit happening like every week or every other week, some homophobic bullshit, some tourist beaten with a baseball bat, or some asshole government person saying gays should stay out of their country. But straight people are just all, you know, la la la," he says, rolling his eyes and pantomiming someone skipping along lackadaisically, "doing what they want."

"Does that bother you? Not being able to go someplace?" I ask.

"Well that depends on where. Do I want to go someplace that doesn't want me? Probably not. Fuck them. I'll keep my goddamned money then . . . but it is still a violation of my civil rights. I have money. I can afford to go there. I'm going to help their fucking economy, right? And so maybe some businesses start to realize they can make more money by being welcoming and tolerant, and they start to realize it's not so bad, and that is good for the gay people there because it's a less hate-filled environment, right? So making it illegal or inhospitable, making it legally or practically impossible for me to visit, is a human rights issue. So whether it's a shithole or not isn't really the issue for me. It's the principle of the thing [that] bothers me."

For Mark and travelers like him, gay travel is a "civil right," and it is discriminatory to use sexual identity to restrict the mobility of someone who has the means to travel. They see tourism as doubly good. For one thing, gay travelers promote greater tolerance of homosexuality by local populations who simply lack exposure to gays and lesbians—at least out and proud ones. Moreover, local people receive more than just a lesson in multiculturalism. Mark and other gay tourists reason that serving the needs of gay and lesbian travelers (or better still—marketing to their niche specifically) provides much-needed economic growth. Thus, gay travel is good for tourists and the toured alike. Tourists in my study such as Mark associated gay consumerism, leisure travel and expenditures, and the acquisition of vacation property with both developing underprivileged communities *and* fostering goodwill toward gays.

Joseph Massad describes Euro-American gays who engage in "missionizing" as a sort of Weberian ideal type that he calls the "International Global Gay."[5] While I discuss his work below, it's worth noting here that Massad assumes these "Gay Internationals" to be highly strategic members of or personally invested in politically focused lobbies and groups such as the Human Rights Campaign. His analysis is apt when one considers men like Mark and his statements about gay rights. However, this complex, self-reflexive framing of gay (sex) tourism as both civil right and social activism was never presented to me by the tourists I know as their primary motivation for travel. Instead, this rationale persistently manifested itself in my data most often as an afterthought or a sidebar, and yet it came up consistently regardless of age, race, or political leaning.

This ubiquitous language of gay rights was no coincidence. It reflects a recent trend in the North American gay community and in gay lobbying groups and NGOs to use the presumed economic privilege of gays or anticipated economic benefits to a community to demonstrate the benefits of recognizing gay rights. For example, in this view straight people should accept "marriage equality" laws not on moral grounds but because it will be good for state and local economies.[6] Gay travel bans should be lifted and gay tourists wooed because they have disposable income. Gay men, who are seen as wealthier, are especially valued because they are the bringers of gentrification and harbingers of rising property values.[7]

As scholars of political economy and cultural critics alike have noted, the excruciating elegance of neoliberalism is that the system appears so natural and inevitable that we seldom notice when late capitalism is at work in our lives. (Or as Margaret Thatcher's policy slogan famously put it: "There Is No Alternative.") Consequently, today one does see gay rights activists replacing radical claims for inclusion with appeals to the marketplace—in effect ceding the moral high ground in an attempt to purchase civil rights without any indication that they understand just how radical this rhetorical shift is or what its consequences are. This line of reasoning appears in gay advertising campaigns for states and cities that encourage travelers to come there to have their gay weddings or honeymoons. It surfaces more subtly in social media as when Marriott launched its #LoveTravels hashtag as part of an advertising blitz directed at lesbian and gay travelers. (This campaign is especially telling because Marriott, which is Mormon owned, broke with church doctrine in its decision to woo gay travelers and their dollars.)

My interlocutors were not just any gay travelers or gay activists, of course. They were tourists who purchased sex from garotos and whose money ultimately helped to support these men and their families. Many fetishized having sex with masculine, heterosexual men, but those who began long-term relationships with their "kept" Brazilian boyfriends often pressured the men to "come out" or at least admit to feeling pleasure, desire, and attraction to the tourist. Robert, for example, was upset when he learned that Wesley cried after doing programas with clients like Robert himself, and he needed to be reassured that he was exceptional and sex with him was not a source of distress for Wesley.

While some experienced tourists were grounded and realistic, offering many deep insights about the complicated nature of transnational sexualities, many more told me quite plainly that they hoped my research and eventual book would reveal garotos who didn't come out to be "closeted" or "repressed" men whose true sexuality was inhibited by Brazil's conservative society. In this way, the gay sex tourists in my study sought to transform the very object of their desire—the unattainable straight macho—into a domestic partner. Not surprisingly, when they dealt with their gringos, garotos I knew eventually abandoned or minimized their use of local terms for sexual identity categories (e.g., *normal,* or "normal"; *homem,* or "man," meaning "straight"). Instead, they would use imported terms such as *gay* for "gay" and *hetero* for "heterosexual" and would often begin to self-identify as *bi* (bisexual) when a client became a full-time boyfriend. The performative labor in which the garotos engage is fundamentally about making one's masculinity and sexuality legible across different cultural frameworks, and so they attempt to perform "gay" and "bi" but instead render these identities as *gay* and *bi*—a syncretic category in which *gay* and *bi* never really take on the exact meanings they have for gringos. In pushing for this shift, however, tourists trap themselves in a queer paradox in which their missionizing in the name of gay identity and transnational community actually require an end to the local figure of the sexually available "Latin macho" that drew them to the Global South in the first place.

Tourists were attached to the object of their desire even as they transformed that object into something that would be banal—sometimes even repellent—to them in its similarity to themselves. This queer paradox of unrealizable wish fulfillment propelled clients back to the *sauna* time and again, always in need of a new *boy* (i.e., rent boy). And it meant that garotos had to become deft at toying, delaying, and playing with tourist fantasies if they were to continue to extract cash for their performative labor.

To be clear, I am not arguing that gay tourism has been a primary means of exporting and popularizing Anglo-European models of sexual identity in Latin America, although that is one implication of Massad's accusation about the "Gay International." Instead, I concur with the queer theorist Eve Sedgwick, who affirmed that conflicting models of sexual identity can coexist or overlap and subjects can move between them.[8] Instead of investigating this phenomenon as a mode of transmission as if identity works virally, I emphasize that these relationships reveal how sexuality influences larger economic processes as gay travel and sexual economies continue to expand and take on new forms. While still nowhere near the value of the enormous heterosexual sexual economy in Brazil, gay commercial sex is nevertheless important to and highly visible in key local economies.[9] Male prostitution and gay sex tourism are now so common in major cities in Brazil that the families of garotos often suspect the men's true line of work, and rumors about which young men in the neighborhood are selling sex now abound in communities far away from red-light districts. No longer unthinkable, male prostitution is increasingly a viable and known path out of poverty, largely because the industry's growth has been so sharp in recent decades.

But even more significant than showing that small interactions are gaining economic and social importance is how gringo-garoto relationships also reveal that economic trends influence everyday sexual practices and processes of identification. As Brazil's growth rate soared in the booming economy of the 2000s, so too did the ranks of the middle classes. Brazilians have had bad experiences historically with inflation and are therefore more accustomed to spending than saving, but highly conspicuous consumption is on the rise, and in 2009 a narrow majority of Brazilians officially qualified as middle class or higher according to the Brazilian government's classification system.[10] Many garotos who work in *saunas* reported that they did so primarily for extra spending money, while others reported that prostitution had lifted them out of poverty and allowed them to maintain a comfortably middle-class lifestyle. These men, in turn, distinguished themselves from street *michês* who sold sex to survive and remained poor.

For example, Felipão described how he came to work in the *sauna*.

"I was out at a club that is more mixed—normal people and some gays. I was dancing, you know, and very sweaty, very hot there, and loud. I went to the bathroom and as I was going to go in, this guy comes up to me and tells me he is recruiting for working in the *sauna*, and did I know what that was? I said I was not interested, but he asked me if I wanted my dick sucked." Felipão smiled, looking a bit embarrassed at this point in his story. "So, yeah, right there in the bathroom and he would *pay* me to let *him* suck *me*. . . . I think it was maybe fifty [reais]. So I did it. I mean, I was high [on marijuana] and I was horny [*fiquei com tesão*]. Then he told me I could have that happen every day, getting sucked and having money, if I came to work [for him]. Then he took my phone number."

"So why did you decide to go?"

"Because I'm lazy!" Felipão laughed, fiddling with a chain around his neck. "Look, I am nineteen so I live at home. I have no responsibilities. I just like to listen to good music, go dancing, go to the mall. I don't want a job; I want to have fun, you know? I am not like these *boys* in the *sauna* who are desperate, who need the money. They have families, you know? Shit. For them, it's serious! But for me, it is more just for fun. So I come two times a week and do a programa or two and that is enough money, and so I do not need to work."

Like Felipão, garotos are quite conspicuous in their consumption, especially of electronics, designer goods, alcohol, drugs, and services at clubs.[11] Many of the older garotos I know lament that they did not save during their early days when they made more money as a "fresh face" in the *saunas*, instead "wasting" all their income (sometimes making in a night what their parents made in a month) on alcohol, parties, and gifts for girlfriends. Similarly, Lucia Rabello de Castro studied consumer culture among poor youth in urban Brazil and found an intense desire on their part to consume as a "mode of inclusion" that achieves short-term gains. Exactly like Felipão, they wear fashionable knock-offs and trendy hairstyles, purchase items they cannot really afford, and "imagine that by trying to imitate the middle-class lifestyle they could become more equal."[12] Thus, garotos are trying to copy, not the tourists' consumer lifestyles, but middle-class Brazilian ones—that is, a refracted Brazilian dream shaped only indirectly by Hollywood and the US culture industry.

Yet the men also gain access to restaurants, clubs, and bourgeois social spaces when they are with a gringo, as in the case of the opportunities Robert provided for Wesley or those Martin described having provided for the garoto he liked on his dinner-and-a-movie date night in the last chapter. Such access is sometimes possible with their Brazilian clients, but local customers (especially closeted men with families) don't party like gringos on vacations. Gringos are in town for a short time, are intent on seeing lots of things and engaging in a lot of leisure activities, are there to spend money, and are often in need of company. And so the garotos are willing to offer exemplary performances of racialized Brazilian masculinity in order to become consumers themselves. Many came into the sex trade when they saw poor friends, brothers, or cousins throwing around cash, getting bottle service at clubs, and buying designer clothes. For them, prostitution is not just a job; it's a process of economic transformation.

Analyzing the role that market-based identity politics plays for gringos and the ways in which garotos adapt to and capitalize on these logics to gain access to opportunities for consumerism reveals just how important economic trends are in linking models of sexual identity with consumerism. In critiquing the logics that motivate contemporary gay sex tourism, I need to be clear that I am not condemning the tourists or the garotos who graciously shared their experiences and insights with me. Rather, I am interested in the inherent contradictions of gay rights claims that retreat from ethical grounding and take refuge in market-based rhetoric instead.

The relationships and ethnographic interactions between gay gringos and garotos reflect on an everyday microlevel the political logics of the gay travel industry—which is an enormously powerful, if diffuse, conglomeration that relies heavily on coupling blunt-force economics and identity politics. Companies produce marketing strategies aimed at gay consumers that define sexual identity as a facet of a coveted consumer demographic, as in the titular TurboConsumers™ campaign that I discuss at length below. Interactions between clients and garotos demonstrate the very real consequences that the marketization of gay identity politics is having at the level of individual relationships and how the imbrications of sexuality and consumerism that affect mobile and moneyed tourists in turn affect masculinity, gender, and even kinship in seemingly remote places.

Tourist Attractions

My tourist interlocutors' sexual interests reflected the wider gay community's valorization of conventional masculinity, or "butchness." They fantasized about having sex with masculine young men, often fetishizing the man's heterosexuality and relishing the idea that they were awakening hidden desires and repressed passions. "He's at least bisexual," they would say of their "boyfriends." Or as a fifty-something retiree from Chicago explained to me of the garoto who had broken his heart, "That one was such a closet case it's no wonder he got married, but he'll always be a *sauna* boy, . . . always go back to turn tricks because at the end of the day he just loves dick." Tourists were well versed in sociological and anthropological views of "Latin homosexuality," in which one's sexual identity is determined by one's role in sex as either *ativo* or *passivo*. In much of Latin America, ostensibly *"normal"* men with wives and girlfriends are free to have sex with homosexual men without compromising their masculinity or sexual identity so long as they are ativo. Tourists use their knowledge of this pattern to avail themselves of the common fantasy of seducing heterosexual men (which is—not incidentally—also a trope in gay pornography, gay fiction, gay television shows, and gay magazines in the United States).[13]

Of the gay tourists who returned to Brazil annually to purchase sex, nearly all of them had at least one experience trying to go on a date with a sex worker outside the strict confines of the *sauna*, and some sought to have relationships and genuine emotional connections. But whenever a tourist grew attached enough to a garoto, he usually would bid him to stop turning tricks, usually offering to support the man financially and visiting several times a year. A few tourists even bought vacation homes and allowed their boyfriends to live in them. These situations were so common that experienced, jaded tourists would warn neophytes about them. Stanley, a very active client who had been going to Brazil for years and who kept close tabs on the rotation of garotos in the various *saunas* in São Paulo and Rio, explained, "These things never end well. . . . I try to warn the new [clients] when they start to fall for a *boy*. I'm like, 'Look, buddy this thing is going to be bad for you. . . . Dating rent boys only ends in heartache.'" Stanley had been married to a woman himself before coming out, and he felt he had lived through a lot. Consequently, he felt he had a knack for "detecting bullshit" in others. "So, yeah, [the garoto] is going to have a sick mother, or he is going to have a debt and some guy in the *favela* is going to beat him up, or he is going to have some online course he needs to take to improve himself or some English class. . . . It's always one thing after another and you just keep handing him cash, and all the while he's doing the same thing to five other dumbass gringos, and he's getting all the pussy [from girlfriends] he can handle because of it, laughing all the way to the bank."

Brazilian clients are quite capable of "keeping" garotos, too, and were doing so long before gringos arrived on the scene. In fact, Brazilian clients would sometimes poke fun at how easily tourists bought into the garotos' hard-luck stories, how quickly they were seduced by Brazilian men. However, garotos take special care to land gringos, preferring them over Brazilians because of the ease with which they can manipulate them and the comparatively little time they need to spend with them. Such ploys (known as *jeitos*) are a common subject of talk among the men, but they also have implications for deeper issues of identity politics.

Upon entering a long-term relationship, garotos often began to identify as "bisexual." They know that they must appear to reciprocate affection and desire, a phenomenon that Bernstein calls (in the context of female sex workers) manufacturing "bounded authenticity."[14] The garotos' gringo boyfriends and the gringos' friends encourage this transformation to supposed bisexuality in both subtle and obvious ways, joking with them and prodding them along. The relationships tourists have with garotos are not superficial, however, and emotional bonds are strong, if complicated. Garotos learned to play out such fantasies with clients decades ago with gay Brazilian customers. It would be wrong to think that gringos are spreading Euro-American gay identity models through sex tourism. However, romantic gringos are far more fascinated with the performances of hypersexuality and the seeming fluidity of sexual practice and identity categories in Brazil than are Brazilians, for whom Brazilian male sexuality is neither exotic nor especially remarkable.

Adilson, with his usual mix of enthusiasm and wry wit, explained this preference for gringos well and, in fact, was enormously proud of having landed "his gringo." Adilson was thrilled with what he saw as "our research project," and we spent many hours talking before or after he went to work at the *sauna*, getting his nicotine fix since the *sauna* had attempted to go smoke free. We were sitting in a seedy bar where garotos hang out, and he took a long drag off yet another cigarette, reflecting a moment before diving in: "It's lucky to find your rich gringo. I've stayed with mine six years, and he comes once, twice a year. This year, he stayed one week and that was all. This is the dream of every *boy* [*sonho de todo boy*]."

Adilson exhaled gray smoke as he talked. "They don't want to bother [*encher o saco*] with a Brazilian. They want a gringo. He comes one time a year or two to three, okay. But he's not around here twenty-four hours a day like a Brazilian would be. Cause if it's a Brazilian, the *boy* is fucked [*fodido*]. He has to see that faggot [*viado*] all day long. Oh no. Nauseating! Gringos are best."

As Adilson continued, he nodded matter-of-factly. "When [the gringo] says, 'What do you want as a present?' most boys ask for sneakers, a phone, a computer, an expensive thing. I asked mine to pay all my studies, both for me to finish school and for English lessons." Adilson leaned back, looking pleased at his own foresight. "He even took me to Switzerland once, but Switzerland is actually a terrible place. *Horrivel!* Swiss people are serious and never laugh. *Horrivel,*" he said, screwing up his face in disgust.

We both laughed at his passionate assessment of how "horrible" the Swiss are before he continued. Despite the negativity evinced by describing gringos as "nauseating" "faggots," Adilson did have some attachment to his gringo. "Today, my gringo and I are all good [*numa boa*]. . . . He comes when he misses me . . . and I never lie to him, never."

I was curious about Adilson's assertion that he never lies to his gringo and how that might square with the question of sexual orientation, which over several years I had heard him describe in different ways.

"I consider myself *bi*, because [my gringo] is a guy that if I see that *he* needs something, and I can help him, I'm always going to help him. Always. . . . Because he's my friend. I like him. I like him a lot."

It's important that Adilson does not frame his identity as *bi* as being about desire. It's about his willingness to engage with the man emotionally, but practically. He "likes" him. He would "help" him. When I asked him if, now that he is *bi,* he would date or have noncommercial sex with men, he said no. *Bi* for garotos doesn't translate as cleanly to "bi" or "bisexual" as the gringo boyfriends would like. Later, when I pressed him about whether he also has *saudades* for his gringo (i.e., roughly, whether he "missed" him), he hesitated a moment before admitting that he did.

Adilson typifies a certain ambivalence among garotos in that, despite boasting about scamming or even exploiting tourists, they also have complex relationships with them. Like Adilson, many spoke derogatorily, but they also defended the men as decent, hardworking, loving, or sometimes as men deserving pity or sympathy but never contempt and certainly not hatred, as commonly portrayed by films or media narratives in which a male hustler attacks or murders a client he secretly despises in a homophobic rage.

Instead, gringo-garoto relationships can be complicated. Adilson moved from poverty to a lower-middle-class status as a result of his relationship and his ability to enact a certain set of character traits. In subsequent conversations, it became clear that these traits included his partial command of English as well as his willingness to identify as bisexual and express pleasure to his gringo in their sexual relationship, performing changes in the contours of his masculinity and sexuality that appealed to the gringo. Meanwhile, the gringo was also a status symbol for the rent boy, and other garotos grew tired of hearing Adilson talk about him all the time. But Adilson also had genuine affection for the man and did not regard him as a client any longer or even see himself as a sex worker anymore, which highlights how difficult it is to define the parameters of commercial sex.

I should also note that several years later, his gringo did leave him. Adilson was crushed. He also, interestingly, told me he was gay, saying that in retrospect he had been wrong to call himself *bi*. "I was always gay," he informed me. I thought that Adilson had used *bi* strategically and temporarily like so many other garotos I knew and whom I describe below, but it turned out that his sexual identifications were even more complex than I had realized and that he really had experienced a sexual awakening through prostitution.

It seems ironic yet also predictable that his gringo—one of the few to actually have his fantasy come true—should dump Adilson, but as Adilson said, the gringo simply "lost interest" in him. "I think he goes to the *saunas* for the *boys* who are *hetero*," he said. "I do not think he has a relationship with any of them like with me." Adilson, absent his gringo, needed to return to doing programas again, his changes in sexual identifications ultimately proving to be what brought him out of and finally back into a life of prostitution.

Enter the TurboConsumer™

Not all gay tourism is gay sex tourism. In fact, "sex tourism" is itself (as I mentioned in the book's introduction) a problematic and ill-defined term that I use rather reluctantly here to refer to a broad range of commercial and quasi-commercial exchanges that can sometimes include "romance tourism," "holiday flings," "green-card dating," and even "sex on vacation" with lower-class Brazilians who mainly date wealthy gringos.[15] While many gay tourists don't self-identify as sex tourists, they did frame sex as an important component of their travel. Some academics support the position that, in the face of adversity, gay tourists may best be viewed as "pilgrims" in search of community and identity.[16] While this may be true for gay men or lesbians visiting San Francisco's historic Castro or the site of the Stonewall riots in New York, when I examine the gay tourist and expat communities in Rio de Janeiro and Bahia, it seems that this search for community and shared sexual identity also includes buying beach condos, starting gay businesses, and frequenting gay bars, clubs, and restaurants.

Perhaps because affluent gay men have already participated so intensely in the gentrification of San Francisco's Castro and New York's Village, it may be easier to see pilgrimage and searches for community there. But in Brazil, the economic development and gentrification accompanying the foreigner's search for gay community is still new. Describing the gratitude of elderly locals when gay tourists produced the smooth transformation of a dangerous neighborhood in Madrid into an idyllic community, Gabriel Giorgi writes that the "gay community neutralizes homophobia by playing the role of urban rescuer: gentrification is the dues gays pay to society."[17] While global gay gentrification doesn't necessarily preclude a larger sense of sexual community or pilgrimage, it does serve as a kind of event horizon—the point at which gay identity inescapably and permanently collapses sexuality and consumerism into one another.

Gordon Waitt and Kevin Markwell insist that gay tourism is *not* neocolonial because "the tourist is not prescribed the role of dominator, imposing an expression of sexuality on the host," and that "the rhetoric [used by academics] of neocolonialism silence[s] the subjectivity of the 'host'" because hosts may have "erotic attraction and fantasy that match the traveler's gaze."[18] While I agree wholeheartedly with their agentive framing, such statements not only assume a low level of incentivization for locals who have sex with tourists but also risk overlooking the myriad ways that sex between gay tourists and locals can be infused with economic difference. This is why determining what counts as a "commercial" sexual encounter is also much more difficult than a lot of the literature on prostitution acknowledges, and without understanding the role of economics in the sex trade it is difficult to approach overarching questions of tourist motivations and rationalizations when it comes to commercial sex.

Most studies of sex tourism have ignored clients' perspectives and their motivations for travel. As global leisure travel increased over the past thirty years, sex tourism has become its increasingly visible adjunct. Despite this, when researchers do write about clients, they do so with little meaningful face-to-face interaction with them or rely on X-rated Internet message boards where a particular segment of the most dedicated sex tourists swap reviews and sexually explicit online stories. Consequently, researchers may perpetuate unhelpful assumptions, arguing, for example, that "prostitute users" are motivated by overt racism. Some feminist scholars quite seriously dismiss clients as "rednecks" who are akin to "the Ku Klux Klan."[19] Even if one is ardently opposed to the purchasing of sexual services, neglecting the rationale and experience of the consumer does not help better understand the nature of the phenomenon at hand.

Gay print media, movies, television, memoires, and magazines in the United States and Europe are particularly fond of the idea of a "global gay consumer." They portray foreign travel as part and parcel of "mainstream" gay culture. As I was beginning research into gay tourism in 2006, CMB and PNO Publishing released the *TurboConsumer™ Out MRI Custom Study* for LPI Inc., which at that time also operated as PlanetOut Inc., published the *Advocate, Out,* and *OutTraveler,* ran websites and a gay travel company, and had many other gay business holdings. The 110-page media kit is devoted to pitching prospective advertisers and investors on the idea of gays as "TurboConsumers™," even trademarking this term for their ideal consumer-subject.[20]

According to the study, 70 percent of readers of the gay magazine *Out* had valid US passports.[21] The figure of 70 percent is astonishing given that the *Economist* generously estimates that only 34 percent of US citizens have a passport, and fewer still actually use them.[22] LPI claims that nearly half their readers take at least one international *and* one domestic leisure trip each year, and 11 percent took nine or more international vacations in the last three years. Because these statistics contradict the fact that other LGBT individuals experience pay gaps and discrimination in hiring, I must stress that affluent gay magazine readers certainly do *not* stand in for gays in the United States on the whole.[23] However, these respondents *do* represent middle-class gay male consumers with the means to travel and are a significant enough substratum of the overall gay population to allow Community Marketing to estimate the domestic gay travel industry's value at $70 billion per year, a figure that is larger than the GDP of many countries.[24] The demographic profile also tends to accurately reflect many (but not all) of the gay tourists with whom I worked in Brazil.[25]

I have argued that the use of economic incentives to promote a global gay identity based on that of the Euro-American gay community is riddled with contradictions. Heeding the warnings of the anthropologist Richard Parker, I do not wish to overestimate the importance of gay tourism for changing Brazilian constructions of homosexuality.[26] However, some tourists do make use of globalization and economic privilege to foist gay identity politics onto primarily impoverished Latin Americans in exchange for patronage, gifts, and payment for commercial sex. Local Brazilian men willing to sufficiently recalibrate their intimate performances of sexual identity may find themselves able to sustain long-term and/or transnational relationships with tourists and expats, thereby gaining the considerable advantages that having a wealthy boyfriend can afford them.[27] However, global gay sex tourism is just one part of a larger "pink economy," or markets shaped by LGBT consumer culture. Appeals to the power of the pink economy rely on the idea that gay civil rights can be won through purchasing power rather than the merits of ethical claims, but the inevitable, if unintended, outcome of making capital the means by which one pursues equality is rampant consumerism.

Anthropologists have long argued that political-economic conditions (re)shape sexuality.[28] Although subcultures organized around same-sex desire long preceded Fordism,[29] contemporary gay identity in the United States owes a huge debt to transformations resulting from the Industrial Revolution, which allowed unmarried young people (especially men) to leave their families in order to live and work in urban areas, giving them greater autonomy and access to sexual partners and nascent communities.[30] This transformation disproportionately benefited white gay men, who—in the ensuing decades—were able to consolidate their class interests and turn "gay ghettos" into thriving upscale neighborhoods. Such white, middle-class gay men increasingly came to represent the "mainstream" gay community, and with subsequent advances in legislative representation, media visibility, and civil rights, they became known as recession-proof tastemakers, gentrifiers, market mavens, and fashionistas.[31] No longer a sign that a neighborhood or venue is a marginal neighborhood or a "vice zone," the appearance of young urban gay professionals—known colloquially as guppies—buying property in the neighborhood now signals the upscaling of a housing market. Meanwhile, guppy diners reveal the increasing trendiness of a restaurant, and guppy fans mark the popularity of an emerging artist or celebrity.[32]

Class-based gay identity in the United States coalesced into "a powerful economic niche through which a range of consumer products and services are marketed on a global scale. It is not surprising, then, that touristic experiences have become increasingly important to the meanings of *gay* in a contemporary world."[33] Within this new pink economy, access to desirable housing, safe neighborhoods, good employment, and other well-deserved rights are all secured through purchasing power. In recent years, this has become an explicit strategy. In keeping with this logic, the Human Rights Campaign, the largest and wealthiest of gay rights advocacy groups, began printing pocket-sized buying guides that rate companies based on their support for gay issues so that readers can exert their political will through their pocket-books every time they go to the supermarket or plan a vacation.[34] This strategy is deemed effective because gay consumer spending is likely at an all-time high.

According to LPI Inc.'s 2002 market research, the annual household income of the TurboConsumer™ is approximately $105,000, over twice the national average. He is forty-two years old (and definitely a "he," as 90 percent of market research respondents were male). He has a 72 per-cent chance of holding a college degree and a 33 percent chance of holding a postgraduate degree. His investment portfolio is worth over $230,000. He drives a luxury car or SUV, frequently dines out, and or-ders drinks by brand when going out to bars or clubs, which is often. He shops at Macy's, Gap, and Banana Republic, but Target is his top stop, although at one moment during the writing of this book there were gay boycotts against Target for its support of anti-gay Tea Party candidates, which the company was notably quick to address. He votes in local, state, and national elections and writes letters to elected of-ficials. Despite his affluence, he is frequently unhappy. Approximately one in four TurboConsumers™ is depressed, one in five has anxiety, and one in six has insomnia. Gay "lifestyle" magazine pages are filled with pharmaceutical ads and ads for other ways to self-medicate or re-lax, including alcohol, sex hookup sites, and travel.

Ironically, all this supposed purchasing power may impede, rather than promote, civil rights. Ann Pellegrini points out that Justice An-tonin Scalia succumbed to the potent myth that all gays are wealthy when he cited the "high disposable income" of gays as a reason why they did not deserve "special rights."[35] Michael Warner positions con-sumerism as inherent to gay identity when he notes: "Post-Stonewall urban gay men reek of the commodity. We give off the smell of capi-talism in rut."[36] For Warner, queerness emerges as antithetical to gay identity precisely in its radical rejection of late-capitalist formations. Jeff Maskovsky takes issue with Warner's claims and asserts that War-ner grants too much credence to the monolithic, white guppy com-munity. Maskovsky also questions whether a queer subject is any less neoliberal. "Gay and lesbian business owners often exploit wider labor-market trends with nary a second thought as to the effect on equality and solidarity within 'the community,'" he argues. "[I]n the name of gay community, employers exercise entrepreneurial spirit on the backs of their workers, thereby reinforcing race, class, and gender divisions within sexual-minority communities."[37]

Martin Manalansan concurs when he notes that "Caucasian gay clones" fetishize working-class clothing styles while simultaneously functioning as both the bearers and the arbiters of good taste.[38] Having fetishized working-class gays and gays of color, they then participate in gay tourism and circuit parties and practice consumer lifestyle choices that tend to exclude these very men, often relegating their participation to service personnel. Gay businesses (e.g., bars, realtors, retailers) also compete for the same clientele and try to drive each other out of business. Gay developers price low- to middle-income gays out of community areas. "This strategy of capital accumulation . . . [has] the consequence that the community [becomes] more stratified along class lines."[39] And amid this rampant consumerism and capital accumulation, gay marketing companies create consumer profiles to sell advertisements and tour packages to gay consumers, encouraging them to leave the stresses of this lifestyle behind and lose themselves in exotic locales like Brazil.

TurboConsumers™ to the Rescue

The TurboConsumer™ is an invention of marketing, as its prominent "trademark" symbol constantly reminds us throughout LPI's report. Tourists I know do not share this vision of themselves. Most did not identify as wealthy or upper class. For many years of my research, they complained constantly about the declining value of the dollar and bemoaned the strength of the Brazilian real, although that trend suddenly reversed near the end of my work, allowing for a resurgence of cheap programas for gringos. Several tourists echoed Stanley's earlier comments and complained that garotos treated them like "walking ATMs" or "G(ay)TMs." The tourists haggled over prices and refused to tip, reasoning that they were already being overcharged because they were gringos. But all this changed when a garoto became a boyfriend. Tourists loved taking them to the Christ Statue or Sugarloaf Mountain, going to dinners and movies and out dancing and shopping. They enjoyed showing off their relative wealth and providing opportunities and experiences for their Brazilian partners.

Tourists whom I interviewed (especially in Bahia, which is poorer and has less infrastructure and a smaller "gay scene" than Rio, but is also much cheaper for tourists) believed that showcasing their purchasing power would not only earn them acceptance, respect, and gratitude from locals (including their boyfriends) but also make the destination safer and more hospitable to "the gay community" as a whole, paving the way for future travelers, and also, they argued, better for local LGBT individuals. Eating at restaurants or hiring local cleaning women became acts of activism in their minds. One tourist, a wealthy African American man in his forties named Russell, pointed to a laundromat in Bahia's Porto da Barra neighborhood that displayed a rainbow flag, saying to me, "Look, if gay people weren't coming here, there's no way that place would have a rainbow flag there. But now the gay people who live here can see that, and the whole neighborhood can see that, and so I think it changes local attitudes not just to gringos and gay foreigners but [gay] Brazilians, too."

Russell believed that the gay tourist presence was creating a gay-friendly community, which he assumed was benefiting locals. As comments such as this accrued during my work, I began to realize that gay travel was, to many of the tourists, a matter of noblesse oblige. According to these tourists, their travel helped make the locations they visited better, safer places for disenfranchised Brazilians who could not help themselves, at least not as easily or as effectively. Such rhetoric overlooks the tremendous amount of local grassroots activism in Brazil, which enjoys a rich array of both mainstream LGBT and radical queer NGOs and groups who fight to diminish prejudice and increase opportunities and living conditions for sexual minorities.

While CMB and PNO Publishing tries to tap gay tourists as a community of consumers, the men see themselves in more heroic and missionizing terms. This incommensurability is a weakness of both marketing research and identity politics. While the marketing divisions of LPI Inc., its consultants, and subsidiaries understand facets of gay men's consumption patterns of which the men themselves are likely unaware, they fail to understand the importance of gay rights and sexual community in the men's lives. Yet the gay tourists in my study occasionally saw how much consumerism also shapes Brazilian lives. They saw that when the garotos put their clothes back on, they were leaving *saunas* wearing designer fashions and carrying expensive consumer electronics. The consumerism had seeped into their gringo travel experience, and the constant requests from garotos for more money, shopping sprees, gifts, and travel took its toll, sullying any romanticized visions tourists had about their travels and their relationships with garotos.

Although the realities of both gay consumerism and the rhetoric of gay uplift affect these relationships, they certainly do not negate their value to those in them. For example, John, a forty-five-year-old highly skilled factory worker, was able to afford to visit Brazil two to three times a year to see his boyfriend, Agostinho, to whom he sent money every few months on the condition that he not sell sex anymore. When Agostinho's mother needed surgery and Agostinho became desperate, John worked overtime to pay her medical costs. As a result of his sacrifices, John could not afford to make his next visit to see Agostinho.

John's story is not unique. Mark Padilla has collected extensive documentation of similar relationships between male sex workers in the Dominican Republic and their "Western Union Daddies."[40] Such relationships can appear benevolent and romantic. Most long-term tourists and garotos are pretty cynical about such relationships, however, and I also became similarly jaded over the years. Yet I also found John and Agostinho's story quite touching. But when I asked John what he got out of traveling to Brazil in the first place, he spoke of broadening his horizons and loving Brazilian culture. Then he talked about how "hot" the men were. Sometime later he explained, "Plus, I think tourism is good for the economy. It's good for the local people, and it helps them become more tolerant and accepting. So it's basically just good for everybody, for us and them. It's a win-win."

This rhetoric of economic uplift is common to both gay and straight sex tourists, especially when the sex workers are young or have children. It is not, as I noted, the primary motivation for gay travel. Yet there is an element of paternalism undergirding many of the stories I heard over the years—which at its most visible involved gay Northerners assuming a global gay identity, prefiguring a global gay community that they are obligated to protect, defend, and foster. Joseph Massad's controversial book *Desiring Arabs* is a polemical but secular screed against the "Gay International," an abstraction fostered mainly by groups like Amnesty International, Human Rights Watch, the International Lesbian and Gay Association, and the International Gay and Lesbian Human Rights Commission. The Gay International unfairly makes special moral judgments against Muslim countries for crimes against gays (a sexual identity that Massad argues is fundamentally Western), pinning assessments of those countries' "development" to their treatment of LGBT individuals.[41] He argues that in bringing all of this "incitement to discourse" about homosexuality, the Gay International is actually creating homophobia and inciting violent backlash by Muslims against the supposed "gays."[42]

I agree with Massad's assessment of the importance of recognizing culturally specific models of sexual identity. And while I have already drawn heavily on his critique of the "missionizing" nature of gay identity politics, he does little to concretize the Gay International. While I am similarly critical of the gay TurboConsumer™—who is certainly a relative of the Gay International—I am interested in critiquing this category by examining the ambiguous and sometimes-contradictory actions and ideas of those who fall under that rubric. Massad allows the Gay International to function so monolithically that he has conjured up a vast occidental conspiracy of human rights organizations guided by a similarly monolithic "orientalist impulse." He also fails to account for or ascribe agency to Arabs and Muslims who fully identify as gay, lesbian, bisexual, or transgendered in defiance of scholarly opprobrium. To be fair, he is not an ethnographer; ethnographers must deal with the world as we find it, and it does seem that the gay genie is out of the bottle, as it were, regardless of whether it was gay rights groups, global media, or grassroots activists who rubbed the lamp.

While my own argument parallels Massad's insomuch as I am critical of European and US gay rights rhetoric that ethnocentrically places its version of identity politics at the heart of its mission, I am more interested in how gay consumers operationalize rights rhetoric. When one turns to the actual, ethnographic details of how conflicting models of sexual identity coexist and how people move strategically between them, we can see that transformations of identity happen through complicated micro- and macroeconomic processes rather than through the collective will of conspiring gay rights lobbyists, underscoring the continued importance of political economy in struggles over identity.

Role Playing

Most of the garotos I knew had in common that they identified personally as heterosexual (or *"normal"*). Only a few heterosexual garotos admit to ever being passivo, although it is a poorly kept secret that many will bottom for the right price. These claims to heterosexuality are based on "Latin homosexuality," in which being passive is synonymous with homosexuality, while men who anally penetrate other men are not thought of as gay or homosexual and can even be considered more manly or virile for doing so.[43] Many tourists spoke in various

ways about Latin homosexuality, an academic discourse that is also circulated in mainstream gay travel guides and travel writing.[44]

Encounters within this model between passive homosexuals and
macho straight men are frequently thought to be nonemotional or
lacking in physically intimate acts like kissing.[45] This form of homosex can also take the form of adolescent boys training themselves for
the "real thing" (i.e., sex with women). For example, Brazilian boys
may play a variety of versions of the game *troca-troca* (turn-taking) in
which slightly older boys penetrate younger ones.[46] In one such varia-
tion, when adolescents move on to penetrating girls and women, the
younger boys are expected to move on to penetrating the next crop of
boys. Any boy who does *not* want to penetrate other boys then risks
being cast as a homosexual, who—when he matures—might then be
visited by men and teenage boys and thus incorporated into the community as providing a socially appropriate sexual outlet.[47] In Brazil,
candomblé priests (*pais-de-santo*) are rather famously associated with
Latin homosexuality and are nonetheless venerated as community
leaders.[48] Latin homosexuality also holds that *bichas* (homosexuals) are
mortified at the thought of having sex with other bichas and are only
interested in having sex with *normal* men.[49]

Not surprisingly, Latin homosexuality isn't a monolithic form consistent across all classes, countries, and people in Latin America.[50] In
fact, the discourse is a deeply problematic formulation. Sex roles of
penetrator/penetrated are nearly always a matter of assumption, and
frequently wrong.[51] Straight-identified men can and do have intimate,
affectionate sex with their homosexual partners, sometimes in relationships lasting many years.[52] Passive homosexuality among pais-
de-santo in candomblé has been vastly overestimated by foreign observers and may amount to a common stereotype.[53] (Moreover, I also
knew of pais using online sex hookup sites, suggesting their sexuality is nothing if not "modern.") There is also considerable debate over
whether men who penetrate other men are in fact free from stigma.[54]
And there are questions about whether the increased visibility of the
Anglo-European "gay identity" model in which sexual orientation is
seen as an identity dictated by the gender of one's object choice (alternately and problematically known as "egalitarian homosexuality")
may be responsible for shifting views and actually increasing stigma
and persecution of men who have sex with men.[55] While variations on
the Latin model are still common among the Brazilian lower classes,
and the "egalitarian" model thrives among middle-class Brazilian gays,

garotos are well aware of both models and can strategically shift between them as needed.

Latin homosexuality has become a point of contention in Latin American gay activist circles. As gay activists began organizing in the 1970s, they looked largely to the United States for their models.[56] Over time, Brazilian gay activism looked increasingly middle class, and sexual identity models similarly reflect disparity in education, wealth, and social position. Thus, *travesti* sex workers (who rely on and relish having penises) may disidentify as *transgêneros* (transgendered persons), seeing male-to-female transgêneros as not only bourgeois but mentally disturbed. (According to Kulick, the travestis believe that people who have sexual reassignment or gender-confirming surgeries will be driven insane, as the semen can't leave and pools in the brain.)[57] Thus, emic categories become classed as low and may be in tension with newer models of gender/sexual identity that are taken up in the middle class. Similarly, middle-class gay-identified Brazilian men with whom I talked tended to be ambivalent about garotos, even though they rarely encountered them except perhaps if they spotted them cruising for tourists at gay night clubs that attract tourists, such as Le Boy. They insisted that garotos were just closeted gay men who used sex work to have the homosex they secretly desired, a problematic assertion that is also difficult to argue with because it sometimes holds, as in Adilson's case, a kernel of truth. These middle-class gay Brazilians saw the failure of garotos to be out as gay (*ser gay assumido*) as uncosmopolitan and backward and ascribed it to the homophobia produced by poverty and poor education.

This narrative of the "deep-down gay" also appears implicitly in anthropological literature about garotos and their corollaries in other Latin American countries.[58] Patrick Larvie, while not going so far as to make any explicit claims about the nature of identity, notes that the garotos he interviewed in Rio in the early 1990s generated almost no profit from their street hustling. "The payment of money for sex is not the chief objective, but . . . [it] provides symbolic insulation from the homosexual desires of his client and the attendant loss of a 'straight' identity."[59] Elsewhere, he writes: "Garotos may go to such great pains to display their virility that their performances cast doubt upon that very attribute. . . . The performance of straightness can reach a level which clearly identifies the performer as something of an imposter, as an actor who is clearly not-straight."[60] Obviously, there is great queer potential among the garotos. It is true that ac-

cepting money can serve as insulation against stigma and as a ratio-
nalization for homosexual experimentation, but the discourse of the
"deep-down gay" also presumes that identity is immutable and that
male sexuality is not fluid.

Further complicating *michetagem's* (hustling's) implications for sexual identity, Paulo Longo, an activist and founder of a now-defunct
NGO doing outreach to street michês, claims that some garotos eventually even have noncommercial sex with each other, a phenomenon
that I never encountered, although garotos did sometimes have sex
with each other during programas or while shooting pornographic
movies.[61] There is evidence, however, that gangs of Brazilian street
children—from which some michês inevitably come—use gang rape to
initiate new boys, which could potentially complicate garotos' feelings
about anal sex, passivity, and hierarchies of masculinity.[62] Moreover,
Parker's gay interlocutors insist that garotos and other garotos may
gradually take on gay friends, move in gay social circles, and eventually become gay themselves.[63] Clients in Padilla's study express their
hope that his research on straight-identified male sex workers will reveal what they "already know" about the men: that "they're all closet
cases."[64] Researchers also describe straight male sex workers who attempted to seduce male researchers, saying they would have sex with
them for free.[65] In Costa Rica, Jacobo Shifter notes that there are many
stories among male sex workers about colleagues who enjoyed the sex
too much or hung out too much in the gay community and became
gay as a result.[66]

Tourist attitudes about the "real" sexual identity and the role of pleasure reflect the ambiguity found in academic and popular sources. This
may also be because the tourists do read a fair amount of academic
and crossover literature and sometimes act as amateur historians and
ethnographers. Those in their fifties and above (i.e., those who came of
age before homosexuality was explicit in mainstream media) were particularly familiar with anthropological studies on such issues as Latin
homosexuality, various "berdache" and "two-spirit" texts, volumes of
gay American history, and a variety of world histories that detail homosexual practices from around the world in lay terms. Tourists were
highly educated; several of the younger ones (i.e., those in their twenties and thirties) with whom I spoke had taken LGBT-oriented courses
in college, and several were academics themselves.

Gay tourists found Latin homosexuality quaint and titillating. For
some, the emphasis on masculine, macho, straight men reminded
them of their own experiences pursuing straight, married, or closeted

men in the United States (i.e., "rough trade"). There was a whiff of danger to having sex with garotos, as male hustlers are often associated with violence and Brazil is no exception.[67] Some older tourists said that Latin machismo made them nostalgic for the 1970s, when gay culture valorized a more rugged brand of masculinity that was more appealing than that of the present. To be sure, tourists are not alone in fetishizing rough trade, butchness, or heterosexuality. Brazilian clients certainly do as well, and many also share tourists' notions of the importance of pride, coming out, and sexual identity. However, the tourist case is interesting because when the tourists insert themselves into the Brazilian sexual context, they imagine it to be a novel sexual adventure even though that sexual context has for many decades been enmeshed with global circuits of sexuality and influenced by the flow of ideas and images from the United States and elsewhere.

Sometimes there was internalized homophobia or disgust at the ubiquity of global gay culture. "The gay guys in the regular *saunas* [i.e., *saunas* where there is no prostitution] are prettier than the guys in Philly bars or the bathhouses in America," said Jordee, a gay man from Philadelphia in his sixties, as he explained why he preferred straight men selling sex in the *saunas* to the noncommercial *sauna* scene in which gay Brazilian men cruise for noncommercial sex. He went on to describe the fashions, clothes, and attitude of the middle-class Brazilian gay men in clubs as strikingly similar to gay men in the United States. "[The Brazilian gays] look just like them. It would be like going to an expensive club, like where the A-Gays [elite, "A-list"] would be. . . . And they're kinda queenie, too. You know what it's like? It's exactly like going to some snooty fag bar in LA where all the boys are models or wannabe soap actors and they're dumb as shit. Brazilian, American, it doesn't matter. Twinks are twinks. Pretty gay boys are the same everywhere. It's a turnoff. I don't like it in America and I don't like it in Rio." Thus, Jordee realized that he preferred the machismo he found abundant in the *saunas*.

I found that a lot of gringos were disenchanted with Rio's gay scene. Pete, a fifty-something lawyer who was a veteran sex tourist, had no patience for it. "These fucking *barbies* here," he says. In Portuguese gay slang a *barbie* is a particular type of elite gay man—named for the doll with her notoriously ridiculous proportions. Barbies are beautiful, muscle-bound, and vain, known mainly for standing around on beaches in cliques. "You've been to Ipanema," he says, referencing the elite gay neighborhood and its gay beach at Farme de Amoedo. "I can't even set foot there. Bitchy, judgy little queens. They have the bodies, but at the end of the day, they're just a bunch of prissy faggots, too, and that's not attractive to me."

This creates an opening for my other question. "So why straight guys?"

"I mean it's hot. In the US, you find supposedly straight guys, but I don't think they are really. What, some straight guy is on M4M on craigslist? A real one? Probably not. So it's the fantasy come true, right? And it's the macho thing. That down here, the straight guys will just do that with no problem. It's ideal for somebody like me . . . who is into the straight thing, that fantasy."

Romanticized feelings about Latin homosexuality also allowed tourists to sort themselves into distinct camps. Specialists in Brazil or Latin America adamantly insisted that "you go east for boys and south for men" or that "only pedophiles go to Bangkok." Erik, a white man from the United States in his late forties, expounded on this point while sitting in a bar, drinking a strawberry *caipirinha*. "Some of these other guys, the rice queens [white gays who prefer Asian men], they freak me out. Like the little Asian twinks, all hairless. I mean, come on, you have to have *some* hair on the guy or else [they look] like they're twelve [years old] or something. And you better hope the boys actually *are* adults. It's creepy. And it's not like they [the tourists] are going to Thailand or wherever looking for tops. They always seem to be talking about how they [the tourists] are tops . . . really strongly identifying as tops—like it's an identity and not just a position in bed, so you get the real dominant types who are into that whole Asian scene."

"But Brazil is different?" I asked him.

"Absolutely Brazil is different. Here it's macho guys working as garotos. They're tough. I guarantee you they could beat the crap out of any gay tourist. And most of the time here you've got gay guys from the US or Europe or wherever who are into the straight aspect of it, and who are pleased as punch to get fucked by a straight guy; that's the allure of it, . . . of being topped by this powerful straight macho guy. So it's just not creepy like the other thing is. . . . It's not at all the same thing in Latin America as it is in Thailand."

For Erik, having sex with masculine men was "less creepy" and had less potential for exploitation than pursuing a young or young-looking Asian man. The potential for power imbalance was further mitigated if the garoto was doing the penetrating, illustrating how gay culture also takes the common heteronormative (and also radical feminist) view that being penetrated increases vulnerability and is a submissive role.

However, not all sex tourists in Brazil agreed with Erik. If Erik was a specialist, then there were also generalists who valued having experienced sex all over the globe. For example, one such man, a professor, framed this practice in terms of his worldliness and positioned the sex as cultural edification, a way of learning about cultures and experiencing them firsthand. "It's like foodie culture," he said. "You can eat at a different ethnic restaurant every night. . . . [Sex] with local guys is a way of getting to better appreciate a culture, get to know its people, immerse yourself." For generalists, sex was a marker of cosmopolitanism and helped them appreciate the broadest possible spectrum of sexuality.

Despite their fascination with various expressions of same-sex desire around the globe, though, gay tourists generally subscribed to teleological conceptions of development and modernity that were predicated on a Euro-American model of gay identity. By combining information from academic and lay studies with that from gay travel guides and travelogues, gay sex tourists were able to use their advanced knowledge of local models of homosexuality and their economic status to increase their access to potential sex partners, while simultaneously looking down on the men as somehow unevolved or unsophisticated. Jasbir Puar accurately describes this situation in which tourists "operate within a missionary framework of sameness and difference, assuming some rubric of queerness that is similar enough to create solidarity around but is different from and, as such, not quite on par with metropolitan queerness."[68]

In keeping with this framework, when tourists hired an escort for a longer period of time, they often took on a very pedagogic role. They taught the garotos English, especially gay slang vocabulary. (In Bahia, African American gay tourists also enjoyed teaching Afro-Brazilian garotos urban vernacular as well as vocabulary from the black gay argot.) Sitting in a *sauna* in Rio de Janeiro, I was talking to a fifty-year-old white American man named Morty while a young *moreno* rent boy named Tomás sat with his arm around him, sometimes twirling a scrap of Morty's thinning hair or caressing his cheek, tugging at his ear in a not-very-subtle effort to assert his presence and encourage Morty to *subir* (literally, "go up," the phrase for going to a *cabine* for a programa).

As Morty explained to me how he had photo albums in which he collected pictures of all his favorite garotos naked, he began telling me in great detail about the specifications of the camera. At some point, he felt this would be a good teachable moment for Tomás and explained digital cameras and how they didn't require film and when to use a flash. Tomás asked in English if Morty had a very nice camera, to which Morty proudly replied that his camera cost more than $500 and that he would very much like to use the camera to take some pictures of him sometime. Morty then began to explain that the batteries were lithium-ion, but even good camera batteries needed to be charged, to which Tomás feigned some interest. "*Tá . . . tá . . . tá,*" he murmured, which is the Brazilian equivalent of "Mmm hmmm." As Morty stood to finally "*subir*" with Tomás, the garoto leaned over and popped his eyes at me behind Morty's back. "*Nossa!*" he hissed, a common exclamation. Pointing a finger at the gringo, he conspiratorially whispered to me in Portuguese: "This bicha acts like I've never seen a camera before! I have one in my cell phone, you know."

When a tourist like Morty found a garoto in a *sauna* whom he liked and trusted, he might take the man on a date outside the *sauna*. Sometimes these garotos evolved into "boyfriends." The tourist might visit only once or twice a year but would send regular remunerations. Such benefactors also lectured the men on the importance of coming out, of being true to one's heart, of admitting that they found the tourist desirable and enjoyed the sex. They cited the men's erections, orgasms, moans, and any hint of affection, pleasure, or intimacy as evidence.

This is not to say that some garotos didn't experience complicated desires and struggle with identity, but Washington, a moreno man in his twenties who had spent several years in such a relationship, was quite candid: "If he knows you're *normal*, then he's not going to give you money every month. So I told him I was *bi.*"

Naldo, another garoto, explained. "It's a job, but I also do it because I like it better than when I worked as an office boy. It's practically as if I was bisexual, right? [*É praticamenete como se eu fosse bissexual, né?*] But I am only ativo. See, one moment I am involved with another man, but I stay with only women outside and only men inside [the *sauna*]."

The men also joked about sexuality's sometimes-strategic fluidity. One afternoon, Cavi and Adilson were discussing this and Cavi told me: "I used to have a girlfriend until recently. But then I also had a boyfriend I met in the *sauna.* . . . I go out with girls for fun, but I only date men for money. I'm single now, but I think I still consider myself *bi.*"

"And next year, he's going to be tri . . ." Adilson said, drolly.

"Penta!" Cavi chimed in, making a pun on a World Cup soccer slogan that was ubiquitous at the time to imply that he was racking up sexual orientations like Brazil racks up championship titles, and they both laughed.

So while tourists enjoyed their own obsession with Latin homosexuality, the garotos were superficially adapting to Anglo identity models, even though their use of *"bi"* remained monetized. And even though tourists loved the idea of straight Latin machos, they simultaneously sought to educate men out of Latin homosexuality as a matter of modernity and civil rights. Yet the garotos saw through this strategy and counteracted it by competently performing the kind of sexual identity expected by clients. The tourists, in effect, commissioned performances. Despite being deflected in many ways, this evangelism of sexual identity models is still problematic, especially when it comes to the importance of sex roles in Latin homosexuality. It's also misguided because, as I remarked above, so-called egalitarian, Western homosexuality is thoroughly "Latin" as well. Fetishizing straight tops is certainly not limited to tourists. Brazilian clients also share this fantasy. However, tourists get caught up in the exoticism of the *idea* of the Latin model as well, not realizing that they aren't having nearly as exotic an encounter as they think, lending further credence to Sérgio Carrara and Júlio Simões's critique of the discourse of Latin homosexuality for the ways that it encourages people to view Brazilian sexuality as an exotic and "backward" latecomer to sexual modernity (*retardatária*).[69]

Most garotos did not want to be passive in anal sex, perform fellatio, or be affectionate with clients. Everything was generally negotiable, however. Garotos who were more convincing at demonstrating pleasure, or who were willing to kiss passionately or cuddle became highly sought after and found providing these services quite lucrative. A few sex tourists—usually those who considered themselves very experienced connoisseurs—considered convincing a garoto to bottom as a conquest.

Occasionally, experienced garotos could turn this particular fetish to their advantage, and I met one such man in Bahia, Gilberto, who worked the beaches. He regularly bottomed, but he would feign his anal virginity when he met a connoisseur who specialized in getting ativos to bottom—thereby dragging the affair out into many days of shopping, eating, and programas in which Gilberto was ativo. As the tourist's departure grew closer, he knew the man would pay almost anything to seal the deal before leaving. He explained to me that if he "gave his ass" (*dar o cu*) early on, the tourist would quickly lose interest in him. Thus, Gilberto used *his* advanced knowledge of Euro-American homosexuality and its fetishization of the straight man's "first time" to maximize his own profits.

When asked why they preferred "straight" Brazilians, many tourists complained that gay-identified Brazilian men were too much like themselves. One explained: "You go to The Week [an expensive nightclub in Rio] and they have DJs who work in New York. They wear the same clothes, same hair; . . . they play Madonna . . . and a lot of them are hot, but also . . . you know, flame-on [effeminate]. . . . I came here to get away from that."

Such gay Brazilian men, being middle class, were also much harder for tourists to attract or impress. Instead, the tourists were caught in the conundrum of wanting to coax a straight-identified man into the familiar social script of "coming out" as gay—or at least admitting to feeling a desire that would betray an inner gay or bi identity—while also being turned off by the commodities, signifiers, and lifestyle associated with global gay identity. This contradiction does more than just throw the practices and rationalizations of gay tourists into question, however. It actually reveals a good deal about how sexual identity and consumerism are beginning to function transnationally and what their relationship is to discourses of "authenticity."

Conclusion

The most famous and enduring sociological theory of tourists and their motivations for travel is that of the sociologist Dean MacCannell, who argued in the 1970s that the main reason tourists travel is that people in the cosmopolitan, Western world lead such superficial lives that they must seek "authenticity" elsewhere.[70] Global consumers may enjoy modern conveniences and fast-paced lives, but sometimes they need a piece of what they see as easy, tropical life—only to end up buying (mass-produced) souvenirs of this simpler time and place to take home and show to friends. Although now critiqued by other scholars of tourism, MacCannell's argument was ahead of its time in that it foresaw the ennui now so closely associated with rampant consumerism, crass commodification, reality television, product placement, and the corporatization of popular culture. In the eyes of the gay tourists I met in Brazil, the superficiality they are so eager to escape from is, rather ironically, the consumerism of the "mainstream" gay community itself. But their newfound object choice is revealing. They go in search of "authentically" heterosexual, working-class, masculine, Latin machismo as an antidote.

However, the gay tourist's very presence—which is possible only as a result of his economic privilege—imbues his interactions with his chosen sexual partners with economic difference and incentivizes particular performances of masculinity and sexuality to suit the tourist's

desires. The longer these relationships last, the greater the incentivization, including the adoption of new nomenclature, vocabulary, and
identity models. When such a fantasy fails to turn into a lasting relationship or—as in Adilson's case—it succeeds only to collapse paradoxically back into itself, the tourist becomes increasingly frustrated and
begin his search for the "real thing" all over again.

As in the case of Stanley, the tourist who was so jaded about romance with garotos outside of *saunas* with their tales of hardship and
perceived desire to fleece gringos, these relationships often fail to live
up to expectations precisely because the gay tourist eventually realizes
he is not successfully missionizing gay identity politics, awakening la-
tent, true desires, or coaxing his partner out of the closet but is, rather,
contributing to the young man's own consumerism through gifts of
phones, clothes, and electronics and increasing his access to trendy
clubs, restaurants, and the like. Eventually, some tourists, such as Robert, realize that lavishing attention and luxury travel like cruises on
someone like Wesley, who is married with children and who seldom
worked the *saunas* but who now does identify as gay and prefers sex
with men, is more likely to yield the desired reciprocation of affection
and pleasure.

Yet many tourists reject middle-class, gay-identified Brazilians as too
much like themselves (and therefore not as authentic as the rugged garotos) to be appropriate objects of their affection. This was the case for
Jordee, who saw Brazilian gay men emulating not just US gay culture
but what he saw as the most superficial parts of it. In rejecting mainstream Brazilian gay culture and its emulation of global gay culture,
the gringo clients consign themselves to the realm of shifting, conflicting, unstable relationships with "straight" men whom such a relationship effectively turns into precisely the middle-class, consumer-
oriented, gay or bisexual men the tourists eschew.

Although a thorough investigation of the overarching rhetorical
frameworks of gay identity politics is beyond the immediate scope of
my work, this case study does offer a cautionary warning about the
contradictions and ambiguity of the individual identity-making practices within the relationships I've described. The great liberal dilemma
in the United States is that consumers understand that consumption
is political, yet remain powerless to alter the march toward marketization. Even as one becomes attuned to "buying green" or "organic," for
example, these terms are co-opted by marketers and advertisers who
collapse political identities into marketing demographics and political
choices into consumer behaviors. Like the tourists in this study, many

progressives may relate to the temptations and perils of mixing identity and consumerism. The gay tourists perceived their travel as an exercising of their civil rights through purchasing power, describing their travel as a matter of economic uplift for local communities that also promoted tolerance of diversity. This rhetoric parallels not only that of major gay advertising, marketing, and media campaigns that promote the image of a global gay consumer but also the efforts of major gay rights groups that privilege economic arguments for gay rights over ethical, moral, and social ones. It is precisely because the men choose to embrace universalizing gay identity frameworks amid wide economic difference that they so often find their relationships unsatisfying. And this combination of consumerism and identity politics is a dangerous brew.

In making this critique of the marketization of civil rights, I want to be clear that I am distinguishing between appeals that valorize consumerism and those that do not. For example, the Montgomery Bus Boycott used the economic leverage of poor blacks to press for civil rights, but it did not assert that they deserved equal treatment because of disposable income. It was an attempt, not to purchase rights, but to draw attention to their moral arguments. This is wholly different from the missionizing rhetoric and noblesse oblige that I have described.

I also want to emphasize that mainstream gay organizations, including Lambda Legal and the Human Rights Campaign, are not unilateral in approach or ideology. There are also groups with long legacies of direct action such as ACT UP and Queer Nation, as well as radical queer groups such as Against Equality, the Sylvia Rivera Law Project, and the Audre Lorde Project, whose ethos stands in contradiction to the kind of mainstream LGBT rights agenda that would map a path toward equality through a morass of consumerism. Nor do I argue that LGBT people should purchase goods from anti-gay companies or that they should not support gay-friendly businesses. But the fact remains that the eagerness with which the mainstream LGBT community endorses the logic of the TurboConsumer™ shows a widespread abandoning of radical strategies by instead suggesting that they deserve rights because they are valuable consumers and good neoliberal subjects. To do so too intimately links identity with consumerism—making the latter a condition for the former and, thus, a prerequisite for equal rights.

FOUR

Godfather Gringos: Sexual Tourism, Queer Kinship, and Families of the Future

Nobody has ever before asked the nuclear family to live all by itself in a box the way we do. With no relatives, no support, we've put it in an impossible situation. **MARGARET MEAD**

Of Brothels and Birthdays

It's "No Towel Night" at the *sauna* and the twenty or so *garotos de programa* cruising its floors aren't happy.[1] Technically, "Hand Towel Night" would be more accurate, given that management replaces the bath towels it usually permits garotos to wear around their waists with small hand towels. The rationale is that they are to sit on these towels for purposes of hygiene, but a garoto can cleverly stretch the rubber bracelet that holds the key to his rented locker and use it to try to bind two corners of the towel around his hip. It never really works. Either his *bunda* (ass) is exposed or his *pau* (cock) is. Often, garotos prefer to cover their *bundas*. Since many of them identify as straight, they don't like to encourage clients to imagine that their ass is available (regardless of whether they are willing to negotiate that point once upstairs in the privacy of a rented room). Given the nature of their work and lack

119

of modesty, I wondered why they hate No Towel Night so much, but a nineteen-year-old named Danilo explained to me that it was about control—being able to choose when, how, and to whom one was exposed and in what ways.

"They do these small towels just to get the *boys* naked. . . . At first it was really difficult, being naked like it was nothing. I felt ashamed [*vergonha*], but you get used to it." He leans back awkwardly, but his tiny towel slips and his flaccid penis falls out. He tucks it away while I pretend not to notice. "[When I began,] I tried to hide behind things sometimes, or to sit, . . . just to have a moment. But I got used to it—now it's fine. Like, look, I sit here with no clothes on now and it's nothing to me."

We're in a tiny *cabine* (rented room) while he says this. It's my first time doing research in this particular *sauna*. The room feels quite crowded. There are clean linens, but the hard, lumpy bed we sit on occupies nearly every inch of space, and because we can't quite sit with our feet on the floor, we sit somewhat cross-legged on the bed as we talk about sex. We look like teenage girls at some perverse version of a slumber party, sitting on this little bed where Danilo has probably had dozens of clients and where he may well return in a matter of minutes to have sex exactly where we're sitting.

The *sauna* has many different social spaces, each resonant with affect, but the awkward nervousness I feel sitting in the cabine with Danilo must surely be a different kind of affect than the sexual nervousness of the clients who have been filing into and out of this room all night. My ethnographic methods coursework hadn't prepared me for the complexity of affective responses I would encounter doing this kind of work. It's precisely because of the precariousness of juxtaposing these two lines of work (sex for them and research for me), of the blending of familiarity and formality, and the discomfort that arises from doing the "wrong" sort of activity in the "wrong" space that I dislike conducting formal interviews in the actual *sauna*. But the manager wouldn't let Danilo leave his shift early to talk with me, so we slipped off to a cabine.

We both seemed to feel peculiar doing this kind of work in this kind of space. The awkwardness settled in like stifling smog, and at one point conversation dried up. I struggled to remember my key questions. Awkwardness became tension, confusion, and embarrassment. I began to feel inadequate as a novice ethnographer. My embarrassment became shame, but of a different affective variety than the shame (*vergonha*) that Danilo described feeling.

Suddenly, a boisterous chorus of more than a dozen men singing

"Happy Birthday" in Portuguese boomed up through the thin floor-boards from the lounge downstairs, interrupting our halting dialogue. We froze. I cocked my head and raised an eyebrow, trying to imagine the scene below. I'd seen Bingo games and campy stage shows before, but who holds a birthday party in a *sauna*? Is it a garoto's birthday? A client's? An employee's? And who is singing? Has the whole room full of strangers stopped their flirting, their cruising, their haggling over who will be putting exactly what where and for exactly how much money just to enjoy this contagious moment of communitas? Danilo laughed at my look of perplexity and surprise—his laughter mirthful and boyish—releasing the tension at last. The affective shift of the rousing chorus permeated our once-awkward little cabine, and soon we were both laughing, relaxing again into a *bate papo*—the easy sort of dialogue Brazilians prize—neither of us ashamed for the time being.

Danilo had hoped to be the kind of *boy* who was snatched up quickly in the *sauna*. This happened quite often when a certain type of guy who had the right mix of traits started working: slightly innocent yet mischievous, good-humored yet serious, uneducated but smart, ambitious but nonthreatening, sexually adventurous but not too experienced. Locals and tourists alike scramble to find such *boys*, "rescuing" them from the *sauna* and turning them into boyfriends they could lavish attention and heap gifts upon. As the sociologist Kerwin Kaye has noted, such rescue operations fulfill a client's Pygmalion-like fantasy of lifting a promising young hustler up out of poverty and helping to refashion him.[2] If a *boy* has worked in the *sauna* for too long, though, he might become cynical or be seen as a less appealing project. Such a *boy* becomes bromidic, mundane, overly used; he is damaged goods. Regular clients talk a lot about the golden boys, though. Vern, a fifty-year-old banker, leaned over to me in the *sauna* one night as we were discussing his years as a client in various locations in South America and pointed out a new guy. "That one," he told me confidently, "will be gone by the end of the week."

"How do you know?" I asked.

"I just do. Handsome, perfect lips, beautiful eyes. Light. Not too cocky. Some local queen will put him in his apartment in Leblon or he'll be left to house-sit a *gringo's* beach house in Copa. Just watch." And he was right. Within a few weeks, he was gone from the *sauna* after a few dates with a client, presumed by all to have been snatched up.

As the birthday party below us continued on in waves of laughter and merriment, Danilo described how he wanted to be one of those kept boys. "When I started, I thought I would only do this work a short time," he said. He had seen other *boys* go outside with clients and not need to do *programas* all day, but this never happened for him.

As we went back downstairs, he slipped into the birthday celebration and seemed to cheer up. His friends were laughing and singing. A favorite Brazilian client that most of them had "gone upstairs with" multiple times was being feted. The guys hung off of him, arms wrapped around him, slapping each other on the back, chatting, and many of them planting kisses on his cheek. There were some clients, mostly foreigners, on the edges of the room, looking a bit excluded as they sat there just beyond the festivities, ignored by the garotos and the Brazilian clients alike. It occurred to me that an enterprising garoto could easily have used the opportunity to get a good programa, but they were more interested in celebrating the birthday. There was a sense of community there and an emotional closeness that I realized I'd not seen described in sensationalistic media accounts of what life in the commercial sex trades is supposedly like. Although Danilo never got to play out his desire for domesticity by setting up house with a client, he was able to enjoy this other camaraderie with his work family.

It's one thing to acknowledge that late capitalism has profound effects on kinship. That fact is undeniable. Free-market capitalism disrupts gendered divisions of labor in locations all along the commodity chain; it forces migration and alters education and labor practices— sometimes in good ways, often in bad ones. As Rio de Janeiro's middle-class economy grows, more men enter the sex trade and pursue different kinds of relationships with clients. I lost track of how many times garotos complained of the tides of new *boys* flooding the market. There are more Brazilian men who can afford to pay for sex and more tourists nowadays adding to demand, but also there are more *boys* wanting access to middle-class consumer society themselves and who want to get there without engaging in violent, criminal enterprises. As crime continues outside, the *sauna* in Rio functions as a safe space and facilitates not only brief encounters but also much more permanent ones.

This question of how globalization reshapes kinship became prominent for me as I met even more tourists and garotos who had a variety of complicated relationships and affective arrangements. Some of these interactions are straightforward programas in *saunas* for a fixed price. Others are weeklong romances that involve gifts, cash, and meals but no outright fee for sex. And some develop into complex, long-distance, long-term relationships in which the gringo becomes a "boyfriend" who sends money regularly and visits a few times a year. He may come to know the garoto's family or support the man's children. The family may even value and cherish him as a member in his own right.

In the last chapter, I described Robert and Wesley's relationship escalating as they went on a global cruise together basking in first-class luxury. Regarding that initial encounter, I even remarked that Robert seemed disinterested in Wesley's children by his ex-wife, struggling to remember their names and ages. In an interesting turn of events, after that cruise, they continued their relationship, sending emails back and forth. Robert wrote to Wesley often, saying that he missed him so much that he cried all the time. Yet Wesley didn't write back very quickly or frequently. When he did, the messages were short and ineloquent, causing a lot of anxiety and distress for Robert, who had returned home and felt disconnected from his lover after their lengthy adventures traveling the world together. Commenting on this to my research assistant Gustavo one day, I realized that I was a hopeless cynic. Having watched similar relationships deteriorate and end in bitter realizations for infatuated gringos, I remarked that the relationship seemed doomed to fail. I waited for it to fall apart, thinking that Wesley was unlikely to prove a strong and steady enough pen pal to sustain Robert's outsized attachments.

However, two years after the interview in which I met these men and in which Wesley learned the details of the lavish cruise he was to embark on, these two men had consistently proven me wrong. Robert visited often and seems to have gotten over any discomfort with the children, instead becoming an "uncle" to them. Wesley's career in gay porn continues unabated and his fan base still clamors for his movies. Recently, Gustavo even received a photo of the whole family— Robert, Wesley, and Wesley's son and daughter—smiling as happily as any other family as they all dined out at a nice restaurant. The children are growing and spending more time with Wesley now, becoming more accustomed to and attached to Robert. Wesley's ex-wife seems unperturbed by the arrangement and is apparently happy for the opportunities provided to her children. It's been a while since I've heard from them, though, and perhaps it won't last in the end. But for these important years, these individuals have collectively formed a queer transnational family and slowly sorted out exactly what this would look like. They don't have a blueprint for this kind of family. But they also are not the first men to find themselves in this kind of kinship arrangement.

Such new family formations in which gay sex tourists effectively queer Brazilian kinship is a side of tourism and prostitution that is almost never considered in the often-sensationalistic stories one finds in newspapers, television programs, and movies. But as Brazil gathers increasing economic and political capital internationally, the state is also showing a marked interest in policing and publicly promoting specific formations of gender, sexuality, and kinship. There are influential evangelical conservatives in some parts of government who press for crackdowns on prostitution and who launch vitriolic hate speech at gays and lesbians, pushing for a return to "traditional family values." However, as gay tourism continues to grow, gay gringos who become the boyfriends of mostly heterosexually identified Brazilian rent boys are forming new kinship systems that the state could never have anticipated.

Serving as godfathers, uncles, and patrons, gay gringos are incorporated into Brazilian families, providing much needed remittances for tuition, medical costs, and child care expenses. They have complex affective relationships with their Brazilian partners, as well as the men's wives, girlfriends, parents, and children. The question of performative labor becomes especially challenging here because the garotos do not just need to navigate affect across cultural difference for a few hours in a *sauna*, but instead, they must perform within a constant and iterative process as they refashion themselves in the new familial relationship. Examining "godfather gringos" and other foreigners who develop long-term transnational relationships with garotos' families, I argue that in an era of sexual regimentation, gay sex tourism is introducing some surprising twists to Brazilian kinship.

Earlier, in chapter 1, I described the history of hustlers in Brazil and the pivotal moment in the evolution of hustling when heterosexual males began to pursue *tias* (aunties), effeminate gay men of relatively more means. Therefore, it may seem strange to devote this chapter to stories of garotos and their gringo clients. Certainly, these same formations exist between Brazilian gay men and garotos. However, by focusing on the relatively recent transnationalization of this kind of informal, transactional relationship, I am highlighting the performative dimensions of sex work, as the garotos must work to make the key features of Brazilian kinship legible to outsiders who have their own ideas about kinship, relationships, and the roles they themselves are to play. To focus on these international exchanges is not to deny the importance of relationships between gay locals and garotos but to show the particular challenges and performative complexities that arise when garotos must move the kind of frameworks shared with local clients to an international one.

These case studies of transnational queer families show that this kind of queer family formation isn't simply an interesting detail or a mere epiphenomenon. On the contrary, it helps us to understand the relationship between Brazilian kinship, sexuality, and global capital in new and productive ways. Moreover, I propose that this form of queer kinship in Brazil is not entirely new and is not an imposition of queer foreigners upon local families but rather exists successfully precisely because it works within existing frameworks of "traditional" Brazilian family values—and as such, it is useful for helping us to think about how to press at the uncomfortable edges of these structures.

Prostitution: A Family Business

When Goldman Sachs famously anointed Brazil as one of the four so-called BRIC (Brazil, Russia, India, and China) countries that could challenge US economic hegemony, Brazil was eager to prove itself worthy.[3] "O Brasil é o país do futuro . . . e sempre será" (Brazil is the country of the future . . . and always will be) goes the old joke. But under the leadership of the then president Luiz Inácio Lula da Silva and bolstered by unprecedented growth, Brazil began to expend its international political capital in new ways, asserting itself in global affairs and angling for a much-coveted permanent spot on the UN Security Council. In a move that surprised many international observers, Lula cast Brazil as the mediator in the coup in Honduras.[4] He cozied up to Iran, to the profound irritation of Hillary Clinton, then US secretary of state, and used his "friendship" with its dictator to urge him to ease up on human rights abuses.[5] Keenly aware that Brazil has its own image problems when it comes to social injustice, he touted his successful efforts at swelling the middle class into a slim majority of Brazilian society and reducing Brazil's Gini coefficient (a measure of income inequality) through the successes of programs such as the Bolsa Família, which pays stipends to poor families for keeping their children in school instead of sending them to work.[6] The Brazil of the future, if it was to perhaps exist in reality and not as merely the punchline of a joke, also needed to be liberal, tolerant, and progressive on matters of gender and sexuality. Consequently, he declared stopping sex trafficking to be a national priority and even proclaimed his personal support of gay rights at length.[7] In the run-up to the 2014 World Cup and 2016 Olympic Games, there were raids on supposed sex traffickers, the closure of brothels, harassment of prostitutes, and the closure of large and well-regulated venues where heterosexual sex tourists and prostitutes could meet, such as Help! and Balcony Bar.[8] Such state responses to sexuality that shore up unlikely alliances between antiprostitution feminist organizations, business developers, evangelical Christian missionary groups, and the state security apparatus are part of what Paul Amar describes—in a lexical mirroring of "paramilitary"—as a "parastatal" formation that typifies the new Brazilian order.[9]

For Lula, homosexuality was to be embraced under the auspices of diversity and tolerance, but mainly through the most normative of optics. Forms of homosexual conduct that benefit the image of a progressive state are welcomed. Thus, São Paulo's gay pride parade—the largest in the world—is a badge of national honor, but it's also consumer driven and revenue generating. More recently, Brazilian courts have paved the way for gay marriage and gay adoption as well. Celebrating gay pride events is commendable in one way, but it is also a nationalist ploy, or what Jasbir Puar refers to as part of "homonationalism."[10] That is, elites hold up a certain brand of gay identity and gay culture (which is—not coincidentally—whiter, wealthier, and more privileged) as an example of good citizenry, often at the expense of vulnerable and disadvantaged populations. Less valued and celebrated are the queer people who do not fit into this "mainstream" gay world of consumerism: the *travestis* and transgendered people, the drag queens, the bull dykes, the *michês* (street hustlers), the aging fairies, the sex tourists, men who have sex with men but who do not identify as "gay," the migrants and poor who do not or cannot participate in the expensive gay club scene or who lack the leisure time and funds necessary or the desire to spend countless hours in gyms like the so-called *barbies* of Ipanema do. At the end of the march toward "order and progress"— which is Brazil's national motto emblazoned on its flag—only an elite group of gay specimens will find a seat waiting for them at the table of *pátria*.

Another way to think about what kind of gay culture Brazil is willing to endorse is to frame the matter in terms of homonormativity, or the "mainstream" gay community's performance of and allegiance to normative heterosexual forms of kinship, love, and social arrangement.[11] The good gay citizen wants to have one lifelong monogamous partner with whom he or she may have children, buy property, and live an upwardly mobile life of consumerism. But as the Brazilian medical psychiatrist and anthropologist Carla de Meis notes, there is a tendency in Brazilian society to view people on the sexual margins of society as somehow being apart from good society and bereft of family, as always and already separate, isolated, and ghettoized, and as very selfish.[12] Thus, studies of sex workers focus primarily on the business of sex (and secondarily on drug abuse) but rarely consider the nonwork aspects of prostitutes' subjectivity.[13] This is especially evident in the literature from scholars of public health, to say nothing of the neo-abolitionist or antiprostitution camps of feminist activists who view sex workers as unagentive victims of false consciousness trapped in exploitation the sex workers cannot see.

Even many feminist activists who are tolerant or supportive of sex work bemoan the example it sets for the children of prostitutes and fret that it creates a generational cycle of prostitution.[14] Prostitution may be a form of sex work, but even among liberal, Marxist, and sex-positive feminists it's not a profession they want to see passed down the way families of doctors, soldiers, artisans, or teachers do. This scholarly tendency to compartmentalize the multiple identities and roles of prostitutes *for them* is problematic because we understand prostitution better when we approach identity as highly intersectional, fluid, and subjective. That is, a prostitute's work life, personal life, family life, spiritual life, upbringing, and racial and class background all interrelate and shape one another—just as they do for everyone else.

Moreover, it's wrong to divorce considerations of family and kinship from questions of sexual labor precisely because prostitutes in Brazil are, as even a cursory material encounter would make plain, not in a social sphere that is the *opposite* of family. In fact, women often choose the profession of prostitution precisely because it pays reasonably well for a smaller number of hours that are fairly flexible, making child care much easier.[15] Similarly, the anthropologist Don Kulick documented that travesti sex workers remained very close to their mothers, and their first major purchase was usually to buy homes for their parents regardless of how their family treated them when they were growing up or when they came out of the closet.[16]

One night, Horácio explained to me that what kept him in "this life" of prostitution was not his irresponsibility or the allure of fast cash but his desire to be an honorable family man. "My mother does not know, but I think she suspects. . . . My father is gone. . . . I do not know him. There is a stepfather, but he is disabled and cannot work. . . . So I come home with meat—big slabs of beef—and I pay for the electricity. She looks so happy when she sees this."

He is looking off into space, positively beaming with pride at some memory he is having of such a moment. "She thinks I work at a hotel in the city and she is so proud! She tells everyone what a good son I am. But I could not do this for her if I took a normal job [as an] office boy, a cashier, a street vendor. Good jobs are not available for *boys* like me. . . . I would need to be in a gang, rob people, or sell drugs, be a bandit to have this money. But if I do this and die, then who is going to pay for her electricity?"

I also found that among migrant sex workers in the United States and Europe, it can be difficult to justify spending money on themselves at local prices when valuable remittances of euros, pounds, or dollars to their families are much more important. One garoto, Vítor, lived in Bahia, having returned there after a vacationing client decided to take him to San Francisco to live with him. "I was so depressed," he explained. "I went there and he said that we did not need to have [sexual] relations, that I was there to study and improve myself because he wanted to help me. But he wanted sex and he did not want me to live [my life]. In California, there are many Brazilians and I had friends. But when I went out, he became angry and wanted me to stay home with him all day." Vítor went on to explain that he did a few odd jobs, including dealing small amounts of marijuana, and he would engage in informal prostitution, asking for "help" or money after hooking up with gay men, which he then sent home to his mother and siblings.

I met Willian in Chicago while he was living with a gay couple. Willian identified as gay and explained, "I knew that I liked men, but where I was from in the [rural] interior of Brazil, this was difficult to realize. But there it is normal to shower together in this big outside [shower stall area] when there is not much water, and I was showering with the husband of one of my sisters and we both became hard. . . . He was very attractive, very hairy and muscular, and had a big dick. We did not have sex, but we came together and I knew I needed to get out because there he is every day, and this is a bad thing to do with anyone, let alone your sister's husband! So I came here to study and immediately found that gay men here give me things . . . like money, presents." Willian was handsome and had a charming demeanor. It was not difficult to imagine him being successful at gaining the favors of older men.

He became animated as he described his situation to me even while he took down chairs, prepping the restaurant where he worked for opening. Then he sat down and unraveled the story of his current woes, speaking mostly in English. "Eventually I went to live with one of them, a rich old *bicha*. He said he wanted to take care of me like a father, but he has a boyfriend, and now they pester me for sex all the time . . . but I am supposed to be their roommate now only! We present a strange image when we go out. Like a little family of these two old men and me. They helped me at first, giving me money, and I helped my family. They fight constantly, throwing lamps and dishes and things at each other. They sleep in separate beds. I hate them; . . . I do not have sex with them anymore and they want to throw me out."

"Where will you go when you leave this 'little family' you've found in the US?"

Willian laughed. "I will go back to Brazil and start my own family. A real one. Find a wife."

"A wife?" I asked, incredulous. "Will you continue to have sex with men?" I furrowed my brow in confusion. "I thought you said you were gay."

"For me, having children is the most important thing in the world. And children deserve a mother and a father. I will always have sex with men, but in Brazil women look the other way when this happens. I will find a woman who accepts this and is traditional and does not challenge my authority. I want to go back and live close to my family."

"Ah . . . and close to your sister's husband," I said without thinking, then realized I was perhaps being a bit too cheeky. But Willian just winked at me in response and shrugged as he stood up, flashing a coy smile as he finished setting the chairs.

Stories like this present complicated family arrangements that are difficult to understand as either normative or nonnormative. Vítor and Willian both sought to use notions of kinship to help lift themselves up and position their families for success by relying on gringo clients who wanted to "help them." But they also wanted to transition those clients from sexual roles into the role of patrons. Here is a moment where it becomes important to think about their interactions not only as being about affects—stirring up desire, feeling contempt—but also as performative labor that transmits those affects. These two men came to San Francisco and Chicago respectively and struggled to make the transition across cultures. They tried and failed to reposition themselves within the kinship arrangements or to transform the kinship relationships outright. The clients were too difficult and the Brazilian men were unable to alter their performances of masculinity in such a way as to transition the relationships into the kind of affective arrangements they hoped for. Their performances of masculinity remained sexualized for the clients, and the clients sought to domesticate them, asserting a homonormative vision of domesticity even within a putatively queer arrangement that still held an erotic charge, which both Vítor and Willian resisted. In this realm of the performative, however, the struggle between affects became visible and sometimes, as Willian noted, even violent.

Although Vítor and Willian both used the language of family and kinship to describe their relationships, the families they describe are unlike those that most anthropologists study. Willian's case especially highlights the murky area between the "traditional" and "queer" family in that he clearly adheres to some very traditional notions of machismo, male authority, and the importance of heterosexual marriage models, but he also wants homosexual relations to be built into kinship as it suits him—be it with gringos or even with his brother-in-law—and normalized. Yet his comment about this being "normal" in Brazil is also quite revealing, which is a subject I will return to at length below.

Prostitution and kinship are so intimately bound up that no responsible study of the former can afford to neglect the latter. And yet we know almost nothing about how families function in the lives of male sex workers, who—owing to their relative gender privilege—are not subject to the same pressure to sell sex in order to ensure survival for their children, at least not in the same way as are young mothers who find themselves with infants, mounting debts, and few other prospects. And yet my own fieldwork data reveal that male sex workers do, in fact, consider their work lives to be vital for their families. I have discovered some general trends and offer some specific cases that rely on the lived experiences of people who are involved in complicated forms of kinship that would not be possible without the advent of mass tourism, gay civil rights, and Brazil's economic growth—potentially offering us new insights into the political economy of sexuality and kinship in an increasingly globalized world.

To do this, I will outline the concept of queer kinship as it has been developed in queer studies and describe some more examples from my own research on gay tourists and garotos who are extending queer kinship transnationally by forging new configurations of affective attachments in Brazil. While gringos execute some of these examples in disturbing ways that reproduce inequality and may even be exploitative, most of these relationships are mutually beneficial to the foreigners and the families. Far from being a case of wealthy foreigners imposing themselves on Brazilian families, the local families and the foreigners coconstruct these new forms of kinship, performing new kinds of masculinities together, relying on practices that are consistent with prevailing conceptual work in queer studies scholarship, but also drawing upon traditional Brazilian kinship forms.

A Queer Kind of Kin

Queer studies scholars have invested a great deal of research effort into studying queer kinship. Most recently, this includes studies of gay adoption, but one need not be quite so literal about "kinship."[17] Precisely because of their sexual desires, gays and lesbians have all too often been rejected by their families and sought new, closely knit communities, or "families we choose" as Kath Weston puts it in her seminal work on queer kinship. As Weston notes, gays and lesbians frequently had to form new families within their new communities to provide emotional support and guidance and to care for them when they were ill, especially during the height of the AIDS crisis. Given this, it's not surprising that words like "family" and "sister" exist in gay slang with alternative, coded meanings. Importantly, though, gay families are not "replacements for" but rather "chronological successors to biological family."[18]

John D'Emilio's classic essay argued that gay identity as we know it came to exist only because gay men (and, to a lesser extent, lesbians) moved to urban areas away from their families as a result of political-economic developments of the Industrial Revolution and capitalism, thereby gaining more sexual privacy and congealing into communities, laying the groundwork for gay communities as we know them today.[19] Later scholars, especially those working within the field of "queer of color critique," refined this argument, noting that many queers of color who either lack financial opportunities or eschew the racism that accompanies a move into wealthier, whiter gay enclaves in the United States may not leave their biological families.[20] These scholars are resistant to the idea that African American communities harbor more homophobia than others. In many cases, African American communities adapt, essentially making a continued place for gay community members within the group. The refrain goes, "He may be a sissy, but he's *our* sissy!" In this way, the community protects its queer members from out-group hostility, but not necessarily from all abuses stemming from within the group.

While poor people experiencing same-sex attraction or expressing nonnormative gender identity may remain stigmatized, they are not *necessarily* isolated from their kin. It's also worth noting that people of color in the United States have often had their own kinship formations that resist canonical white formations. For example, African American families have, as Weston says, "never held to a strictly biogenetic interpretation of kinship" and are accustomed to forming a variety of types of biological and "fictive" families to find support in a white-supremacist society.[21] This strategic adaptation in the face of adversity is something for which they have been subjected to racist attacks from right-wing politicians such as in the infamous 1965 Moynihan Report, which argued that the lack of solid nuclear-family structures among poor African Americans was a threat to the nation.

More recently, queer theorists have argued that rural queer youth are increasingly adept at making a place for themselves, disrupting popular and scholarly assumptions that happiness is contingent upon escaping the rural family and seeking fulfillment in the city.[22] In Brazil, one finds similar trends. While cosmopolitan areas such as São Paulo and Rio de Janeiro remain sites of visible gay entrenchment, there is also a history of creating social spaces for queers in poor urban and rural areas, perhaps most famously in the case of "gay" men rising to positions of prominence in *candomblé* communities—not incidentally including the role of "priests," or *pais-de-santos*, who have many "children," or followers, whom they mentor and care for.[23]

With so many emic forms of queer kinship already thriving in Brazil before it became a popular gay travel spot for foreigners, it's not surprising that gay gringos' kinship systems would acquire a transnational component. Sometimes, this is overt. It can also be a negative and colonial enterprise. Consider the case of Dale, a wealthy gay American attorney from California who adopted a Brazilian girl in the mid-1980s. In 2008 he brought her to Rio de Janeiro to show her the *favelas* (shantytowns) that might otherwise have been her home. In between bringing high-end male escorts to luxury suites for himself, he took his daughter on a favela tour, during which they gave money and toys to the children. During this well-intentioned but paternalistic bout of spectatorship, he became enraged when the guides talked about the happy, normal lives that *favelados* lead despite what the gringos might have learned from news reports and watching films like *City of God*. Dale complained that this was terrible information to give people because poverty is not a happy condition in which to live.

My assistant, Gustavo, knew Dale well and heard his stories of rescuing his daughter from what he imagined was a terrible fate: being poor in Brazil. The guides' accounts of favela life as being normal and generally peaceful disrupted the tourist's own narrative, in which he was a benevolent interloper who had rescued his daughter from her fate through legal adoption and naturalization as a US citizen, wrapping her in a cocoon of financial privilege. This is the kind of example of transnational queer kinship that some find troubling: an American purchases a Brazilian child in a private adoption and then denigrates impoverished Brazilians when their reality inconveniences his liberal vision of kinship-as-rescue.[24]

But this case is far from the norm. Instead, what I encountered most often were tourists who formed relationships with a particular garoto. They usually met them in *saunas* or on beaches, and when they found themselves growing attached to them, they would beg them to leave prostitution. In exchange for this, they would send money and come to visit a few times a year. For those who owned vacation homes or property, the garotos could also serve as caretakers. Whenever a garoto wanted more money, he could email details of particular hardships and threaten that he was considering returning to "the life." Often, it was at this point that the garotos who were heterosexual would begin to identify as "bisexual" in order to make themselves appear as appropriate objects of affection capable of affective reciprocity.[25] Sometimes the gringos would let them continue to date women but insisted that they must not date other men or do programas. Garotos I knew in these relationships usually did occasional programas anyway, but they also saw this arrangement as the best of all possible situations.

For their part, many tourists in these relationships tell me that garotos are "closet cases." Michael, an account executive in his early thirties, explained his take on the situation. "Here in Brazil, see, there's a lot of homophobia, especially in the poor communities, the favelas, and so on. You can't just be gay. But if you take some money for it—well, that's different. There's an excuse because you can just say, 'Nah, I'm not gay. I'm only in it for the money.' So it's a good way to explore your sexuality and have it be more acceptable."

While it is generally true that garotos downplay any pleasure they feel or attraction to clients, I don't find it particularly useful to fall back on reductivist notions of "closet cases." Such a conceptualization relies on painfully outmoded visions of "true" inner selves and simplistic, fixed identities. Garotos' performative labor of constructing masculinity and navigating their relationships with their clients is fundamentally about the transference and manipulation of affect. So rather than falling back on discourses of the closet or even of sexual orientation, I prefer to think about the work that goes into creating these families using the rubric of performative labor because it reveals how ambiguous and mercurial pleasure and desire are and how this performative difficulty contributes to garotos' feelings of ambivalence toward their gringo boyfriends. The garotos feel emotionally attached and sometimes they may feel pleasure, but this does not mean that they are obscuring or denying an immutably gay (or bisexual) identity. So while the gringo boyfriend may not be the ideal partner or one that a garoto's mother or girlfriend or child would have envisioned wanting in the family, they nonetheless learn to accept, value, and empathize with the boyfriend—even to love him sometimes, although kinship's complexity sometimes far outstrips language's capacity.

Generally, garotos were not eager for their lives with their gringos to bleed into their primary family lives. But they did like to make sure clients knew about them—either to emphasize their heterosexual status or to motivate business, tips, or gifts. One man, Túlio, worked in a *sauna* in Rio. Túlio had a nice, high-end phone with a large screen and a camera. He turned it to face me. "This is my daughter," he said, showing me a sleepy-eyed infant in a pink jumper. "Her name is Ana. She has a brother, Samuel, who's three." Túlio flips to another photo to show me a picture of him, his common-law wife, and Samuel at nearby Copacabana Beach together. The next photos in the lineup are naked snapshots of himself and close-up shots of his erect penis, which he sends to prospective clients. We decide to do a follow-up interview in a week, but he says his phone hasn't worked in months because of his cash flow problems so there's no point giving me the number. "But don't worry. You can find me at the *sauna* again no problem. I need to work if I am going to get the phone functioning again."

During his early days on the scene when he would do two to three programas a day and worked every day, Túlio could clear the equivalent of $2,000 in a month, whereas a minimum-wage worker earned around $270 per month for the same hours. But Túlio, like other garotos, didn't want to work every day. He spent the money on expensive clothes, cologne, and electronics. He takes his friends to clubs and buys liquor by the bottle. He buys gifts for his wife and kids and—I later learn—his mistresses. But Túlio's hair is starting to recede. He looks closer to thirty-five than the twenty-five he tells people. Túlio knows that street hustling may be in his future if he doesn't start saving in earnest soon. Now he's trying to buckle down and work more hours again, but some days he does not get a programa. And he knows that he needs his expensive phone working again if he is going to provide for Ana and Samuel.

That these photos were adjacent in the lineup actually revealed a lot about the tendency for compartmentalized parts of garotos' lives to rub against one another. No matter how much the men tried to keep their family lives separate from their professional lives as prostitutes, the two can bleed into each other. A few garotos I knew did enjoy talking to gringos about their kids, but this tactic also ran the risk of alienating clients. While having sex with a "macho Latin daddy" is a common fantasy, making the connection that the man is—as one tourist put it— "only fucking you to feed the kids" whose photos you just saw can be a fatal dose of reality for the fantasy and a major turnoff.

At the other end of the spectrum are sex workers who are eager to incorporate their gringos as much as possible into their lives. I briefly knew a man in Bahia named Paulo who had worked as a *porteiro* (doorman) and who had become the boyfriend of a gay tourist. In the past, tourists who rented apartments in the large building had propositioned him, but he had declined (in part because he knew he could lose his job). Yet with the seed of the idea planted, he sought out one particular tourist from the neighborhood who seemed to him like a reliable boyfriend. Paulo had a common-law wife and a baby, and eventually the gringo even got to meet Paulo's wife. She made sure he held the baby, and though she must have suspected that her husband's "special American friend" had markedly sexual interests in her husband, she kept silent about these and focused on his role as a potential benefactor to the child. The gringo was never affectionate or sexually suggestive with her husband in front of her, but he would stop by to pick Paulo up and enter the house to say hello and perhaps leave a small gift for the baby or the household. In my admittedly limited interactions with her, she seemed to bear no ill will toward him and was never cold but instead quite enthusiastic about participating in her husband's calculation, playing the gracious host.

While I don't contend that this kind of relationship is the norm, it's common enough that gay tourists often warn one another to stay out of family dramas. They offer jaded advice to neophytes about any garotos who have "sick grandmother stories" or—worse still—"want you to meet their kids and get involved." One tourist, Arthur, a fifty-something expat, told me about a serious relationship he had with a policeman named Guilherme who also did programas at a *sauna*. After several programas, they began to see one another outside the *sauna*, and Guilherme began visiting Arthur at his home in one of the nearby island villages, where they stayed with a landlady and her son "like a little family," in which Arthur cooked dinner, and they all played cards and watched the evening telenovelas together before retiring to bed, where he and the sexually versatile policeman would have passionate sex every night. Guilherme came and went periodically, and the arrangement worked well for them both. Some months later, however, Guilherme sent Arthur an email inviting him to his wedding. Although Arthur knew that Guilherme was sexually interested in women, he nonetheless confessed to feeling surprised and even a bit jealous.

Arthur explained, "My best friend, she would tell me, 'You know Guilherme really loved you.' But I didn't love him. He didn't even really like living with me. He liked being in my house. He liked fucking, sucking, doing all that. He liked *sacanagem* [sexual stuff], but he didn't like [life in that town]. He was a policeman, and he needed more action, to be in the city."

Arthur says he didn't love Guilherme, but he does sound hurt even all these months later. "And so then later on . . . the policeman, my policeman, my *boyfriend* . . . invites me to *his* wedding, and he even invited my mother as well because he knew she was here visiting me for the month of January. But I thought that would just be sacrilege to have her go into a Catholic church and have her be there, knowing that he's there marrying a woman! And how to explain things to people afterward at the party at their home in the Zona Norte?" The Zona Norte is a comparatively poor part of Rio de Janeiro. I try to imagine Arthur in a favela with his aging mother, awkwardly making their way through the crowd of jubilant wedding guests.

Arthur continues, "And [even though] my friend is telling me that he really did love me so I should go, but I'm imagining myself sitting there in church when I've had my dick up his ass! Can you imagine? The whole concept of that, and then having my mother there as well was too strange to comprehend for me, actually. But he really wanted us there."

For Arthur, who prided himself on his intelligence and who had spent many years living in Brazil and thinking a great deal about the nature of sexuality in Brazil and its sexual economies, entering into a complex, queer kinship arrangement was not a new and exciting way to strengthen an affective community. Ironically, it was Guilherme who was pressing to expand *his own family* in this way. It's especially interesting because, in most other cases I know of, the gringo is incorporated into the Brazilian family, but the Brazilian is not incorporated in any meaningful way into the tourist's family. But in this instance, Guilherme even wanted to include Arthur's aged mother and, moreover, to host both of them at a religious ceremony whose express purpose was to seal Guilherme and his girlfriend into a formal, monogamous bond. Despite this fact, Guilherme pressed for an expanded and queer family with his on-again-off-again gringo boyfriend. From time to time, the two men ran into one another in Rio in the *sauna* or on the street, but Arthur declined to continue having a sexual relationship with him, to Guilherme's apparent disappointment.

There are several rather-reductive readings of this story. A cynic would say that Guilherme was being conniving, enacting a virtuoso ruse the entire time. An essentialist might say that Guilherme was a closeted gay or bisexual man who succumbed to societal pressure and left Arthur for a woman. I think it's more ambiguous than that. While material motivations may have played a role, Guilherme spent a lot of time with Arthur without even informal remuneration and seemed to enjoy himself. I would still take the cynic's line if it were not for the wedding invitation, which I cannot imagine any garoto doing for any man whom he still viewed as purely a client. The invitation made Guilherme very vulnerable to outing and stigma, potentially disgracing his family and his bride and ruining perhaps the most important day in their lives. It was a profound act of trust that was not necessary to securing material benefit. In fact, Guilherme had relatively little to gain with the invitation and everything to lose. And so I am inclined to believe that Arthur's best friend was correct: that Guilherme did love the gringo—even if in an unconventional way—and wanted to keep him in his life. The fact that he and his children might benefit is not incidental, but it doesn't invalidate the bond the two men had or Guilherme's feelings for Arthur.

Not all tourists are as reluctant as Arthur. Some tourists actually have several such families. One gay traveler, an anthropologist and academic, confided to me that he has "at least one family like that in every port" across a span of several continents. He was proud of this—and perhaps rightfully so—as he was as close to some of them as he was to his own biological family. Moreover, he genuinely enjoyed his time with each and understood them to enjoy this relationship as well.

I don't want to suggest that tourists are overly eager to insert themselves into families. Forging new kin is not a motivating factor in sex tourism. Nor are garotos' children necessarily the focus of such arrangements. Sometimes the garoto's mother is the most important part of his family. Few mothers knew the men's profession, but many suspected. They didn't ask, because they didn't want to know where the money came from. "My mother begged me not to tell her what it is [that I am doing], but only to [reassure] her that it was not drugs or stealing," André, a garoto who had worked in the Rio *saunas* for six years, explained.

As this case demonstrates, the family can loom large over a programa. The performative labor of prostitution involves compartmentalizing and managing certain facets of identity, including family life. But even when compartmentalized, these various aspects of subjectivity influence one another profoundly. The act of maintaining secrecy around his profession signals the importance of family to his work by both protecting his own privacy and sparing him their possible condemnation, but it also protects *them* from the stigma and shame they would be forced to bear.[26] Moreover, family motivates and spurs the performance of masculinity in everyday life, contributing to machismo and, ironically, to the "macho" character that the garoto uses to appeal to gay clients. Thus, family life motivates and crosses over into the garoto's professional life even as sex work eventually influences family life and spurs new potential forms of kinship.

Neither New nor Naive

For the conservatively minded, these queer kinship formations may seem newfangled, unnatural, or threatening to "family values." Despite Brazil's significant advances in gay rights and the government's attention to reducing homophobia, promoting gay marriage, and investing in things like gay tourism and gay pride, there are powerful conservative voices, such as that of the controversial minister and congressman Marcos Feliciano, who used his congressional committee role as human rights commissioner to lambast gays as a powerful threat to traditional family values. Even for the socially progressive, the transnational queer kinship formations I am describing may seem foreign or invasive. These configurations of kinship are not wholly new, nor are they neocolonial formations visited upon an unsuspecting and powerless "native Other." As several of the cases above demonstrated, the "natives" are far from naive and are, in fact, usually the ones inviting foreign men into the family. And so what looks novel (and perhaps liberatingly queer to some) at first glance is actually a mere adaptation of traditional frameworks and understandings of family in Brazil. To better explain this, I want to briefly revisit three (of the many possible) figures of Brazilian family life and read them in a queerer context—the *padrinho*, *patrão*, and *coroa*.

To begin, one of the key features of Brazilian kinship is the unique role of *padrinhos*, or godparents, in *compadrio*, or godparenthood. Gringos who are invited to serve as godparents may be surprised to learn just how different the role is in Brazil than it is in places like the United States, where it is often honorary and may be as simple as acting as the principal witness at an infant's baptism. The role can be so cursory that many baptized people in the United States may not even know who their godparents actually are. Moreover, godparents are frequently close blood relatives of the parents, such as siblings, meaning that they do not bring any particular advantages or expand the kinship group in any meaningful way.

Conversely, Brazilians have a long history of using compadrio to expand and/or solidify existing social networks. Although not as strongly observed as in some other Latin American countries such as Mexico, compadrio is nevertheless important throughout Brazil, even though Brazilianist scholars tend to focus on compadrio among the poor, *nordestinos* (northeasterners), indigenous populations, and—more historically—slaves. As Marshall Eakin notes, elites use compadrio to retain social distinction and privilege, while the poor may use it to incorporate somewhat more powerful actors into their fictive kinship systems, providing not only for children but also for the parents, who acquire their own kinship bond with the padrinhos.[27] This tradition goes back most visibly to the colonial slave era. Alida Metcalf argues that slaves in Brazil used compadrio to forge "vertical networks" of more powerful people, such as freedmen and slave owners—including some slave-owning biological fathers who served as godfathers to their own children.[28] According to historian Ana Maria Lugão Rios, free godparents could represent slave families in legal matters and disputes with their masters and provide substantial social assistance. Some slaves even secured freedom for their children through careful selection of godparents.[29]

Marcos Lanna has argued that compadrio is not (as the famous 1950s anthropologists Sidney Mintz and Eric Wolf would have it) a way of expanding or intensifying social relations "but rather one of the very foundations of community life" from the moment a village is established.[30] While Lanna is correct about the latter, compadrio certainly still accomplishes the former, and in a neoliberal era of increasingly global flows that can form affective and commercial linkages between gringo travelers and sex workers, it is being deployed in ways far outside those encompassed in his study of compadrio-as-foundation in a small, rural town. One can build upon Lanna's conceptualization of community foundations to suggest that compadrio now can and does incorporate transnational elements that were simply outside the scope of his analysis.

Another particularly adept point of Lanna's is the slippage between *padrinho* (godfather) and *patrão* (boss, patron), with the former occupying a murky space that may include interactions between an individual and his or her customers, bosses, or even friends. Traditionally, anthropologists such as Nancy Scheper-Hughes represented the realm of compadrio and padrinhos as an "egalitarian and collectivist" one that "siphons off the most minimal surplus to redistribute it among those even worse off" in the community.[31] But the world of *patrões* (bosses) and *donos* (benefactors) is hierarchical, locking people into "relations of servility, dependency, and loyalty to those who oppress and exploit them."[32] It is a nasty holdover from the ethic of patronage, or *paternalismo*, part of "self-colonizing dependencies" begat by the *casa grande* (plantation system) and, ultimately, slavery. Lanna, however, finds interesting and productive potential convergences between Brazilian padrinhos and patrões, eloquently observing that "even though my padrinho may live thousands of miles away from me, there is a shade of his presence, but not of him as a person or necessarily a shade of his person, in each one of the several patrões I will have in my life."[33]

In my own work, I frequently find myself sifting through Lanna's murky overlap. The gringo tourist who becomes involved with a Brazilian family is always marked by his past status as a client or customer. This can create some tensions, as in the cases of Vítor and Willian, who traveled to the United States and tried to turn clients with whom they had a sexual relationship into nonsexual patrões who would still have an obligation to assist them. They imagined that by shifting their roles and taking the erotic element out of their own performances, they might alter the affective exchange and transform the basic nature of the client-worker relationship.

When a garoto manages to forge a relationship with a client outside the context of their original encounter, the client may transition into the role of a patron. That is, he calls the shots in most of the basic economic aspects (i.e., where they will go, how much he will spend). But he also has obligations to take care of the garoto should misfortune befall him. At least that's how the garotos understand it, but as Willian discovered when his hosts were ready to evict him, gringos don't always play by the same rules. Working from the Brazilian perspective, the garoto imagines that the client who moves into the role of a patron should help those who work for him. Such a client may loan him money rather than give it to him, assist him with paperwork for travel or student visas, help him to receive medical checkups or emergency treatment, and even help him to find work and attain his *carteira assinada* (i.e., official working papers). That is, he fulfills many functions of not only a patrão but also a padrinho. Consequently, it is not surprising that when a garoto finds a good patrão who is especially attentive and helpful, he may invite him into compadrio as a padrinho to his child or, to a less formal degree, a *tio*, or "uncle."

Making godfathers out of gringos is not a new strategy or even a clever ploy. Gringos may fret that garotos who expect all these things from them are maneuvering or manipulating them. This is another moment where garotos' performative labor can fall short. What the gringo may fear is manipulation, the garoto sees as a *jeitinho*, a clever work-around to find a solution or improve one's condition. Brazilians often talk about these *jeitinhos*, and such ploys need not happen at the expense of patrons as some gringos cynically fear but are instead a perfectly rational way of relating to someone with more class privilege for whom a garoto de programa has a particular, albeit-complicated set of attachments and affinities. When a garoto tries to reconstitute his relationship to a client in this way, he is engaging in a particular type of performative labor in which he is struggling to transform the relationship from within even as both actors have drastically different conceptions of the relationship and the roles available. The attempt to render the roles intelligible and have a long-term successful outcome poses high risk but also high rewards.

Lastly, I want to draw another murky categorical figure into this brief analysis. Up until now, I have spoken primarily of sex workers who are incorporating gay gringos into systems of *parentesco*, or kinship. Although some conservative evangelicals may espouse prejudices against prostitutes that cast sex workers as being incompatible with traditional family life or somehow outside "good" family formations, the fact that sex workers do incorporate clients into family life (be it as *patrões, tios, donos,* or *padrinhos* or using less formal ways and nomenclature) conflicts with these prejudices. In fact, part of the reason a certain segment of conservative Brazilian society is so uncomfortable with prostitutes in the family sphere is that they themselves are on some level aware of the role that money plays in their own sexual lives. Indeed, the idea of an older, wealthier man in the house—a *coroa*—is probably one that they, their sisters, mother, or friends are quite familiar with. The idea that heterosexually identified Brazilian men might have coroas as well may be doubly uncomfortable because it threatens traditional gender roles and personal allegiances to machismo, but it's also a mere permutation of traditional Brazilian kinship.

In her piercing analysis of the subject, Donna Goldstein describes how many women from poor communities in Rio's Zona Norte share a common fantasy of seducing a coroa in what they called a *golpe do baú* (treasure chest coup). Indeed, stories of this kind of *golpe* are a genre unto themselves that the poor women in her ethnography trade. They use a "fairy-tale" formulation in which "a poor, clever, and seductive dark-skinned woman finds her rich, old, and white 'prince,'" although the stories contain many humorous elements because "the old man will not be able to satisfy the passions of the younger *morena* seductress."[34] The women saw these scenarios as entirely possible and realistic, if rare, and one common version was for a diffident gentleman to grow fond of his domestic cleaning woman. In this way, good *patrões* are not only ideal godparents but also potential suitors.

Goldstein argues that while such stories may merely invert old conceptualizations of the master-slave relationship or offer a problematic version of discourses about the benefits of "whitening" society through interracial intimacy, they are regularly created, told, and enacted by poor women as a legitimate means of coping with oppression.[35] They also obscure the racism and abuse that employers may inflict on the women they employ in their homes (which is almost certainly more common than golpes are). Goldstein concludes that the fantasy of the coroa is not "democratic, nor egalitarian, nor idiosyncratic" and is instead predicated on the economic correlations of race.[36]

While I agree with her final assessment, what I find interesting is that the fantasy of the coroa is held by women who are not sex workers. In fact, many female sex workers choose prostitution precisely because they do not want to be *empregadas* (live-in maids) even while many empregadas and housekeepers are proud that they at least have an "honorable" profession and are not *putas* (whores). Yet when I have visited Copacabana's *orla* (beachfront) area or heterosexual sex tourist bars, I find that a great deal of what the media and government consider prostitution consists of cases of women who are looking to find gringo coroas for economically beneficial dating or for possible immigration opportunities (rather than for programas per se). Looking for gringo coroas may bring them into the sexual economy, but landing one is how they get out.

Interestingly, garotos de programa whom I know well also talk of coroas as ideal boyfriends because they believe them to be lonely clients who often crave affection more than sex. Being very skilled at caressing and cuddling, they say, is a better ticket out of the life than having a big penis. It's all about the performance of desire, and if one can find a "good guy" whom one can think of as a friend and patron, then it's easier. This is their own version of the golpe do baú, except they have no desire to enter into a gay marriage. Instead, they tap into the refrain so familiar to the women from their communities, deploying it in homoerotic contexts. As with the women, the line between coroa and client is blurry at best, but the coroa is a ticket out of full-time prostitution and into a better situation with more opportunities even if garotos may still continue selling sex informally or occasionally. However, for the mostly heterosexual garotos, life with a coroa is not seen as happily-ever-after because they do not want to be in a life-long relationship with a gay man. But they also do not necessarily want to lose the man financially or emotionally, and so moving him from being strictly a coroa into another, more honorable form of kinship such as a padrinho may be the best way to accomplish this.

The Family of the Future

In Brazil, as the anthropologist Linda-Anne Rebhun has noted, rhetoric of "the family" signals a moral claim about "virtue, stability, and loving relationships associated with the home" and is actively deployed as a defensive attack against prostitution and loose morality.[37] It is not surprising that much as it is in the United States, gays, lesbians, travestis, and transgendered persons in Brazil are discriminated against, beaten, and killed in the name of family values.[38] The figure of the heterosexual garoto de programa or the michê who has sex with men is especially threatening to family values because in addition to combining prostitution and homosexuality—the two great sexual boogeymen of our era—it also raises the specter of AIDS and fears that garotos and michês are a "bisexual bridge" between bad people who invite or even deserve AIDS and unsuspecting *moças de família* (good girls, "family girls") who do not.[39]

But when conservatives argue that "the family" in Brazil is under threat, they forget that gays and prostitutes are *already* members of families and are well versed in the systems of kinship and the nuances of Brazilian family life. Therefore, it should not be surprising to find gays and prostitutes deploying the same structures, patterns, and systems of kinship in new transnational contexts, queer and otherwise. And yet, these relationships are far more threatening than the comfortable and homonationalist visions of respectable homosexuality associated with pride parades and cosmopolitan gay life. Those gays are respectable by virtue of their very separateness.

The queer families I have described risk splitting a married heterosexual couple by appending a gay gringo and involving him in the raising of a child or the maintenance of a family. Despite the Brazilian state's considerable and sometimes-successful efforts to reduce inequality, the fact that some sex workers rely on and even prefer the financial and emotional patronage of gringos draws attention to the remaining shortcomings of the state and its inability to provide for some citizens, even though others may be able to improve their lot. Moreover, while garotos can have Brazilian boyfriends as well, the reliance on foreigners for economic support also mirrors the kind of geopolitical relationship of dependency from which Brazil has often struggled to free itself. The gringo's presence highlights the lack of opportunity and the continued inequality that many young Brazilian men face. This dependency is no way diminishes the complex affective and emotional exchanges the men share—including desire and love—but framed this way, "godfather gringos" may be harbingers of a new kind of kinship system that Brazilian men are seeking out for themselves across national, class, and sexual difference. By focusing attention at these queer edges of kinship without losing sight of the new kinship system's origins within traditional family structures, we also better understand such queer kinship as simply another formulation of these sex workers' families that—like all kinship structures in Brazil—is forged on the basis of the dual and inseparable desires for economic opportunity and strengthened social networks.

FIVE

Ecosex: Social Misremembrance and the Performance of Eroticized Authenticity

The Indigenous Rainforest Spa is about connecting with the ancient and native world. Satisfying natural curiosities. Being rewarded. Having a meaningful and memorable experience. Discovering the truly authentic.
LA SELVA JUNGLE LODGE INDIGENOUS RAINFOREST SPA

In Manaus, an industrial city of almost two million people located a thousand miles inside the Amazon rain forest, it rains almost every afternoon. People plan their daily schedules around this. "Let's meet up tomorrow after the rain," they'll say. As I explored the dingy downtown, having what was supposed to be a bit of a respite from fieldwork, I realized I needed to hurry or I was going to get caught in the daily downpour. Everyone else seemed to know better and to have taken shelter, but there I was out in the open like the naive tourist I was.

Suddenly, I was no longer alone. A somewhat-disheveled man was approaching me. He had a dirty face and open shirt that set loose his big paunch. "Hey amigo! You want to see the jungle? You want a tour?" he said in thickly accented English.

It's very common in Manaus for unscrupulous and importunate touts to try to sell trips to tourists. When not outright frauds, these men refer tourists to only slightly

145

more scrupulous companies who overcharge them for mass tours that load hundreds of people onto uncomfortable, outmoded boats and drag them out to take pictures of the polluted nearby waters, deforested shores, and impoverished indigenous children who sell mass-produced souvenirs. I brushed him off and briskly walked past him.

"My friend, wait!" he shouted after me, picking up his pace and walking along beside me. "No jungle? Do you want to fuck Indian pussy?"

He gave up his pursuit with a shrug. It took a few seconds more to fully register the implications of this question. Because I am a gringo, I realize, I was just hailed as an ecotourist. And a sex tourist. By the same guy.

This was my first real inkling that the ecotourist industry might also help support the sexual economy in the area. I thought about ecotourists and their desire to explore the jungle, to see wildlife and swim with river dolphins, to visit indigenous tribes and so on. And I wondered, are these two forms of tourism related on some affective level?

To be clear, the sex tourism in the Amazon is not a vast phenomenon permeating the jungle. There are, however, some interesting cases of organized, packaged sex tourism there that I do take up below, and there are rich, if diffuse, connections between informal sexual economies and the ecotourist economy. Despite the level of sex tourism in Manaus being lower than it is in many other cities in Brazil, the booming ecotourist industry with its lavish ecoresorts, spas, and folkloric shows does use the erotic to introduce and orient tourist clientele to indigeneity and to manipulate their desire for authentic encounters. It's for this reason that I'm choosing to focus on the rain forest in this chapter.

Ecotourism in the Amazon deliberately teaches tourists to interpret their experiences within an erotic framework as they apprehend locals and fasten meanings to their encounters. Although this is more visible for heterosexual tourists because of the abundance of sexualized imagery of indigenous women presented to tourists, gay tourists also relate sexuality and ecology in similar yet complicated ways. Therefore, this chapter takes up (*a*) the general eroticization of performances of indigeneity within an increasingly mass-marketed version of ecotourism that proliferates in Brazil and that sometimes overlaps with overt sex tourism and (*b*) the issue of how the homoerotic functions in this ecological realm.

The ecotourism industry uses the erotic to construct a narrative about the authenticity of tourists' travel and to create a memory for them in which their interaction with locals and their experience with nature benefited local people and the environment. Sexual intimacy is a marker of this authenticity, and so the major industry players incentivize particular performances of indigeneity, making them legible to tourists through the erotic realm. This leads to a restaging of colonial encounters that encourages mass-market travelers to imagine their ecotourism as good for the planet while also using performances of "authentic" indigeneity to increase tourists' own cultural capital as cosmopolitan consumers.

Throwing Stones

"When I was a small girl, about seven years old, the tourists used to take pictures of me," Andréa says, covering her mouth to stifle a giggle that the mirth in her eyes betrays anyway. "I hated this so much that one day when a tourist snapped a picture of me, I picked up a rock and I just *threw* it at him!" She mimes throwing the rock and laughs again. "And sometimes I would spit at them! Oh, I was an angry little Indian!"

I smile at the mental image of a tiny, ferocious Andréa and ask her if she ever imagined that she would grow up to be a tour guide for these *gringos*. "No, but I love my job. And I always tell all the guys, 'Don't take pictures of the native people unless you ask first!' Usually, it's okay, but they appreciate you asking, and sometimes then you have a conversation. That is better, I think. And if you don't . . . well one day, you never know . . ." She hefts another imaginary stone menacingly for emphasis.

For Andréa, tourists' obsession with capturing properly performed indigeneity is not only about the ethics of taking photos of people who may not want to be photographed. It's also about the ethics of taking photos of some who do. "The children should be in school, but parents know they will make a lot of money if the child stays in tourist areas in their native clothes and poses for pictures. . . . They can ask the tourist for a few dollars for posing in these pictures. It's very bad. Tourists do not think. They do not realize that their pictures actually are keeping poor children [from] going to school and improving their lives. They just click, click, click . . . always, click click click."

Andréa grew up in the highlands of Peru. "I'm the wrong kind of Indian for this weather," she later lamented as she shepherded a gay international tour group out of our canoe and up a riverbank in the sweltering heat to an ecolodge in the Amazon basin, close to the Brazilian border. Even with luxury amenities, Andreá and the tourists alike wilted in the humidity and suffered from the insects. It's little wonder the nickname stuck when explorers began referring to the Amazon rain forest as the "Green Hell." A few years earlier, Andréa had taken her children and left a philandering husband to live with her uneducated and impoverished mother. She nonetheless carved out a career as a tour guide, working for an international gay tour company that kept her apart from her children for weeks at a time but that paid her quite well.

Despite tensions with her family, she loved her job, and she loved working in the gay community, not just with the gay tourists—though she conspiratorially whispered that she found them much more fun than most of the heterosexual ecotourists she'd worked with in the past—but also with the many LGBT guides, restaurateurs, waiters, and bartenders she had met and formed long-lasting friendships with while taking her gay foreigners out for nights on the town. For young lesbian and gay people, the ecotourism industry proved a viable path out of small-town life and a chance to travel and to meet new people, including foreigners from all around the world. Andréa herself flirted with the idea of trying a relationship with a pretty, young woman she found attractive but concluded that she would just never be able to put aside her desire for burly, macho men, even though she felt that attraction was what led her into a disastrous marriage.

Andréa loved introducing tourists to her culture and taking them out with her gay friends, but she was also strict with the clients. No litter. No upsetting the animals. No uninvited photos. Sex was fine, but not with rent boys—a rule that the gay travel company even included in the fine print of an agreement its clients signed, warning them they would be ejected without a refund if they paid for sex, regardless of whether it was legal in the host country. The gay travel company was so keenly aware of the association of gay travel with sex tourism that it sought to distance itself overtly and litigiously.

When I accompanied Andréa on that tour, I'd already been into the Amazon twice. I was initially baffled at the ecotours I saw gay travel agencies advertising, and I wondered why there would be so many. Certainly, acquaintances have asked me to account for the appeal of packaged gay tourism. Why would you need a separate tour just for gay people? When this happens, I patiently explain that gay travelers must worry about things that never enter into most straight people's minds. In some locations there can be difficulties finding hotels that let LGBT couples share a bed or a room or even let them stay at all. Gay couples may book rooms only to find themselves turned away and scolded. Even if they aren't denied service, they have a perfectly reasonable desire to vacation among people from whom they needn't worry about receiving sermons, glares, or snide comments. And sometimes they want to vacation with gay groups or go on gay cruises because they hope to find some romance with their fellow travelers.

On Andréa's tour, all the men I met were single. They ranged in age from the late forties to the sixties. Among their ranks were a successful restaurateur, a lawyer, an accountant, a business consultant—all white, upper-middle-class to wealthy professionals. They hailed from the United States, Australia, and Ireland. A few of the men would go into town to cruise at gay bars for local men, but they didn't seem interested in purchasing sex outright. They were more interested in traveling and hiking but didn't want to risk encountering homophobia by going with a non-gay tour. Their trip was identical to the tours Andréa took straight people on for other local companies with the exception of choosing gay venues for nightlife options. They visited markets, where Andréa sought permission from the local indigenous women to take photos. They visited a village to bring food to indigenous children, watch weaving demonstrations, and purchase souvenirs—with Andréa again receiving permission for the tourists to take photos. They stayed at a jungle lodge in the rain forest and snapped photos of a few of the hunky male guides. But it wasn't all that gay a trip. I wondered if these gay travelers perceived their experience differently than did the heterosexuals I went on tours with. Did they orient themselves to their surroundings in queer ways?

Social Media and the Performance of Authenticity

As Andréa noted above, tourists take photos constantly. With today's technology, one can take thousands of photos on a single memory card and can upload them to Facebook, Instagram, Tumblr, Flickr, and dozens of other social-networking sites or apps for sharing photos. The phenomenon of travelers photographing themselves with native people has become widespread enough that the genre has spurred many parody sites in which bloggers collect hundreds of actual photos and post them for ridicule. One Tumblr that was popular when I was in the field was called "Gurl Goes to Africa," which offers scathing articles like "The Four Cutest Ways to Photograph Yourself Hugging Third World Children." The satirical news site *The Onion* also poked fun at the photographic trend with its headline, "6 Day Visit to Rural African Village Completely Changes Woman's Facebook Profile Picture."

Many of the tropes of the genre that these media outlets are sending up are artistic in nature (e.g., a small black child's hand in an adult white one) and bear a striking similarity to the style of images produced by *National Geographic* and the Travel Channel. While mocking the perceived paternalism of white tourists' fascination with interacting with and helping "Third World" people, what these satirical sites reveal is the failed attempt to capture what for the tourist felt like an authentic moment of transformation. These parodic sites' existence points to the fact that the photos are documenting an interaction that was, in all likelihood, more meaningful to the tourist than to the local while also deflating the altruism of the tourist by virtue of the fact that he or she so quickly and publicly broadcast the moment. Although I appreciate the barbed response to those whom the satirists perceive as missionizing foreigners, what these types of photos and the sites that parody them hint at is something much grander: there are large economic and political structures in place that create the conditions and contexts for these photos, and these structures are what make signifiers of "authenticity" have value in this social realm. The promotion of the "authentically" indigenous category is what commissions performances of indigeneity, which are paradoxically both desexualized and erotically charged.

Dean MacCannell's influential 1976 book *The Tourist: A New Theory of the Leisure Class* suggests that tourism is a failed attempt to stave off alienation in an increasingly superficial world and that tourists search for authenticity because it is now in such scarce supply. Consequently, tourist spaces now manufacture "staged authenticity" for tourist consumers, as in the case of the indigenous children Andréa referenced whose parents dress them in traditional garb and make them pose for paid photos with tourists instead of going to school. Tourists feel they must always be wary of "tourist traps" that are inauthentic and must seek out ever more exotic locales to find the truly authentic, behaving in MacCannell's view like pilgrims on a quest for a holy site or relic. During the 1990s, the sociologist John Urry updated MacCannell's theory by describing the importance of the tourist gaze in cultural/heritage tourism and by arguing how local populations such as the indigenous children in question perform and reflect the expectations of tourists (generally based on cultural stereotypes) for financial gain.[1]

For Urry, governments and media deliberately manage and manufacture "authenticity" to create and sustain the industry itself, which often spurs the revival of ethnic pride and reattachment to identity. The anthropologist Ed Bruner, however, draws on fieldwork among tourists and Maasai warrior-performers in Kenya to argue that tourists are often skeptical of staged authenticity. He presents locals as agentive in their self-presentation, creating possibilities for more-nuanced and syncretized modes of performance. Nevertheless, although tourists may be skeptical of the inauthentic, they may still be able to enjoy such an experience, replete with "all the comforts and luxury of home, and a good show."[2] That is, for Bruner, tourists know that a good deal of the indigeneity they encounter is fake, but they enjoy it anyway.

The search for "authentic" indigeneity is frustrating for ecotourists arriving in Manaus. Downtown Manaus does not feel as if it's in the middle of the Amazon rain forest. Surrounding an impressive opera house built in the nineteenth century when Manaus was awash in money from the rubber boom, the downtown now features store after store selling cheap electronics and plastic goods. Manaus is the heart of Brazil's free-trade zone (FTZ), so production costs are low here, and the city has swelled despite being surrounded by a thousand miles or more of jungle in all directions. The standard of living is low here, too, with squalid shacks lining the waterfront posing a risk for outbreaks of tropical diseases.[3] Manaus seems worlds away from the beaches and cosmopolitan nightclubs of Rio. It has the feel of a border town like Tijuana or the crumbling urbanism of Detroit, and not at all of the lush exoticism tourists expect when landing in the middle of the rain forest. That happens later after transferring deeper into the jungle to their ecolodges and resorts.

Ecotourism is now a huge industry, and it is not necessarily the bastion of altruism and environmentalism that those who profit by it may pretend. In 2009 the American owner of Wet-A-Line Tours, which operates bass-fishing vacations in the Amazon jungle, was held in Brazil on charges of operating a house of prostitution, corruption of minors, domestic trafficking, and rape, it having been alleged that since the year 2000, the Georgia man recruited young indigenous women as prostitutes for his clients (including several who were alleged to have been underaged teenagers).

The men circulated photos of themselves with the women in fishing boats and at restaurants and allegedly of themselves having sex. In these photos, the prostitutes pose, smiling, sometimes giving the thumbs-up sign so ubiquitous in Brazil, alongside the men, who appear to be in their fifties and sixties. Many of the men were apparently friends from Masonic Lodges. They smile happily with the prostitutes in the photos, wearing Hawaiian shirts and looking every inch the gringo.[4] Although the Wet-A-Line case was eventually dismissed in part because the statue of limitations had been exceeded and the proprietor continues to deny wrongdoing, it is another example of eco-tourism's fraught relationship with local sexual economies in the Amazon. But it's also important to remember the structural issues at play in the FTZ. In a region where jobs are available in manufacturing and, increasingly, big-budget ecotourism, young people may find the provision of sexual services to be one of the few employment opportunities available if they don't want to or can't get hired to work for the big hotels, lavish ecoresorts, or major corporations.

Brazil's Amazon jungle region has been the beneficiary and victim of an enormous spike in so-called ecotourism in the last twenty years. Meanwhile, young men and women, many of them of indigenous descent, try to scrape out a living in the shadow economy that big-budget ecotourism and the FTZ have wrought. But just how extensive is this sexual economy? To be sure, the sexual economy is not devoted to ecotourists. Businessmen of many nationalities are involved. And there are locals to sell to, and these make up the vast majority of clients. The sex tourist industry is also small compared with the economies in places like Rio, Bahia, and Recife. If we focus even more narrowly on male prostitution, the industry is smaller still. Yet Brazil's racial mythology invariably hinges on the symbolic figure of the *branco* (white), *negro* (black), and *índio* (indigenous person). This triumvirate is essential to understanding intersections of race and sexuality, and so a consideration of gay travelers' fascination with and eroticization of racialized masculinity in Brazil ought to consider how indigeneity plays into the gay traveler's imaginary.

Although gay tourists are a minority among ecotourists, many gay tour groups visit the Amazon every year. Concierge Travel, a gay travel company, is beginning to offer gay luxury cruises of the Amazon River, and Olivia Travel currently offers similar cruises specifically for lesbians. The large and opulent ecoresort Ariaú Amazon Towers even decked itself out with rainbow banners to host a gay pride celebration organized by Fontours, the largest (and gay-owned) tour operator in Manaus.

In order to encourage more gay tourism, the local gay pride group invited LGBT activists and journalists from gay magazines and websites to travel to Manaus to tour hotels and ecoresorts and meet with their business and sales managers. Olando Câmara, president of Manaustur (the city's tourism bureau), told the group, "We have no prejudices. Manaus is democratic and the city is ready to receive you with open arms." Raul Sampaio, a travel agent specializing in trip planning for foreign, as well as domestic, tourists, added, "Manaus is a great destination for tourism and is a gay-friendly city." Meanwhile, an official from Ariaú Amazon Towers informed the gay travel professionals that the hotel planned to offer a new LGBT suite in the style of *casa da boneca barbie* (Barbie Dream House) for vacationing or honeymooning gay couples.[5] Domestic and foreign gay travelers are now being wooed by the ecotourism industry, but ecotourism in the Amazon carries with it an erotic—and often homoerotic—imprint, which does have implications for the sexual economy.

Gay tourists and business travelers in Manaus tend to avoid the street-hustling scene. They prefer higher-end *garotos* in order to avoid the violence and drug problems that they presume to be endemic among street hustlers. They stick to *saunas*, escorts, and informal hookups with local men at gay clubs where remuneration may be a small cash gift or even just a bar tab for the man, pressing at the edges of what might still be defined as commercial sex. Some gay sex tourists I met in Rio had brought along their own garotos as escorts on their Amazon vacations. These men wanted the romance of the Amazon adventure but were reluctant to explore the markedly more downscale world of prostitution in Manaus.

Hal was a fifty-something gay man who had come to Manaus with a thirty-year-old garoto named Rafa, one of a few favorite garotos whom Hal would call whenever he was in São Paulo for work. Rafa normally prided himself on his cool exterior, trying to appear so unflappable that he often came across as arrogant. But his utter excitement about seeing the Amazon would bubble through this veneer and erupt in gasps and brief, joyous laughs and exclamations whenever we encountered wildlife. Whenever this happened, Hal would shoot me a conspiratorial wink, but he never teased Rafa about it. In truth, nothing seemed to make Hal happier than watching Rafa's excitement over getting to explore this part of his own country. But Hal was dismissive about Manaus in general. "It's disgusting," he pronounced glumly. "Just really gross." When I asked why he didn't pick up a local guy in Manaus, he shrugged. "Rafa has decent English, and I figured that would be harder here. The boys here are *hot*, as I'm sure you noticed . . . but I wanted this to be special and so I went with a known quantity. . . . Rafa has wanted to come here for years. I'm a little afraid to see what the *saunas* here are like. Probably disgusting . . . but I thought maybe I'd go with Rafa, . . . maybe find a third [man for a threesome] there or just go see who we find at [a gay club]."

One garoto I met, a gay-identified twenty-four-old named Anderson, had defined, yet delicate facial features. With his long, dark locks of hair framing his big, brown eyes, Anderson read to most as indigenous. He lived in Manaus, where he was a student and worked as a go-go dancer at a gay club. Only occasionally did he dabble in *programas* with local guys he met there, but every once in a while he would find a foreign business traveler or tourist to go with. "I really prefer those," he said with a laugh, "because they pay more money. . . . One of the tourists, who was young and very handsome, very nice, told me I should move to Rio de Janeiro because I could make so much there if I went to a *sauna*. . . . I think I would like to go there. I've never been there, never seen [it]. . . . It's funny, really, I think because all the tourists I ever meet have seen more of Brazil than I have. They know more of my country than I do! Incredible."

But Anderson was likewise disconnected from the Amazon. "One time I met a gringo and we went through town . . . together all day long. [Then] he took me on a [boat] tour, which was really strange. And he kept pointing," Anderson told me, laughing so hard that he almost could not finish. "He pointed at trees and would ask me what it was, or at flowers or things like that. And I kept telling him, 'I don't know, man, I don't know,' until finally he said, 'You're the worst Indian ever.'"

I can't say to what extent the tourist was being ironic or joking about Anderson's poor performance of indigeneity, but the fact remains that the client assumed that Anderson would make an excellent local guide despite the fact that he was born and raised in Manaus and had had a lower-middle-class and fairly urban existence. Throughout my research in Manaus, Rio, and Salvador da Bahia, tourists struck me as being in various states of inevitable disillusionment. They almost always imagined their garoto companions as racialized ideals and stereotypes—suave Latin lovers, beefy machos, thuggish *favelados* (slum residents), hypersexual black bucks, noble savages—thereby forcing the men to either perform accordingly or, in the case of Anderson, disabuse them of their romantic visions of Brazil. More broadly, I came to learn that the tourists *wanted* to be fooled into taking an optimistic posture, especially in the beginning, before they'd learned from a broken heart, a stolen credit card, or a sob story that it's hard to live out a fantasy without being affected by the material realities of inequality. They wanted to be swept off their feet and weren't as skeptical about the tall tales the garotos would tell them to get more money or as incredulous about the garotos' sometimes-fantastic backstories. Much like Bruner's tourists watching the Maasai warriors perform in Kenya, they were willing to suspend their own disbelief in order to indulge in a bit of staged authenticity that they found pleasurable.

Most tourists in Manaus were likewise willing to suspend some disbelief in the service of having a good time. On a tourist river cruise, I saw would-be ecotourists horrified by the garbage floating in the water carefully advising each other how to frame their photographs to crop out the trash. Later, at the Ariaú Amazon Towers ecoresort, I watched people crop out indigenous children who were wearing Western T-shirts so they could focus on the more traditionally dressed ones. Unfortunately, all too often, "ecotourism" isn't very ecofriendly. But ecotourists' ambivalent relationship with authenticity is relevant to their encounters both with nature and with local men and women, signaling a similar underlying structure that provides insight into the ways in which ecotourists conflate nature and natives.

Greenwashing the Green Hell

Much of what passes as ecotourism doesn't function sustainably or ecologically. Indigenous laborers are underpaid and given limited opportunities, and commercial tourist operators have inequitable and unreliable relationships with local partners. In fact, some experts maintain that the ecotourism industry may be doing more harm than good.[6] Many of the most visible businesses traffic in highly sexualized images of indigeneity, including luxury hotels that offer sexy versions of "folkloric" dancing that include G-strings and tassels, souvenir shops that sell erotic artwork, and luxury spas emphasizing traditional healing and rain forest remedies provided by beautiful indigenous women and men.

The great contradiction of mass ecotourism is that the ecotourist impulse is predicated on a desire to experience "virginal" spaces of nature before they are destroyed by global capitalism and, ironically, by their growing popularity with other tourists and by the ecotourism industry itself. Diverting attention from this paradox, large-scale players in the ecotourism industry—most visibly Ariaú Amazon Towers as the largest player in the ecoresort industry—encourage interactions between tourists and locals that rewrite colonial encounters in new ways. Some tourists purchase sex in formal venues or through informal transactions, but this is merely an extension of the same principles and phenomena. In an era when ecotourism in the rain forest is increasingly popular, affordable, and mass-marketed, the whole industry is shifting to accommodate the kind of tourists who care more about their jungle lodge's air-conditioning and its souvenir stores than its ecological principles. It feels increasingly difficult to experience the "real" Amazon. The industry, however, depends on tourists to restage and reenact the titillating colonial encounter between explorer and native Other, creating a false memory in which the modern tourist's shared interaction was beneficent to the perpetually static local person's existence. Through these restagings, the tourist is able to reimagine neocolonial undertakings as vital to saving the planet.

When I arrived at Ariaú Amazon Towers, the jungle's most famous hotel and resort, I had already been in contact with staff members with questions about research. I had also been warned. Nearly every guidebook screams out some variant of "Just don't go!" and describes the resort as teeming with tourists who are mostly interested in luxury and cheap titillation. This meant it was exactly where I had to start in my efforts to understand mass ecotourism and how it incentivized and eroticized performances of indigeneity. Staff with whom I spoke at Ariaú were enthusiastic and genuinely loved what they did, which they saw as helping to save the rain forest. But after an indigenous man hoisted my suitcase up over his head and climbed some eighty feet up steep stairs that looked more like ladders, he opened the door to reveal an air-conditioned suite among the treetops with an enormous bed, expansive balcony, fully equipped indoor plumbing, plush sofa, and a computer.

In between his piranha-fishing trip and swimming with the pink river dolphins, Solomon, a business executive in his fifties, sat down at Ariaú to talk to me. He traveled to Manaus regularly for business and had decided to extend his stay for a few days to take in Ariaú. "The girls in town are amazing," he told me. "They see you're an American guy—a gringo—and they just throw themselves at you. I go out all the time with guys from work and we walk into a place and—bam!—five, six, seven girls are on us. . . . I told my son in San Francisco he needs to come down here because he is really into nature stuff, but he might leave with a wife, too, if he isn't careful!"

When I asked if the women asked for money, he looked sheepish. "Sure. But they're not prostitutes!" he objected. "These are nice girls. Local girls!"

"Indian?" I ask.

"They look like it. But all of the people here are at least part, . . . but yeah, you give them something at the end of the night, but it's just like a tip. Like just a little more than the cab fare is . . . so they go away, go on home." Sitting near the main lobby area in the resort, we were surrounded by sultry paintings for sale of naked Indian women, legs splayed, casting decidedly come-hither looks at Ariaú's guests as they perused the lobby gift shop.

Ariaú and its 205 guest rooms spread among nine towers have played host to many famous guests, including Bill Gates, Jimmy Carter, Bill Clinton, Kevin Kostner, Jennifer Lopez, Susan Sarandon, Ice Cube, Martha Stewart, Charlton Heston, Roman Polanski, Neil Armstrong, and Arlen Specter, among many other Hollywood celebrities, politicians, pop stars, and royalty. It is the largest and most famous hotel of its kind in the world, and it is difficult to underestimate its role in the ecotourism industry and local economy. Its massive lobby is covered in placards identifying the various celebrities and groups who have been guests, with dozens of university student groups and business school cohorts represented. Ariaú staff are fond of claiming they did not tear down a single tree to build the hotel.

I tried to work in good faith with the folks at Ariaú. But in truth, the staff seemed perplexed by my questions about sustainability and downright uncomfortable when I asked about eroticization, fetishization, and the like. I got the distinct impression that they were more accustomed to travel writers and journalists writing puff pieces about the sheer wonder of this most famous of the jungle hotels. And when I observed other tourists asking questions about conservation, these guests were usually satisfied with only the vaguest of claims and replies. No one seemed to mind much that the space designated on the resort's map as the conservation and education center was now being used as a garage and had nothing in it except for golf carts that were used to zip around the man-made pathways that stretched for miles—all the way out to the launch pad for alien spacecraft that the wealthy and eccentric founder had built to welcome extraterrestrials who might wish to visit the rain forest if they came to Earth.

Friendly monkeys swarm visitors at every turn, providing a constant sense of close proximity to nature. Patrick Tierney, a business travel writer for *Forbes*, describes a highlight of his stay at Ariaú: "On a moonlit night I climbed the highest observation tower and found a man from Oregon blanketed by a troop of woolly monkeys, who were all hugging and grooming him while he kept telling them how much he loved them. One deck down, a female woolly jumped into my arms. When I put her down after what I thought was a sufficient display of affection, she threw herself on the floor and . . . I think this is the right word . . . blubbered. I was disconcerted and strangely touched."[7]

He's right. The monkeys are terribly endearing. It's hard to deny. But the boom in ecotourism and the constant flow of food and soft drinks from tourists have effectively domesticated them more thoroughly than any zoo. Tierney goes on to tell readers that his guide was a middle-aged French expat who told him how "there are seven women for every man" in Manaus and how you have to fight them off.[8] The man had just married a twenty-year-old woman, which, he assured the *Forbes* writer, was quite normal in Manaus. Hordes of woolly monkeys *and* voracious mobs of indigenous Brazilian girls make for a glowing review for *Forbes*'s intrepid business travelers and struck me as perfectly consistent with Solomon's assessment of the situation.

Tierney can't conclude his profile, however, without taking a jab at a French anthropologist he met who bemoaned that tourists "think they are doing a great service to the rain forest by going to a resort when their presence alone is causing damage." Tierney takes umbrage. He points out that the resort employs eighty locals from nearby. Other guests told him "this was one of the most unforgettable experiences of their lives, and that kind of enthusiasm may ultimately do more to save the forests than severe scoldings from scientists" like the prickly French anthropologist.[9]

Tierney assumes that remembering the experience fondly translates into some kind of environmental action or other tangible good. *Forbes* thus encourages readers to ignore the expert's warning and patronize Ariaú freely. *Forbes* readers are free to misremember their encounter as they see fit and to imagine that it was as beneficial and enjoyable to the locals and to the rain forest itself as it was to them. But the real action that excites Tierney is a proposed $1.5 billion theme park that the state government would like to build in the state of Amazonas, "a sort of Disneyland of the wild."[10]

Local guide Mark Aitchison takes a dimmer view of Ariaú, noting that local journalists "described its much publicized eco-program as nothing more than a front aimed at sucking in starry-eyed foreign tourists with false promises of social projects and reforestation plans. The state's official environmental watchdog, IPAAM, slapped Ariaú with an unprecedented US $40,000 fine for not correcting waste disposal inadequacies identified a year earlier."[11] Thus, it came to pass that Ariaú was fined for dumping its waste in the Amazon rain forest month after month while selling itself as the foremost in ecoconscious jungle-based luxury hotels.

Although Aitchison worries that ecotourism, even greenwashed eco-tourism but especially real and sustainable ecotourism, is dying out, he does single out one area of strong growth in the Amazon: cruise ships. "Coupling an aging client base with group pricing has proven to be an unbeatable combination. Companies catering to the business and events sector here are [also] doing well."[12] As I noted earlier, the cruise ship industry has grown large enough to diversify into gay-specific and lesbian-specific Amazon cruises. But these kinds of industries consolidate profits among the few, and the community receives much less benefit than when it is actively engaged. In fact, Aitchison concludes, the industry does not "benefit the underprivileged and deprived local populations we are forever reading about and are supposed to be assisting."[13] It's small wonder then that young men and women would enter the sexual economy of Manaus. It's one of the few industries with job opportunities, flexibility, decent wages, and minimal barriers to entry. After all, all those catered special events prevent tourists from eating at mom-and-pop establishments or shopping locally, but prostitution is one service that the ecotourism industry has yet to bundle into the package directly (Wet-A-Line fishing expeditions notwithstanding).

Ariaú may be the most famous, but there are around two dozen other such operations, most of which offer far fewer amenities than Ariaú. Nevertheless, a study by Luciana Coelho Marques found that of all the lodges in the main hub area around Manaus, only one uses alternative energy. She also found problems with some lodges not re-cycling, lodge sizes increasing over time, deforestation surrounding the lodges, inappropriate building materials that included plastic and asbestos, and completely ignoring regional handicrafts and artists for decoration in favor of materials like plastic, Styrofoam, and fiberglass.[14] There is also a lack of international guidelines governing ecolodges, ecohotels, ecoresorts, and the like.[15] Such businesses also often provide little quality information to visitors and take a "paternalist attitude, donating food, fuel, toys, and other items" to grateful local communities, but they almost never engage them as partners or involve them in meaningful ways.[16]

I would be remiss if I did not point out that there are a few notable exceptions, particularly on the Peruvian side of the Amazon, which actually has a more robust ecotourist scene than Manaus. Kurt Holle's award-winning Posadas Amazonas, for example, is now studied at Harvard and Stanford's business schools as a model for preserving the rain forest while providing careers for local people.[17] In this case, the community partners are the Eseeja people, who no longer poach endangered wildlife, destructively pan for gold, or sell illegal timber to the Chinese and instead handle every aspect of the lodge from managing operations, accounting, hospitality, education, and employee training to conservation and wildlife protection. At Posadas Amazonas, the Eseeja run the business using their own indigenous decision-making practices, which emphasize consensus and discourage top-down management approaches, and have received 60 percent of all profits since its founding in 1996. After twenty years, Holle and his investors handed over the business and its profits completely, fulfilling a condition of the original business contract. It's not a charity or an NGO but an ethical ecotourism business. What it lacks in domesticated monkeys, air-conditioned suites, and sexually available young people it makes up for in sound labor and conservation principles.

Ariaú, on the other hand, takes a different approach to including Indians in the business: they relocated what *Forbes* describes as "an impoverished remnant" of the "Satura Mawé [*sic*]" tribe to "a patch of land next to the hotel" to which they shuttle tourists who "want to see real, live Indians," a practice that has caused much conflict within the struggling tribe and that also prompted hotel workers to complain that the hotel is making the Satere-Mawé into "exhibits for the tourists."[18] In this way, Ariaú demands the performance of proper "authentic" indigeneity as a condition for the continued existence of a tribe. In the cutthroat world of ecotourism, large companies force local people into high-stakes performances in order to fool tourists into thinking they have had a meaningful brush with the cultural performances and traditions of locals, and that their touristic presence actually helps to preserve local life instead of making it even more precarious.

Ariaú also hosts private events, including a gay pride party hosted by Fontours and featuring imported go-go boys, which travel writer Ernie Alderete described in a piece for a gay travel website in which he also informs gay readers interested in staying at Ariaú that the services of a rent boy in nearby Manaus run about ten dollars. Gay-owned and -operated Fontours (the largest tour company in Manaus) also owns "a fleet of gleaming new motor coaches, sea planes, speed boats and private chauffeured cars as well as Lago Salvador Lodge and Resort."[19] Fontours is conveniently located in the Amazonas Tropical Hotel, the behemoth resort in Ponta Negra where I easily found sex tourists roaming around its three swimming pools and the hotel's "zoo"—a cluster of jungle animals kept in tiny cages, from which they stare at the vast forests and the uncaged monkeys who freely venture onto the property and sit on the tree branches staring back at them, just out of reach.

The Lay of the Land

Walking along the revamped Ponta Negra boardwalk, where families go for fun and where semiformal prostitution and gay cruising occasionally happen, I overheard three middle-class locals, who appeared to be in their late teens or early twenties—two effeminate men and a woman—talking about me. "Look at this gringo, probably a *viado* [faggot]," one of the men said in Portuguese, speaking loudly not two feet away from me, assuming I wouldn't understand. Then the other, mocking me with his imagined version of my interior monologue, said, "It's like this, 'Oh, I really want to fuck a Brazilian.'"

"No, no," said the first, howling with laughter and flapping his wrist excitedly in a fanning gesture while clutching at his throat with the other hand. "Wait, wait," he said, gaining composure. Then in English, putting on his best impression of an American accent. "Oh please, oh please. I really want to fuck an Indian guy." The men cackled while the girl looked at me, giggling until she caught my look of surprise and comprehension at all this and then she blushed. I was used to being mistaken for a sex tourist in Rio and Bahia, but I hadn't expected this in Manaus and it took me off guard.

The next night I resolved to give up my leisure plans and investigate further. I sat at the bustling lobby bar of the touristy Hotel Tropical, nursing a drink and catching up on field notes. Short of going into a brothel, hanging out alone in a touristy hotel bar is, I have learned, the best way to find heterosexual sex tourists in Brazil. Despite traveling halfway around the world, single men traveling in foreign countries like to talk to other single men traveling in foreign countries. "So," they'll say, "can you believe how hot the women are here?" Or "Hey, buddy! Quick! Get a look at *her.*"[20]

If the conversation goes well enough, they can even go look for women together. It often surprises colleagues, especially those who don't often travel alone, when I tell them how easy it is to find clients. On a return trip three years later, my research assistant, Gustavo, set up camp by the pool of this same Manaus hotel and was almost immediately solicited by a Brazilian sex tourist who wanted to go out looking for women together. So it wasn't a huge surprise that, in about an hour,

I met a heterosexual sex tourist as easily as if I'd been hanging out in Copacabana's red-light district.

His name was Bill and he was originally from Oklahoma. He came to Manaus every few months on business but had also spent a lot of time in São Paulo and had vacationed in Rio. "Mongers" tend to be a chatty bunch. Mongers—who take their appellation from the term "whoremongers"—are members of the loosely knit heterosexual sex tourist "community," which consists of anyone who reads or shares stories, news, or advice on any of the dozens of sex tourist websites online. It didn't take long for Bill to give me the "lay of the land." Manaus was his favorite city because of the indigenous women. Bill preferred his women young, usually around sixteen, which he was quick to point out to me is the legal age of consent in Brazil. Eighteen is actually the legal age of consent for prostitution, but he waved away this distinction because he preferred to find individuals who sold sex informally and did not necessarily consider themselves prostitutes. Mongers use the term "semipro" to describe these women who like to "party" with gringos but who expect meals, drinks, and usually a bit of cash or a gift of clothes out of the date.

Brazilian girls in Manaus, he explained, were less "fake" and more "genuine" than girls in Rio. But more importantly, Manaus was a good place for semipro action. "The girls aren't whores. They just do a trick now and again. . . . I like this place outside this hotel with the folklore show. You can usually get some there, local types, you know, who don't whore for anybody except the occasional guy like me or maybe one of these Japanese they got poking around here, the businessmen, you know, and [the women near our hotel] aren't even really doing it for money or coming out looking to turn tricks." When I ask about the dancers and if they are available, he shakes his head. "The girls dancing *in* the Boi Bumbá [folklore show] don't turn tricks, although I wish they did [because] they look incredible in those outfits."

The Boi Bumbá (Bucking Bull) is a several-day theatrical folkloric competition based in the Amazonian town of Parantins (many hours from Manaus) that uses dance, ritual, and large animatronic puppets. In a Boi Bumbá show, two competing teams take turns telling and retelling the story of a poor farmworker whose pregnant wife (often played by a man in drag) gets a powerful craving for beef tongue, but when the worker kills the bull, his boss is angry. Various characters try and fail to resurrect the beast until a shaman succeeds at last, saving the man from prison and leading to a massive party.[21] Hotels and bars in Manaus have seized on the idea and offer their own much smaller

Boi Bumbá shows, featuring beautiful, young, scantily clad women and muscular, fire-breathing men in loincloths who all perform a kind of sexed-up version of "folkloric" dancing that, as Bill accurately put it, "involves some major booty-shaking."

"The Manaus girls aren't refined or blonde or whatever like I get in São Paulo, but you can find some who aren't Indians if that's your thing, but I like the Indian girls. Or partly indigenous, most of the girls here have the look even if they aren't full-blooded [Indian]. . . . They also come cheap in general here, cheaper than Rio and São Paulo by far. And there are ten of them for every guy so they practically jump on your fucking dick." Although he's overstating the gender disparity, this is a common refrain in Manaus, as both Solomon and the *Forbes* business travel writer described above. The gender disparity they have picked up on is actually the result of the labor market in the FTZ factories and the surrounding areas, which has spurred emigration and reorganized the demographics in Manaus as men look for work in logging and cattle industries and women remain in the capital looking for work in retail, manufacturing, and service economies.

Bill got his start as a monger a couple of years earlier when his company began sending him to Manaus every few months. He had been to São Paulo on business and Rio on vacation, where he purchased sex for the first time. Once he realized that, in the end, "gringos all pay for sex, whether they realize it or not," he made his peace with the idea, although he preferred paying indirectly because he found semipros to be "less pushy" than self-identified prostitutes. In Manaus, a taxi driver offered to take him to a brothel or to arrange an escort for him, which is a common service that taxi drivers throughout Brazil offer to gringo men traveling alone.

"The whole business district is red light at night, with the brothels on Lobo de Almada. Those can be filthy. Girls go for about fifty reais [thirty dollars (2007)] for an hour. Right near the hotel here, by [Avenida] Turismo near the airport, is a nice *termas* [bathhouse serving as a brothel]. Those girls get one hundred reais [sixty dollars]." The prices are less than half what they are in Rio, but the income can also easily be enough to live a middle-class life in Manaus.

"The girls that hang out next to the hotel [watching] the Boi Bumbá mainly just want to go out with a tourist," Bill concludes. "They're not really pros. They're just bored locals looking for something different, exotic. That means people like me. . . . That's one of the great things about Manaus: Oklahoma is exotic and sexy." He laughs a big, toothy laugh. He's also not entirely wrong about the reverse exoticism. Manaus is removed from Brazil's other major metropolises. Young people here need opportunities, and an American or a Japanese businessman can draw more attention because he is perceived as wealthy and well connected. But there are so many gringos in Manaus nowadays that they can hardly be considered a novelty.

Bill is a good example of one kind of client in Manaus: the business traveler. But it would be wrong to fully separate business travelers like Solomon and Bill from the ecotourists who visit Ariaú or other large nearby resorts. Most businessmen have at least been out on some of the day tours to see waterfalls, spot caiman, or visit the "Meeting of the Waters," where the Rio Negro flows into Solimões River (the two waters, each a markedly different color, flow for miles before they fully mix, becoming the Amazon River). Many of the tourists I met on such tours were businessmen on their downtime.

Although the heterosexual prostitution scene is larger, it's a bit surprising how much male prostitution there is. It is also largely overlaid atop the general LGBT nightlife scene, creating a nuanced erotic landscape of commercial, quasi-commercial, and noncommercial encounters that exist in tension with one another.

The Queer Landscape of Manaus

During my time there, the male street-hustling scene in Manaus centered on the southeast side of Praça Matriz but then extended upward along Avenida Getúlio Vargas, where there were various corners and pockets where *michês* would concentrate on a street otherwise occupied by *travesti* and female prostitutes. There was even a married couple I knew of there who worked on opposites sides of the street, both husband and wife leaning into car windows to negotiate with men looking for sex. Sometimes michês worked as pimps or provided protection for girlfriends or wives working in the area. Programas on the male street scene cost about twenty reais (ten dollars [2008]), and the street-hustling scene was marked by vigorous displays of masculine posturing, with michês often hurling homophobic epithets at one another to police the masculinity of the area. Most men were from Manaus, but about a third came from the Amazonian interior. The men usually worked for only a year or two before exiting the industry, and very few had worked more than five.[22] Some of them also worked in a movie theater that screened heterosexual pornography, the back rows of which were known as a site for local gays looking for commercial or noncommercial sex. Tourists rarely picked up guys from the street or cinema, which they perceived as dangerous, preferring instead to go to *saunas* and nightclubs.

Manaus had two *saunas* during the time I was there, and there was intense competition between them. As cultural geographer and ethnographer Jean Moreira Alcântara observed in his research on male prostitution in the area, to protect business secrets, management does not allow garotos to work in both locations. Unlike the gay scene in Rio, where *saunas* were neatly divided into those with garotos and those without (i.e., where clients had sex with one another), in Manaus garotos could find themselves competing with clientele who would have sex for free. Prices were low, usually around fifty reais (thirty dollars [2008]) for a programa. The house sometimes cut into that fee directly but also made its money in the legal manner of door fees of a few dollars for clients and garotos. Garotos never worked the streets, but they did go to the city's gay nightclubs to cruise for programas, where they competed with street michês, something that made the nightclubs a unique space.[23]

The two main LGBT nightclubs were similar in that they had multiple floors and spaces for socializing and dancing, stages for drag shows and go-go dancing, and dark rooms for sex. Garotos and michês who usually worked the *saunas* and streets, respectively, preferred to enter early in the evening to avoid the cover charge. They were largely indistinguishable from other guys unless clients recognized them from commercial sex venues. However, tourists could still spot them because in addition to their muscularity and aggressively forward sexual demeanor, they would often remove their shirts and grab or stroke their penises through their clothes while playing "the game of eyes" with potential clients. According to Alcântara, many of the michês do programas inside the club and use the money to purchase drugs on-site.[24] Although gringos were rare, they were not such an anomaly as to be particularly remarkable. Despite tourists' romantic notions of sexuality in the Amazon, the lived experiences of male sex workers there show they were a population at risk for violence and a group that often struggled economically and psychologically. Few knew this better than the outreach workers at the Boys of the Night Association (Associação Garotos da Noite, or AGN).

In the mid-2000s, AGN set out on an ambitious project that surveyed 89 male sex workers in downtown Manaus. In reviewing the raw data with Dartanha Silva, the project's director, a profile became clear.[25] Garotos ranged in age from fifteen to thirty-four, with the majority (76 percent) being between the ages of eighteen and twenty-five, and 12 percent being under the age of eighteen. Seventy-eight percent were born in the state of Amazonas. Around half had made it to middle school, with the other half making it into or completing high school. Around half had also attempted some sort of professionalization course (e.g., a basic computer class, English lessons). A small percentage, 16 percent, were married and lived with their wives. Many more, 57 percent, lived with their parents, with the remainder divided between living alone or with nonfamilial roommates. A little over half, 57 percent, had no other source of income, while 43 percent worked another low-wage job. Most (62 percent) were Catholic, but 22 percent were Evangelical Protestant. About a quarter had experienced violence on the job, with 11 percent of the total suffering abuse from clients and 16 percent from police. As for place of work, 21 percent worked from home, 31 percent worked the streets and plazas, and 48 percent worked out of *saunas* or sex motels.

Interestingly, business was steady. Over half (58 percent) turned one or two tricks a day. Just over a third (34 percent) had three to five *programas* a day. The remainder (8 percent) said they did six to seven *programas* a day. Of those who responded to the question, a vast majority (77 percent) reported making between 40 and 100 reais (USD 25–64) a day, while 19 percent made 110–200 reais (USD 70–128) a day. Although male sex workers have been known to overestimate their incomes and the prices they charge for various acts in an effort to boost perceptions of their masculinity and virility and to justify their participation in homosexual activity, the numbers in this study seem reasonably reliable when examining AGN's methodology vis-à-vis that of other scholarly studies.[26] If we take them at face value, this means that the typical garoto in Manaus would be making around 32,000 reais (USD 20,000) per year, which also happens to be the median per capita income in Manaus.[27] Thus, prostitution is a pretty effective way to attain a middle-class income in spite of a lower educational status, a feat that may be especially valued when other family members may not be earning above the levels to which their educational status would normally predict.

Unfortunately, that's where most of the good news stops. Although 91 percent said they "always" use condoms, only 36 percent actually showed they were carrying them even though they were working and should, in theory, have been carrying them. Dartanha complained to me that he keeps giving out condoms, allotting each guy sixty condoms a month, but the garotos sell most of them instead of actually using them. This situation parallels, but is actually even more egregious than, that in Rio and Bahia, where I found men trying to give the "right" answer and therefore overreporting condom use to avoid researchers' disapproval or lectures or to prevent more outreach workers, researchers, or health officials from nosing around. Sixty-eight percent said they did not usually use additional lubricant. Many garotos, especially the least privileged ones, do not understand the importance of lubricant or that using improper lubricants such as spit means that condoms are more likely to tear. This may be especially true if condoms are not of high quality, and activists have reported a problem in Brazil with condoms of low quality illegally smuggled from Uruguay.

Drug use was high. Around half of the men used cocaine on a regular basis; 20 percent reported using *pasta base*, an addictive and destructive drug that is essentially the cheap, freebased leftovers of cocaine production with crack added to it; 27 percent reported using marijuana. A small number reported huffing, or glue-sniffing, which is a common habit among homeless children who grow up on the streets. Only a third, however, reported using these drugs before programas. One-third did not know what a "sexually transmitted disease" was, while one-fourth had already contracted one. This STD was gonorrhea 80 percent of the time. Only around half of the garotos who contracted an STD went to the doctor; the rest tried to treat it using remedies from pharmacies or other kinds of traditional, folk, or at-home remedies. Sixty-seven percent said they wanted to leave prostitution for another line of work.

According to Dartanha, the sexual health situation for male sex workers in Manaus is dire. "This fact that the prevalence of STDs in Manaus is 7 percentage points more than the national average is very worrying. We have to strengthen our work . . . because the michês don't have the habit of using condoms. We talk, do the workshops, but at the time of the relationship, perhaps because of drug use, they end up putting aside the condom. Or sometimes the client provides drugs in exchange for him to not use condoms, or they offer more money for a programa with no condom." In Dartanha's experience, the industry's shift indoors into *saunas* has been a good thing because *saunas* provide and encourage condom use. "The owner has to maintain a quality establishment. I call it 'selecting for health' [*seleção de saúde*] because he doesn't want the garoto to go back to the street and stop using condoms and then get an STD that he could pass on to the *sauna*'s customers." But while the *saunas* are generally safer, one of them is alleged to illegally take the garotos' money, putting the NGO in a tight spot because it doesn't endorse this kind of exploitation.

Although media depict escorts who do house calls as high-end workers, Dartanha warned that this was dangerous for the michês. "They shouldn't do a programa in the house of a client or in their own house," he says with a sigh. "Many killings occur for this reason. When it's the client's home, there are boys who steal and kill. On the other hand, in [just a few months] there were five garotos de programa murdered by clients because they stole from them. But when the case reaches the police, they record the victim as a 'student' because the family doesn't want it to come out in the open that the boy was a michê." In this way, shame and stigma about prostitution and same-sex intimacy combine to perpetuate violence against men who sell sex.

Alternative Sources of Violence

Many media depictions emphasize violence directed against sex workers, especially street prostitutes, in order to portray life in the sex trade as inherently dangerous and victimizing. However, some male sex workers described violence in their lives that originated outside the sexual economy. Carlos had spent several years in the army, which has a large base in Manaus and, he said, conducted a lot of jungle operations in the surrounding states against drug traffickers and smugglers. "I've worked [as a garoto] in the *sauna* since I left the army. My mother works selling pastry snacks, and my [half] brothers are still small. . . . It was always my dream to be in the military, but I didn't know those in charge of the military are corrupt. For me, there was this ideal that the army was to defend the country. There are battles on borders. . . . And other [officers] say if we invade this camp, they may have weapons and money and drugs. We'll take the drugs and sell them someplace. . . . It's a big business."

Carlos looked distraught as he unraveled his tale of woe, glancing around nervously. "Then I got angry because I was very dedicated . . . and I would be shot at for this? [Another time], these [traffickers] were making a place to process cocaine, and we invaded them, but the commander negotiated a bribe . . . but later there was an inquiry and I was pushed out of the army. . . . In the army, I was respected, many soldiers respected me, I won awards; . . . there I was something!" He clenched his fist and pressed it against the table of the little *boteco* where we were having a beer one evening.

"Now here outside, you're playing football or flying a kite [*soltando uma pipa*, a common pastime in poor neighborhoods], and here comes a *funkeiro* [thug], wanting to put you down [*querendo te diminuir*]." But Carlos felt frustrated living under the rule of the gangs in the *favela*. "You know the guy is nothing. I could kill him with my bare hands! And still you have to lower your head. I find it so strange out here sometimes. . . . There are also times I wake up and I'm frightened . . . from bad dreams, . . . then I remember that I am no longer in the military. . . . I dream a lot; it disturbs me greatly [*me perturba muito*]."

Carlos was very animated as he described his glory days. He was full of bravado, and I wondered how much of his story was embellished for effect. Even if he was exaggerating, his desire to beef up his masculinity with tales of violence resembling an action movie reveals a great deal about his need to present a suitably masculine front while working in the stigmatized role of a prostitute who has sex with other men. Yet when I asked Carlos about how he went from being a soldier in the Amazon to working in the *sauna* and how these lines of work compared, he became downcast.

"After I left the military, a guy I knew told me, 'I see you're going through a hard time. I worked in a *sauna*. . . .' He explained everything to me, and I said, 'No, no, I'm not going to do work like that!' But at home I'm the only man. There is my stepfather, but really it's just me, my mother, and my little brothers. So I'm the man of the house. I'm the one who works to help [my mother] out."

Carlos's voice swelled with pride and defensiveness as he mentioned his mother. "I needed to do this and go to the *sauna*. . . . I worked one time and in less than five minutes, I made 100 reais [USD (2009) 60]. I made a purchase at the market, and I went home. . . . I felt guilty. I worked too hard [in life] to be in a situation like this, but at the same time I looked back and saw that my mother and brothers needed me. And that's what gives me the strength to continue working in the *sauna*." He drained his small glass of beer and looked dismissive. "Over time you get used to it. Not that you start to find it very natural, but you are not as afraid any more. At first, I was embarrassed. I didn't take my penis out to show it as much as other people there . . . doing obscene things. I stayed put in my corner. It's still a strange thing. I prefer not to think about it, you know? Just get there, do [the programa], take the money, and do what I want with it. I'm not thinking about what I do, reflecting on it, because it makes me feel bad."

When I asked why he felt bad about the work he did, he replied, "People think you're denigrating society and your self-image [*está dene-grindo a imagem da sociedade e a sua auto-imagem*]. So I don't have the courage to say, 'Mom, I do this work.' It would be the biggest disappointment for her. And as I try to do everything for my family—I live for my family—so I do not want her to have such shame."

Sex workers often use military jargon such as "battling" to mean "turning tricks" or "name of war" for "street name," illustrating that they understand their work to be difficult and that they are frequently under threat (in their case, from economic forces and state security such as police, who may harass or extort them). Carlos treasured his time in the actual military, but it was also a life of disillusionment and violence—far more violent than his next career as a prostitute. When antiprostitution activists cite bleak statistics from studies of sex workers (even those from sex worker rights activists such as Dartanha) to argue for the abolition of prostitution, they often forget that the other forms of work available to poor men and women are often violent in their own ways. And yet, antitrafficking organizations don't concern themselves with, say, Brazil's mandatory military service (which in Brazil is, de facto, for poor people only), even though compulsory service is *also* the forced movement of people into dangerous and degrading low-paid situations many of them do not wish to be in.

It was unclear to me exactly what Carlos's role was in the corruption scandal in his Amazonian unit in which he became embroiled, but it is entirely possible that, as a young man from a poor background, he would have made an easy scapegoat for commanding officers who were on the take or have been subjected to more severe punishment than a more privileged person. Regardless, his dream of a military career was shattered, and when I met him, he was selling *programas*. He was also incredibly successful and sometimes had a line of clients so long that he could barely find time and energy for them. He had gone on to work in Rio, making enough money to support his family and entertain girlfriends. He was smart and charming, very lean, with boyish good looks that attracted no end of attention from men and women. Six months after our last interview, though, I heard that he had bulked up and now paraded around the *sauna* in Rio confidently displaying his intensely muscled body. No longer shy about nudity, he even joined the other guys in doing stripteases in various costumes, including military fatigues, which was, so far as I know, the closest he has come to returning to his dream career in the army.

Virgin Forests

It's clear that the lives of male sex workers in Manaus do not match the romanticized images of indigeneity projected onto them by eco-tourists. Ecotourism is undergirded by a titillating desire to relate to indigeneity, but differences between gay and straight tourists' use of the erotic were less visible, although the gay tourists seemed to have a more romanticized view of nature. Both gay and straight tourists' experiences were informed by common viewing practices, a common "tourist gaze," the search for (even cynical) displays of authenticity, and a rush to upload images on social media. Both relied on tropes from travel magazines, documentaries, and reality television competition programs—tropes that were largely the same although also marked by a homoerotic undercurrent.

The admittedly small number of gay tourists I knew touring the Amazon were there primarily for the ecotourism, and the sex was folded in as just another facet of exploration. On the contrary, most of the heterosexual sex tourists had no such romanticism on their minds. Consider the following summary from Bacchus, a writer on *Roosh V Forum*, part of a cultish and explicitly antifeminist "pick-up artist" site that includes a global sex tourist forum.[28]

"I worked as an English teacher in Manaus for a year, and for that time, it was my pussy paradise. . . . I don't want to make too much of this point, but there's no way around it. Simply put, they *love* white people here. They just don't get many gringos visiting the city. If you have light eyes or hair, you will get stared at during the day and approached at night, sometimes even by attractive girls."

Bacchus goes on to explain the racial typology in question. "The typical Manauara [native of Manaus] has light brown skin, long black hair, a great ass, a disappointing chest, and Indian features. . . . They are easy to lay, and are phenomenal in the sack, . . . very feminine, but also kind of dumb and flakey. A lot of them have funny-looking faces. . . . Not all of them, but it's a common enough problem. A surprising number of them have braces."

Bacchus then proceeds to advise the other men on the forum how to perform their gringo masculinity to succeed in their sexual conquests. "For best results, I would run Uncle Roosh's world game. When I first arrived, I used asshole game, as I would on American sluts. That didn't go over well. After turning it down, I started crushing ass. Compliments work here, as does waiting an hour to kiss her. All the dudes practice caveman game, so if you wait, your girl will inch closer and closer to your face."

Mongers on this forum constitute a speech community with a shared linguistic code, which serves not only to effectively communicate but to instill a sense of fraternity and insider knowledge. Uncle Roosh is an author of books on how to get laid, and he offers various travel guides for picking up women (typically not sex workers) in various countries. Thus, Uncle Roosh's "world game" is a pickup tactic that consists of things like "drop all cockiness and teasing" and "relax your rules on buying things for girls"; that is, it is the opposite of the "American game," a mode of performance consisting of projecting a "bad boy" image. These "games" are repertoires of masculinity performed by the sex tourists. Their success depends on performative competence and the ability to select the appropriate performance of masculinity for a particular cultural forum.

Within Bacchus's misogyny and the conversation that followed among the other sex tourists, one can see the men consciously constructing a gringo masculinity using specific actions and performatives that they believe will be intelligible to women in Manaus and successful in the Amazonian context. The men debate the merits of indigenous women, with many deciding that they are not attracted to that racial "type" but they are turned on by the perceived hypersexuality of these native women. While the residents of Manaus may have the aura or exotic sense of the Amazon about them in their indigeneity, the mongers were more ambivalent about ecological activity or even derided it.

Consider the following advice from a US citizen named Quasi taken from another Roosh sex tourist forum on Manaus: "go see the jungle its awesome. . . . Go to Remolus (the whorehouse) . . . and enjoy a cold bear at punta negra . . . (place near the amazon river with lots of locals) . . . the indian women are really pretty and exotic . . . dark skinned petite, long slender hair, their eyes like deers [sic all]." Quasi makes a bestial metaphor, linking the women to nature, but this is as "romantic" as he gets.

He then goes on to suggest other recreational ecoactivities but is less enthralled at the actual proximity to nature required, as he says, "Maybe tray the acaii stuff, and maybe try to smoke some of the visionary stuff (drugs) in the jungle . . . would have liked to do more jungle stuff, but know that traveling in the jungle is a pain in the AZZ, so traveling by water is a lot nicer and then make short trips into the jungle [sic all]."

This suggestion isn't well received by PartyTime, who responds, "Are the girls hot? I'm not into indigenous looking girls. Is that what they look like? Many people are saying it is super easy to get laid, Is this true? Can anyone confirm this from personal experience [sic all]?"

Another poster assures him that "Manaus is the best place in Brasil for non pros and hooking up with girls. . . . There is a majority of girls there who only live to party and have sex. . . . In Brasil . . . your chances of hooking up with a *quality* non pro are next to nothing. Unless you're talking about gringo chasers/gold diggers who speak English or the bottom of the barrel faveladas or down right prostitutes. Only exception in Brasil would be Manaus where girls are notorious for 'having fire in their ass. . . .' Let's put it this way, when you live in the middle of the biggest jungle in the world, where it's oppressively hot and rains like hell most of the time, what else is left to do other than having sex? . . . Manaus is filled with fly girls who just live for partying and having sex. This is not a place to look for a serious gf/wife, so don't kid yourself [sic all]."

For mongers, ecotourism isn't the main item on the agenda. They may take short trips to do ecological things, but these tend to focus on recreational drug use or casual sightseeing. Some of them complain about ecotourists and backpackers who will not go out looking for women with them. Ideally, they do not want to pay for sex because they believe resorting to "paying for it" makes them less manly, but "world game" allows for relaxing rules on buying things. As with Bill, the sex tourist quoted earlier, "semipro" women are acceptable, but they prefer *informal* prostitution or exchanges that are easily rationalized as noncommercial because these allow the man the status of being a "player" who has "game."

The motivations and actions of straight sex tourists were markedly different from those of the gay tourists described above who visited Ariaú and took jungle tours but who incorporated a romantic vision of nature and their exploration into their narratives of personal and sexual discovery. Yet for both populations there is a creeping eroticism in the performances of indigeneity that the tourist industry and popular cultural forms promote.

"Warning: This Program Contains Indigenous Nudity"

As a tourist, the first thing you see after Ariaú's private boat transfers you from your Manaus hotel to the jungle resort is an indigenous couple in tasseled loincloths who are standing in front of color-coded recycling bins and who wrap a necklace around your neck. They are young and attractive, with face and body paint on their taut and muscled brown bodies. As another Indian woman hands you freshly made fruit juice, you may notice the life-sized plastic statue of a bare-breasted, shapely Indian woman with dark nipples and luxurious hair, holding a spear and standing next to a jaguar while her hand slides downward toward her vagina for reasons that seem to have little to do with hunting. Behind her, in front of the gift shop, is a large, framed oil painting of a naked Indian woman with a waterfall in the background. She is bronzed but has intense tan lines from a string bikini and is sitting with her legs splayed around a hammock, shooting a sexy look at the viewer, a single nipple peeking out at the viewer. From the moment you arrive at Ariaú, eroticized indigeneity abounds.

The anthropologist Jane Desmond focuses on the corporeality of "staging authenticity." In her framework, tourist sites such as the Boi Bumbá folkloric dance show, with all its G-strings and tassels, and the indigenous presentations at Ariaú foreground the relationship between performers and audience as inevitably rooted in colonial relations predicated on difference and otherness. She also argues that this way of structuring tourist encounters between locals and nonlocals serves to benefit commercial business interests such as, in this case, Ariaú and the hotels along the Ponta Negra.[29] In *Ethnicity, Inc.*, the anthropologists John Comaroff and Jean Comaroff observe that the performers themselves participate in the manufacture and maintenance of "ethno-commodities." Even as the commodification and performance of ethnic identities produce profits for major business interests, "those who would (re)claim their ethnic 'nature' by means of grounded ethno-preneurialism appear to do so, more or less often, with a good measure of critical and tactical consciousness."[30]

Certainly, this is the case not only for the Boi Bumbá but also for the indigenous groups in the forest who welcome boats of tourists to their rituals, which they stage on demand. Yet the industry also encourages tourists to praise themselves for having come all this way and having seen such "real" performances and having had such authentically staged encounters. The industry's way of ordering the encounters also allows the tourist to gain social cachet by posting photos of the events on myriad social media sites while also affording them a comfortable, idealized, and greenwashed misremembrance of the meetings that negates any postcolonial guilt.

When tourists circulate these photos, sending them to friends or to the online world at large, they are accruing what Pierre Bourdieu calls "symbolic capital." It is a material marker that demonstrates their worldliness and carries with it the implication that the person is wealthy enough to engage in leisure travel in hard-to-reach places. Because the images capture relatively rare encounters, they have more prestige. Within Bourdieu's framework, most people may have photos of run-of-the-mill trips to iconic vacation spots like Disney World or the Grand Canyon, but the Amazon carries more cachet by virtue of its attendant exoticism. When tourists take photographs of their Amazonian adventures, they are also engaging in what Bourdieu calls "symbolic violence," which is an often-unconscious form of quotidian social domination that furthers, in this case, racism and ethnocentrism.[31]

One important marker of authenticity that I encountered on tourist excursions that involved encountering native people was the indigenous nudity. Tourists eschewed pictures of themselves with indigenous people selling souvenirs or welcoming them to the village if the natives were wearing any Western clothing. Better to have feathers or tribal markings. Women who had bare breasts were especially popular. I observed many tourists—male and female, Brazilian and foreign, sometimes whole families—purchase some small souvenir item so that they might speak with such a woman and then pose for pictures.

Even though tourists seem fascinated by indigenous nudity, they often have a peculiar relationship to it. *National Geographic* specials and similar documentaries have provided tourists with a template for understanding the photographing of indigenous nudity. *National Geographic* titillates viewers with images of naked indigenous people whom it simultaneously construes as primitive and sexual while objectifying them and rendering them as inappropriate objects of civilized desire. Such programs have even invented a special phrase to use in their viewer advisories: "This program contains indigenous nudity." That is, they will display naked people, but viewers should *not* be aroused by them as they might be by the sight of other naked people, because the natives are primitive and too unlike them. Despite this, as Trinh Minh-ha has explored reflexively in her early film *Reassemblage* and subsequently examined in *Naked Spaces: Living Is Round*, the camera in ethnographic documentaries lingers overly long on all those pendulous breasts, allowing viewers to take pleasure in the viewing while imbuing their gaze with an aura of objectivity.[32]

The Amazon is constructed in this erotic realm in other products, too. Consider the popular Travel Channel series *World's Lost Tribes: The New Adventures of Mark and Olly* (originally *Mark and Olly: Living with the Tribes*), in which two dashing and rugged Brits—a journalist and a former soldier—"go native" with a different "uncontacted tribe" each season. The men eventually adopt native garb, which includes wearing little else but a gourd over the shaft of their penises. Should their white penises flop out, the producers pixelate them. As Catherine A. Lutz and Jane L. Collins noted in their study of *National Geographic Magazine*'s photos of people of color, the magazine traffics in the sexuality of women of color but is "less comfortable" with men's.[33]

In *World's Lost Tribes*, viewers can redirect their erotic gaze to the white, English, and appropriately masculine figures of Mark and Olly, the show's real stars, as they lose their Western clothes and put on the same scant coverings that their indigenous hosts wear. Mark and Olly look like models plucked out of Central Casting on a great homosocial and sometimes downright homoerotic buddy trip. For viewers so inclined, the men make an "appropriate" outlet for potentially discomforting erotic affects that viewers may experience when seeing the "indigenous nudity" they were warned about. In a heterosexual male context, this need not be discomforting or threatening, as the hosts can function instead as avatars who stand in for the male viewer and allow him to relate to the native women through these men, just as in the case of heterosexual pornography, where male actors can stand in for the male viewer and thereby bolster, rather than threaten, his heterosexuality and masculinity.

However, *World's Lost Tribes* ran into major problems when its maker, Cicada Productions, came to film a season of the show in the Amazon and allegedly caused a flu epidemic that killed three children and one adult in the Matsigenka community. According to a government spokesperson, "They were warned not to go upstream, but were unhappy with the tribe in Yomybato—the village they were permitted to visit—as the Indians appeared too westernised. So, in searching for a more stereotypical tribe, they came into contact with a vulnerable community. . . . We even have people working on the ground who claim that the crew offered the tribe more traditional costumes. . . . Through their indiscriminate chasing of so-called witch doctors and head hunters these reality TV crews are jeopardising the future of indigenous communities across the world."[34] Although Cicada Productions vehemently denies all wrongdoing, the case points to the potential for reality television to commit violence that is far more than symbolic (in Bourdieu's sense of the term) precisely because of the producers' desire to find and commodify the performance of "authentic" indigeneity for its armchair anthropologist viewers.

Tourists have taken the lessons of reality television to heart in their own pursuit of "authentic" indigeneity, pressing companies for increasingly "authentic" Indians. I've listened to dozens of tourists grumble that the only natives they meet are operating souvenir stands in the jungle or demanding money from them for pictures. And I once saw a female Brazilian tourist become irate with her tour guide because the Indian children in the village were playing soccer. She deemed their fun too Western for her photo collection and wanted them to go play another game away from the field so the shot would not be contaminated with any sign of soccer, even though it's Brazil's national sport.

Conflating indigeneity and nature is another way of making rhetorical claims of authenticity. For example, reality shows like *Survivor* film in the Amazon, using vaguely indigenous motifs to structure games of "skill" for mostly white American contestants, occasionally featuring visits to local tribes to emphasize the authenticity of the jungle setting. Predictably, when *Survivor* filmed their Amazon season, the producers and crew lodged at none other than the ritzy Ariaú ecoresort for the duration of the season. Such representations teach tourists certain expectations about what an authentic Indian is supposed to look like. So when tourists photograph indigenous people, they are banking authenticity that they will later circulate. Sufficiently unique tourist experiences are a marker of status and a means of accruing symbolic capital. Photographs of the encounter are far more valuable than the mass-produced souvenirs they purchase from the Indians because photos are performative; they make a claim about the self and provide evidence of personal experience. Unlike a souvenir, which is merely a fetish object for the tourist that he or she may imbue with memories of the encounter, the photo of the tourist and Indians is a fetish object of a different sort. It allows the tourist to symbolically take home a native for her or his friends to gaze upon. But there is a scopophilic exchange that happens when tourists collect these photos of themselves with indigenous people (with or without clothing) and post their collections online for friends.

Social Misremembrance and the Queer Paradox of Ecotourism

The mass ecotourist experience peddled by Ariaú is fundamentally an attempt to offer the most "authentic" nature and indigeneity available for the least amount of inconvenience. And yet, I don't believe that the whole encounter between tourists and the indigenously nude is as asexual as *National Geographic* or *World's Lost Tribes* might have us believe. When the guests arrive, they are surrounded by sexualized imagery of indigenous people. All of this is part of a long erotic history between natives and visitors to the Amazon. Colonial accounts going back centuries contain accounts from sailors, missionaries, and explorers describing the sexual licentiousness of indigenous women and the rampant sodomy indulged in by native men.[35] One can read Uncle Roosh's sex tourist devotees' accounts of indigenous women who are "easy lays" because of the "fire in their asses" as part of this lineage of travel writing.

Europeans believed the Indians were hypersexual through and through, closely associating them with base animal instincts, sexual licentiousness, sodomy, and low morals. Having an encounter with an indigenous person offers the tourist a unique experience and cachet. This Indian may be a naked one with whom the tourist can be photographed, the Indian may be one upon whom the tourist may practice his own *National Geographic*–inspired photography skills, or the Indian may be a sexy dancer in the Boi Bumbá or perhaps a semipro who does the occasional programa with a tourist or even an escort who will provide sex as well as go bass fishing with gringo clients.

The real issue here is not the sexualization of indigenous people or even the creeping erotic within ecotourism but rather that these modes of encountering indigeneity conjure into existence an alternative memory of colonialism and exploration. In the case of Ariaú Amazon Towers and the big-budget ecotourism industry it represents, they plant a false memory that enables the trope of the noble savage to endure and they perpetuate a potentially false memory in which the modern tourist's shared interaction was beneficial to the indigenous person, stimulating the local economy and helping to preserve the rain forest the Indians call home. Meanwhile, the advent of social media and the desire to craft one's self-image through performative curating of one's adventures encourage others who see these photos or who read or hear about the programas to go and get their own.

Such renderings freeze the indigenous person in time. The tourist continues on, returns home, reminisces about the holiday, shares the photos or stories. For the tourist, the indigenous person does not live beyond that photo or that sexual encounter and is no more real to the viewer for having been seen. The Indian is static, locked in what Johannes Fabian has called an "allochronic" orientation.[36] This tendency to discursively lock indigenous people into the past and impose a view of time as a long, steady, upward slog toward modernity, culture, and enlightenment is an organizing principle of the ecotourist industry.

For some would-be progressive tourists, their visit is a form of activism that helps save the planet. And while there are some truly good companies and people in the Amazon who are genuine conservationists and who know how to partner with local communities, the sad truth is that ecotourism is a multibillion-dollar-a-year industry that often squashes local industry and economic development by forcing indigenous people to commodify and perform ethnicity for tourists. The ecotourism industry also makes it hard for ethical operators to be successful and is part and parcel of neoliberal capitalist globalization, which most truly eco-minded tourists and backpackers would decry as immoral. And it isn't sustainable because the more the ecotourism industry in the Amazon grows, the more it degrades the area and moves on to new territory. After all, when the authentic native is disappearing, the economic principle of scarcity dictates that the encounter becomes only more valuable.

The lingering question remains: why does sexuality make such encounters with indigeneity more valuable? Sex is an epistemology, a way of knowing a place and its people. In the context of contemporary tourism, sex is just one facet of travel that tourists may engage in alongside other activities like shopping, eating, and sightseeing. But it is a special form of knowledge marked by a presumed authenticity of experience. The authenticity is linked to physical and emotional exposure because societies conflate sex with vulnerability. Yet there is a paradox here: at the point of knowing, the knowledge collapses in on itself. In an earlier chapter, I described gringos who pursue authentically heterosexual men and then want them to reciprocate pleasure, thereby negating the masculinity that attracted the client in the first place. This was one queer paradox of desire. Similarly here, the ecotourist's own presence renders the encounter with the vanishing Amazon inauthentic. In the tourist psyche, the indigenous body is a proxy for the environment and a way to know and experience nature intimately, but the object of desire is then never really accessible. Thus, there is a queer paradox in this form of tourism as well.

Tourists—be they sex tourists, ecotourists, or both—project many things onto indigenous people. In the next chapter, I examine this in the context of African American gay men in search of Africa and the black diaspora who purchase sex as part of their cultural tourism. In cases such as this, black and brown bodies are asked to stand in metonymically for other objects and ideas as the recipients of desires and affects. Tourists in the Amazon use the familiar tropes of exploration and exotic primitives popular in social media, reality television, magazines, and anthropologically inspired documentaries to refashion their relationship to nature, but they access their romantic vision of "nature" through the native. In this way, they bolster their own social standing among their peers through an erotic reorientation to the native body.

SIX

Sex Pilgrims: Subjunctive Nostalgia, Roots Tourism, and Queer Pilgrimage in Bahia

Nostalgia. *Noun.*
From the Greek: *nostos* (a return home) + *algia* (a painful condition)

We don't see things as they are, we see them as we are. ANAÏS NIN

On the Hunt

A beach vendor passes us, selling cheap oil paintings of various *orixás*, who are the gods or—more precisely—spiritual entities honored in the Afro-Brazilian possession-based faith of *candomblé*. I look over the quickly rendered paintings and smile, but shake my head. Brício, a *garoto de programa* sitting with me, thinks this vendor is new to the scene. He suspects that the man is already selling sex to tourists. Garotos who work Salvador da Bahia's beaches sell everything from henna tattoos to sunglasses to fresh fruit as a way to supplement their income selling sex to men.[1] Not all *ambulantes* (mobile vendors) sell sex, of course, but many garotos I met in Bahia do just a few programas a week so they tend to have other jobs. Working as an ambulante is common because it allows them to make contact

181

with tourists. Brício, for example, has a board of beaded necklaces that he goes up and down the beach selling.

"Well, if you don't want this, maybe you see something else you like?" Brício will ask the *gringos* sunbathing on the small gay section of the beach. He'll run a hand over his bare chest, caressing his dark skin, or maybe adjust his cock with a stroke. Then if their eyes linger: "Maybe you want a massage? I know a place nearby . . ."

Brício prefers American clients because they pay more than Europeans, and in Bahia, American more often than not means African American. These tourists often want him for a whole week and take him to restaurants and clubs. If the client wants only one *programa*, Brício can still hire himself out to the man as a guide for the week because he speaks some English. He can also arrange encounters for tourists with other reliable garotos, taking a finder's fee. "It's lucky you found me. The other guys around here will rob you, but I'll introduce you only to safe guys," he tells them.

He also sometimes takes them to a *terreiro*, which is a candomblé house of worship. The religion is known for being gay-friendly, and—owing to stereotypes—is sometimes mistakenly thought to allow only women and gay men to serve as priests. Many garotos I know are active in the faith and talk about candomblé a great deal. Tour companies take small groups to ceremonies for a fee and a promise to follow certain rules, so when a garoto shows up to a terreiro, he can always just say he is a guide.

Brício laughs loudly and gestures to two passing sunburnt men, calling out to them in a booming voice: "*E aí, turistas?*" ("What's up, tourists?") They smile nervously and hasten their steps away from us in response, murmuring in what sounds like Italian. Brício's eyes follow them. "I am a *caçador*," he says, more to himself than to me. *Caçador* means "hunter." It's also derogatory slang for a street hustler in Bahia and a term that beach garotos usually use to refer to garotos who work the historic district of Pelourinho, whom they regard as pushier, more violent, and without moral fiber. "Caçador" refers to the way they cruise around their territory looking for clients.

"A caçador," Brício repeats. "And I am on the hunt." He mimes notching an arrow and drawing the bowstring to his cheek, taking a careful, squinting aim at the tourists' backs.

"Does Oxóssi have your head?" I ask, wanting to know if the orixá of the hunt is his patron. Brício talks a lot about orixás. Oxóssi seems to occupy a special if unofficial place in the lives of quite a few garotos I know. Brício lets fly the invisible arrow. I imagine it sinking into sun-kissed tourist flesh with a thunk. He doesn't take his eyes off the tourists, but lets go of the invisible bow after a moment. He stares at the other garotos now beginning to circle his prey and flirt. "Oh yes, Gregório. I think he has all of us."

Roots Tourism

In Rio I encountered mostly white gay men who relied on *saunas* to provide a range of often-diverse partners. Bahia hosts many more visiting African American gay men (and some living as expats) in the touristy areas of the Porto da Barra, Pelourinho, and Rio Vermelho neighborhoods. This is not to say that African American gay men don't go to Rio in large numbers; many started out there before "discovering" Bahia. As Edward, an African American tourist in his forties, explained to me, "Who has the money for Rio? There is a recession on in America. Your money goes a lot further here, and as soon as a friend turned me on to Bahia, I was like, 'Bahia? What's that?' But then I came here once and now I wouldn't dream of going back to Rio."

My focus in this chapter on African American men doesn't mean that white gay men, especially Italians and other Europeans, don't go to Bahia. However, the sheer numbers of African American sex tourists are noticeable to scholars and locals alike. In her book-length ethnography of sex tourism in Bahia, the anthropologist Erica L. Williams describes her sex worker interlocutors' view that white people from the United States were not interested in Bahia because they did not like black people. However, they believed that Europeans and African American tourists—including sex tourists—did like black people and liked them not incidentally but out of *specific* interest in the black bodies and black culture on display in Bahia.[2] In choosing to focus on mostly black tourists in Bahia I hope to highlight how sexuality, money, and travel interrelate in often-racialized ways.

I will also provide information on sex tourists of color. Because so much of the literature on sex tourism emphasizes that the sex worker is a racialized Other, nonwhite clients risk appearing as mere statistical outliers or epiphenomenal johnny-come-latelies. Because some feminist literature on sex tourism has critiqued the industry as fundamentally racist, the assumption has developed that sex tourism is something that only white people engage in.[3] That clients of color exist in large numbers and that they might have a different set of motivations, views, and experiences within sexual economies is a basic fact that has gone relatively unexplored until only very recently.[4]

Just as the mainly white tourists in *saunas* in Rio illustrate the contradictions of consumerism and of exporting gay identity frameworks, black gay tourism in Bahia shows contradictions in how communities relate to their pasts across time and space. African American gay tourists I encountered in Bahia engage in more than "sex tourism." They undertake a form of black sexual pilgrimage that allows them to recuperate black spirituality through what I term *subjunctive nostalgia*. Subjunctive nostalgia is the practice of tapping into alternative, imagined racialized histories in the diaspora by asking other subjects to stand in metonymically for an originary source so that one may experience a broader sense of shared community.

That African American gay men in Bahia are after far more than just sex is readily apparent by their interest in attending candomblé ceremonies and demonstrations of, or even learning, *capoeira*, a popular Afro-Brazilian martial-art form disguised as dance that survived slave times and is now thriving internationally today. Because capoeira most often involves shirtless, muscular young men sparring together in a close rhythmic dance, some perceive a sexual undertone. Many tourists now come to Bahia to study capoeira, and some tourists bring Bahian *capoeiristas* abroad to tour or teach. According to Williams's informants, this has led to "situational bisexuality . . . because many of those [foreigners] who have the resources to bring capoeiristas to Europe and North America are gay men."[5] This informal sexual exchange was not something I encountered in my own research, but capoeira *is* the source of an entire subgenre of gay porn, most notably the series *Capoeira* by French Connection, a European gay porn studio, which has found these films popular and lucrative enough to have produced twenty-seven sequels by last count, mostly shot on location in Brazil using local garotos rather than actual capoeiristas. (Thus, each scene begins with a rather clumsy display of capoeira as a pretense for physical contact, followed quickly by rather more expert demonstrations of sexual abilities.)

Many African American tourists take an interest in Bahian cuisine (which relies on many West African traditions), the history of slavery in Brazil, Afro-Brazilian musical forms, including samba, and local experiences such as the distinctly untouristy outdoor "African market," where residents buy everything from soap to implements for magical spells to animals for sacrifice. Here tourists can also see a small slice of local gay life. As one gay tour guide pointed out, "I like to bring the black Americans here because this is where all my gay friends hang out. We stand in the market to look at all the handsome men, so it shows the tourists what real gay life here is like." Taking in all these sites with a garoto on one's arm is much more in keeping with what is sometimes called "romance tourism," in which sex is just one part of a larger journey, but in Bahia it is a nostalgic pilgrimage that is as spiritual and emotional as it is sexual.

To be sure, not all African American gay men in Bahia engage in commercial sex. And some who do have no interest in cultural heritage. Williams quotes a gay tour guide, Tiago, whose clients mostly consist of African American gay men whom he helps navigate the gay scene, including Bahia's *saunas* and the street *michê* cruising scene. According to Tiago, only about one in three clients did *not* have an interest in cultural history to go along with their sexual liaisons, and 60 to 70 percent of the clients ended up purchasing sex, usually with heterosexually identified men. Williams's interviews corroborate my own findings, and while not all the gay African American tourists who do want programas want extended sessions or to directly mingle their cultural tourism and sex tourism, the commingling of these activities is visible enough to make this a valuable case study for examining transnational performances of race and masculinity in a unique context.

For some African American tourists, the romance of Bahia was a transformative experience. "Rio is just so fake. Those *sauna* boys are ridiculous, . . . very fake and not very good at connecting," explained Tony, an African American man who was in Bahia to celebrate his fiftieth birthday with a couple of friends. "And Rio is just expensive and touristy. . . . Bahia is more authentic. You feel like it's the real Brazil." Tony had been to a candomblé ceremony and loved it. "I don't buy this whole thing that black people are more homophobic," he said over a beer one afternoon. "But I do think the Black Church [in the United States] is. There's a lot of homophobia [when you're] growing up in the Church, . . . people saying that you can't be gay and black because homosexuality is a white thing. . . . So here it's very nice to see the candomblé because everyone is so accepting. . . . It felt like you belonged here. Here, it was like being accepted." Tony's experience of candomblé was that in that faith blackness and homosexuality are both valued, and for him that was profoundly moving. He felt the Bahians accepted him. Sometimes, however, Bahians did not appreciate the terms upon which tourists asked to be accepted.

Rivelino, a dark-skinned Afro-Brazilian garoto who worked the streets and beaches of Bahia, explained. "There are many [African Americans] who come and who want a guide as well as sex. . . . They like me because I am very muscular, because I am a man [*homem*]. The truth is, it is like this, okay? I prefer these men because if I ask for a hundred dollars—American dollars—they will pay it no problem. And I am proud of my culture." When I ask about the sex, he smiles a bit bashfully. "Yes, that part is okay. I can do that part because I am young and strong, because I am a man [*homem*], like I said. But they call me 'brother,' and this thing I do not understand . . . because we are not the same. . . . [T]hey are light, they have money, they fly here on airplanes, they are gringos. . . . It makes me angry sometimes, truly. But because of the money, I call them this way, too."

It may seem confusing that Rivelino thought of the African Americans as racially dissimilar, but in Brazil one's race is perceived not only by skin color but by other characteristics such as facial features, hair, and even self-presentation. Categories can be very slippery, but even rather dark-skinned people may identify or be identified as a category other than *negro* (black).

Performing masculinity across cultures was not an issue for Rivelino. Although he was heterosexually identified, he did not experience anxiety or guilt about attracting and pleasing clients. That part of the work—the performative labor of masculinity—came easily to him. He also had done numerous pornographic movies and had become accustomed to kissing and physical affection, which pleased clients. He could perform desire and pleasure with other men. It was the performative labor of race, however, that he struggled with. He felt obligated to accept the clients' claims to sameness and to perform that sense of commonality back as part of the commercial exchange, but he found himself angry about it and resenting them.

Bahia, which was Brazil's capital when slavery and sugar reigned, remains the center of Afro-Brazilian culture, and the government consistently markets Bahia's "authentic" blackness to tourists. Thus, it's unsurprising to hear Tony complain of Rio's inauthenticity and to highlight Bahia as the "real Brazil." Historian Anadelia Romo is skeptical of all this tourist interest in Afro-Brazilian culture in Bahia, however, stressing that it has not really economically benefited black people in Bahia.[6] So what does this tourism actually do and what does an examination of black gay sex tourism in Bahia show us about the complexities of performing competing ontologies of blackness across cultural difference?

Race in the Subjunctive Case

I take as my starting point for exploring subjunctive nostalgia Renato Rosaldo's now-classic analysis of *imperialist nostalgia*, or the tendency of cultural imperialists to become nostalgic for the traditional ways of life that they themselves helped to destroy. In his essay, Rosaldo writes with righteous anger about films such as *A Passage to India*, *Out of Africa*, and *The Gods Must Be Crazy*, all of which portray white colonialists as orderly and civilized, with their racial domination seen as innocent and even pure. He goes on to critique agents of colonialism (missionaries and the police loom large in his essay) for waxing nostalgic for a simpler time. That is: they miss how local life in the colonized society was when they "found" the natives. "Nostalgia," Rosaldo writes, "is a particularly appropriate emotion to invoke in attempting to establish one's innocence and at the same time talk about what one has destroyed. Doesn't everyone feel nostalgic about their childhood memories? Aren't these memories genuinely innocent? Indeed, much of imperialist nostalgia's force resides in its association with (indeed, its disguise as) more genuinely innocent tender recollections of what is . . . an earlier epoch."[7]

Rosaldo explains that this contradictory sentimentalizing by mostly white elites is part of the same impulse that allows white people to view Native Americans as "noble savages" and stewards of nature even though, prior to exterminating most of them, whites used to see them as ferocious rivals and dangerous subhumans. Only once the "bad Indian" was gone was it safe to opine for "good Indians." Imperialist nostalgia is when yuppies gentrify a neighborhood and then mourn the loss of mom-and-pop ethnic restaurants. Or when hipsters make an item of clothing or a musician popular only to abandon it for becoming too mainstream. Or when tourists go to a trendy vacation spot only to complain about how touristy the destination is becoming. And it's what happens when gay tourists go to Brazilian gay clubs and complain that gay culture in Rio is too much like that of Europe and America. Imperialist nostalgia is, in fact, so commonplace nowadays that readers can no doubt furnish their own favorite examples.

But what's happening in Bahia is not imperialist nostalgia—at least not yet. The African American gay men who go there are not disappointed in Bahia. They do not wish it back to a prior state of "authenticity." They are enamored of it. It feels, as so many of them have said in one way or another, "like coming home." This is also why nostalgia is a particularly apt term for diasporic tourism, evoking as it does the Greek words for "a return home" (*nostos*) and "a painful condition" (*algia*).[8] Part of the allure of "home" is that "traditional" and putatively "authentic" West African culture is alive and well, especially compared with the United States. Some women wear the old-time clothes of colonial *baianas*, Brazil's version of the mammy figure. People walk with enormous loads balanced atop their heads. For tourists caught up in the romanticism of Bahia, the old gods of Africa still live and they descend into bodies to walk with their people. Bahian children "play" capoeira, and in so doing keep alive something quintessentially Afro-Brazilian in that capoeria was a form of physical resistance designed to be not only effective in combat but also a beautiful dance-like "game." The state of Bahia is where escaped slaves fled into the backlands and built mighty settlements and fortresses for themselves called *quilombos*, from which they could attack slave masters. Such a scenario is almost unimaginable in, say, nineteenth-century Virginia or Mississippi. Blackness in Bahia is an embodiment of resistance with much romantic allure.

The African American tourists I know talk about how "it's like time stopped" in Bahia and how they are able to understand something new about the black diaspora because in Bahia it is so rife with examples of resistance. Black tourists see Bahia and they feel reverence for this kind of resistance and subjunctive nostalgia for the possibilities that this entails. They also see in Bahia another possible life that might have been theirs. What if their ancestor had been put on this ship instead of that one? Sold to this slaver instead of that one? Moreover, what if the Brazilians around them are cousins—their mutual forebears having been split up and sold in different directions? Nostalgia borne from this collection of "what ifs"—all those might-have/could-have/would-have-beens—is what I mean by a *subjunctive* form of nostalgia. And in the absence of historical or biological evidence, tourists are left with nothing but the subjunctive case and err on the side of imagining Bahians as part of their community.[9]

The Afro-Brazilian anthropologist Ana Paula da Silva, however, has little patience for this notion of shared community, which she sees as taking place on African Americans' terms rather than those of Afro-Brazilians. She argues that in Bahia middle-class African American tourists' "imperial eye rearranges the landscape according to its North American satisfaction and, in so doing, creates interpretations which are widely seen as 'more authentic' than native realities themselves . . . [thereby erasing] the diversity, ambiguity and complexity of Brazilians' own views of themselves and their country." She balks at the idea of African American tourists in Bahia rejoicing in "our shared history" and makes a biting critique:

Wait a minute: "our history?" Listen, I am down with the idea that there is a Black Atlantic, but it is a diaspora and disaporas are defined by cultural, political and historical diversity and yes, power imbalances. Though I may be deeply inspired by the history of the US Civil Rights Movement, it is not my history. If it were my history, I wouldn't need to be interrogated by immigration agents every time I visit New York, now would I? And yet Brazil's history—which most Americans, black or white, can hardly be bothered to learn—is now somehow a part of black US heritage. . . . The idea of "heritage" is itself . . . a myth-making attempt to fix claims to certain elements of history as personal or collective property. [Bahian blackness] makes no useful sense on its own terms and holds little interest for Black foreign tourists, except as it fits into their personal mythologies of identity. . . . Imagine Afro-Brazilians flocking to the Carolina Sea Islands and declaring the Gullah to be the only "real" black culture in the US.[10]

Subjunctive nostalgia might seem a likely target for critique, but it is also productive in the political affiliations, affects, and networks it creates for travelers exploring the diaspora, as in Tony's transformative experience finding black queer community in candomblé. However, I am diverging from Rosaldo in calling this nostalgia *subjunctive* rather than imperialist because, in the end, it is based on a fetishizing of Bahia and risks caving to the neocolonial tendencies of mass tourism to diminish nuanced local particularity into mass-marketing generic versions of religion, dance, performance, and other cultural forms—into "staged authenticity."[11] Just as garotos must perform race and masculinity across the span of cultural difference in order to transmit affects, subjunctive nostalgia is a tool through which tourists seek to perform sameness and render legible the Other and themselves. Finally, nostalgia is common to both gay and straight African American sex tourists in Bahia, but African American gay men use it to somewhat-different effect to marshal affective attachments to performances of racialized masculinities.

Black Sexuality and Diasporic Travel

African American "roots tourism" in Bahia began in the 1970s when groups of friends began making small, informal trips from the United States. Over the decades, as anthropologist Patricia de Santana Pinho has demonstrated, this transformed into a lucrative and organized market of networked travel agents.[12] Tour groups now come for the food, music, spiritual traditions, and performing arts such as the Balé Folclorico da Bahia (Folkloric Ballet), which uses ballet, modern, and traditional dance to bring to life capoeira circles and a veritable chorus line of orixás to audiences both in Bahia and across the United States.

Tourists—straight and gay—also come for sex. Many michês I know who worked the streets and beaches view African American female tourists as especially good targets for seduction, and while they never charge them outright, they may try to guilt or sweet-talk them into giving some money. These women seldom realized that the men were also targeting gay tourists.

I met one such michê, Heitor, near the beachfront one day. Taking me for a sex tourist, he began his con, speaking in English. Only later would he walk me through the steps of his routine: First, ask where the gringo is from. Next, ask what the guy thinks of the beautiful Bahian women and their *bundas* (asses). If his enthusiasm (the author's) is not forthcoming, switch the conversation to how beautiful the beaches are. Then begin the tale of woe, emphasizing one's own promise and exceptionality. "It is beautiful here for you, but it is hard for us," he said. "I, myself, am a medical student. But I cannot afford to buy books."

During our initial conversation, his shabby clothes, general appearance, and comportment had seemed inconsistent with this story, but he quickly pressed on, noting how hot it was and asking if I wanted to join him for a drink. I was used to being solicited as a client on this street, but I'd barely gotten a word in when he changed the subject in an unsubtle move toward sex. "Yes, America is very different. There are many gays there, I hear. Me, I have always been curious about this. I am not a gay, but I have wondered what it would be like to—how do you say this?—get a blow job from a guy?"

The speed at which he marked the paces of this script was remarkable. His character had evolved from broke college student to bi-curious rough trade in mere seconds while he quickly ushered me to a table and locked me into a conversation that was clearly aimed at a programa. At this point, I began to explain my research to him, deciding that it was high time for us both to come clean. Suddenly, an African American woman he recognized walked by and he jumped up to run after her. "One minute!" he said to me and went to try to woo her, complimenting her and asking what she'd bought in the market that day. "Nothing for me? You are breaking my heart," he said. "When will we have dinner?" She rebuffed him but did so politely, touching his arm and smiling coyly.

Eventually he wandered back, curious about the idea that a researcher would be interested in writing about his pickup artistry. In the interview that unfolded that afternoon, he explained that the woman who had passed by was a foreign exchange student and that he was, in fact, no medical student but a "guide." Heitor was also known in the area as a *caça-gringa* (hunter of female foreigners). Female foreign exchange students were especially popular targets for hustlers on the beach. He explained that he saw the women as young, inexperienced, easy to seduce, around long enough to be worthwhile conquests, and likely to be loose with their parents' bank cards. They were also seen as bestowing cultural capital, and he liked to walk around the neighborhood with a pretty gringa on his arm. As Williams explains in her ethnography, a gringo-hunter or "tourist grabber" (*pega-turista*) may link these activities to a desire to become cosmopolitan and meet people from different cultures, as Heitor did, rather than to sex work per se.[13] This disidentification with sex work was also important because many Bahians thought "sex tourism" to be synonymous with *child* sex tourism and pedophilia and did not see consenting adults purchasing sex as "sex tourists" but simply normal tourists engaging in a normal behavior.[14]

Heitor was not the only man to run out in the middle of a conversation with me to pursue a possible liaison with a gringa. None of these foreign women seemed clued in to the fact that Heitor and the beach michês who just romanced them derive most of their income from selling sex to men, and my relationships with my interlocutors and ethical commitments to them prevented me from disabusing the women of their fantasies.

Roots tourism and study abroad programs are just two examples of types of travel that overlap with sex in Bahia, and they show that sexual economies do not always consist of heterosexual white men pursuing local women. A colleague also once told me of an academic conference of mostly African American scholars hosted in Bahia that included condoms with the welcome packets. She was torn between dismay that scholars would be interested in finding sexual liaisons— including commercial or quasi-commercial ones—in their downtime in Bahia and concern that this was not an assumption on the part of the Bahian hosts but a sensible precaution based on experience. Whereas white sex tourism for straight and gay men originated with the European tradition of the Grand Tour and developed through European colonialism, black diasporic sex tourism could not emerge until the rise of a black middle class with the means to participate in leisure travel. Despite this very different genealogy, it remains the case that with economic prosperity for a segment of the African American community has come black sex tourism in the diaspora as a phenomenon in its own right.

Black heterosexual male sex tourism in Brazil got a big boost in visibility through a number of popular movies and videos produced by hip-hop stars. Pharrell Williams starred in 2003's *Dude . . . We're Going to Rio*, a film in which three African American tourists travel to Rio to pursue sexual adventures with Brazilian women. Meanwhile, Snoop Dogg's music video for "Beautiful" (featuring Pharrell) opens with Snoop lounging high up on a *favela* rooftop and tossing around Portuguese expressions before interspersing shots of popular tourist sites and sexy Brazilian women "with big fat booty" who "wanna do it" and get his "pimp-pimp fluid." Meanwhile, Ja Rule's video for "Holla, Holla" shows off a seemingly endless array of scantily clad women on Rio beaches. Citing these videos, feminist theorist Tracey Denean Sharpley-Whiting notes that this popular media attention prompted many black sex tourists who were already regulars in Brazil to lament that hip-hop was letting the cat out of the bag.[15]

Jewel Woods, a licensed social worker and self-described "gender analyst," collected interviews with dozens of heterosexual African American sex tourists who visit Brazil and published them with coauthor Karen Hunter, a journalist, in their book *Don't Blame It on Rio: The Real Deal behind Why Men Go to Brazil for Sex*.[16] The authors never mention having visited Brazil, and the book—which includes chapters such as "Eight Signs Your Man Is Traveling for Sex" and "The Frigid Black Woman"—aims to heighten concern (if not induce a moral panic) among African American women about what their men are doing while also sexually shaming the women with a bevy of quotes from black male tourists in Brazil about how angry black women in the United States are and how feminism has ruined them for African American men. On the other hand, the book is a marvelous advertisement for Brazilian sex tourism, and the quotations seem handpicked to function as a user's manual for African American men interested in hopping on this bandwagon. Woods's coauthor, Karen Hunter, also coauthored J. L. King's book about black men "on the down low," which led to a host of articles and books after Oprah Winfrey featured King on her show, creating not only a sex panic but rampant and unfounded speculation that closeted black men "on the down low" served as the "bisexual bridge" that allowed AIDS to turn from a gay white man's disease to a scourge on African American women.[17]

Although Woods and Hunter's book on black sex tourism in Brazil did not get picked up by Oprah, it speaks to a disturbing media tendency to use black sexuality to sow suspicion and misogyny among African American men by teaching that strong black women are a threat to black masculinity. Meanwhile, authors like Woods and Hunter seek to profit while simultaneously policing black sexual practices under the guise of promoting respectability and health. Their work also encourages subjunctive nostalgia on the part of tourists. For example, Woods and Hunter refer to Brazil as a "Black Womb," a framework that "erases the existence of the very real effects of racial inequalities in Brazil," as anthropologist Williams rightly points out in her work on sex tourism in Bahia.[18]

I cannot speak for Woods and Hunter's tourist interlocutors who frequent Rio, but sex was not the primary reason for roots tourism among African American gay men I met in Bahia. It was only one facet of travel. Despite sex tourism's growth in Bahia, my interlocutors have almost never disclosed that sexual experiences were part of their diasporic tourism to other places, even though many had been to West Africa, particularly Ghana and its nightmarish "slave castles" through which their ancestors may once have passed.[19] As Tony, the African American tourist quoted above who had found inspiration in candomblé, explained, "I went to the Door of No Return [at Elmina] and to a lot of places in western Africa and also South Africa. . . . I hooked up with a guy in Cape Town once." When I asked him if he had likewise hooked up with someone or paid for sex in Ghana, he looked shocked at the suggestion. "No way! That would just feel wrong."

Although Tony had trouble elaborating on why it felt natural to pursue sex with locals in Brazil yet "wrong" to do this in Ghana, Pinho argues that the difference between roots tourism in West Africa and in Bahia is pain and joy. In West Africa, tourists are confronted with the horrors suffered by ancestors and may experience catharsis or cry out empathically in pain. By contrast, in Bahia, "tourists feel the joy of reconnecting with a culture that, in their view, dared to survive, having been capable of resisting oppression and maintaining cultural ties with Africa." However, she also explains, "African American tourists also experience frustration and disappointment during their visits to Brazil, especially when they realize that black Brazilians conceive of blackness and Africanness differently" than African Americans do.

As in the case of Rivelino mentioned above, this can create tensions between guest and host. For example, one of the directors of Ilê Aiyê, a large *bloco afro* (black cultural organization), bemoaned to Pinho that African American tourists put her and the members of the *bloco* in a difficult position when they want to come to rehearsal and parade with them at carnival, because although the tourists say they're black, "to us, these people are *white!*"[20]

Bahian Heat

By the time gay tourism became popular in the 1990s, commercial tours and tourist infrastructure were already forming in Bahia. UNESCO had declared the historic downtown Pelourinho area a heritage site and was in the process of displacing residents, effectively turning it into a Disneyland-like area filled with tourist police, costumed mammy figures, expensive tourist restaurants, and Afrocentric souvenir shops.[21] As African American tourism in Bahia grew alongside a general rise in gay tourism in Brazil, so did opportunities for further market diversification. In 2006 a club promoter in New York organized "Bahian Heat," a packaged tour for gay African American tourists. The company had undertaken similar endeavors in the past in the Dominican Republic with its "Dominican Island Heat" events, which garnered hundreds of African American clients, and its subsequent "Nubian Dreams Cruises" to the Caribbean. For its fifty or so clients, Bahian Heat included opportunities for clubbing, drag shows, go-go boys, private cruises to nearby islands, and other venues for socializing. Tourists even made donations to a local orphanage. The company did not include sexual services in the tour price, but participants I interviewed confirmed that some participants purchased sex formally or informally. Some participants posted photos on the web of the African American tourists at male strip shows with sex workers.

Bahian Heat's advertisements (figs. 2–4) were slick and professional, featuring well-muscled black models in suggestive poses with come-hither looks, clad in white Speedos, on beaches or under waterfalls (including one woman, possibly transgendered, in a less visible position in one ad). Organizers also advertised the event in Portuguese, encouraging Bahians to "come and welcome the Americans to Bahian Heat in Salvador" for a cover charge of just ten reais (six dollars [2006]) at a gay club that also featured DJs and go-go boys. While not explicitly inviting sex workers to mingle with the clients, this ad was aimed at the sort

FIGURE 2   Advertisement for Bahian Heat

of person for whom meeting comparatively wealthy gay tourists would be an appealing investment opportunity rather than an irritation. (In Bahia, as in much of the rest of the world, a high density of tourists is not exactly known for making a nightlife spot "cool" among locals.)

One of Bahian Heat's attendees, a sixty-something man named Wilson, told me it was one of the best experiences of his entire life. He made amazing friends on the trip, and he felt a kinship with the other tourists that younger black gay men living in cities may take for granted, he said. For someone his age who did not live in a city with a large black gay cohort, this trip provided a new sense of community and affirmation of his identity as a black and gay man. "[Purchasing sex] is not at all the most important part of the experience. You have to understand that it's about so much more than that. Sex is just one part. . . . You have to see the bigger picture. For me . . . it was a larger experience, and it was like that, I think, for almost every man there."

As we talked, Wilson seemed to find my focus on the sexual aspect of his trip frustrating even though he seemed to understand that I wasn't

FIGURE 3   Advertisement for Bahian Heat

judging anyone for purchasing sex. He was correct that when people travel, they experience cultures through more than just sightseeing. They also experience through food and drink, through didactic learning by visiting museums and reading books, and through interacting with locals like shopkeepers, waiters, and (sometimes) other residents who are outside any direct commercial interaction. Why not, Wilson wanted to know, through sexuality as well, assuming one is respectful in one's interactions? For him, Bahian Heat provided a sexual means of apprehending diasporic black culture that was no more important than the other modes of experience provided by Bahian Heat and may have even been less important, but it was part of his overall experience nonetheless and something worth validating.

Feeling the Spirit

African American gay men gave me rapturous accounts about their experiences in Bahia. They generally did not know much about Bahia's history when they arrived, except sometimes some general background from friends who had been there and recommended the destination. Candomblé was especially meaningful to those who had ventured out to the terreiros, usually accompanied by their dates or as part of a tour group. Those who learned that the "priests," or *pais-de-santo*, are often gay men and that the religion is accepting of homosexuality found that this affirmed them as both gay *and* black in a way that their own often-homophobic experiences growing up in the Black Church had not. In so doing, they draw on a long tradition of African American gay men appropriating alternative spaces of blackness as subversive sites for reclaiming black queer spirituality, as E. Patrick Johnson has observed in the case of such men finding the sacred within black gay urban nightlife.[22] Moreover, candomblé is highly syncretized with Christianity and there is no need to abandon one's Christian faith to honor the orixás—at least from the candomblé perspective. (From the Christian perspective, this is another matter.) This tolerant attitude was appeal-

FIGURE 4   Advertisement for Bahian Heat

ing to most of the men I met because they usually considered themselves faithful Christians.

Early on in my work, I attended a pilgrimage to the Bahian town of Cachoeira for an annual ritual that is put on by the Irmandade da Boa Morte (Sisterhood of the Good Death) each August and that draws many devotees, including large numbers of African American tourists. On the bus, three lower-middle-class Bahian women asked if I was traveling alone and, taking pity on me, decided they would adopt me for the day. They took me to the ceremony, to lunch, to the open market, to visit one of the women's cousins who was recovering from dental surgery, and to buy a live chicken to take home on the bus to sacrifice later at their own terreiro—this last matter prompting a passionate argument about whether the chicken would be especially powerful because it was obtained on pilgrimage and also whether it would get loose and defecate on the bus. (The eldest among them decided the powerful chicken should ride inside my backpack to prevent this possible difficulty, but thankfully she lost the argument over whether to buy the bird.)

Almost as soon as we got off the bus in Cachoeira, the women asked if I was married or had children. When I said no, one of the women asked if I was a gay and quickly assured me that this was no matter for shame, as she had a gay nephew who was active in the candomblé. That afternoon, while we carried all their purchases in one enormous bag, the eldest woman—perhaps seventy years old—chastised me for trying to carry it myself. Bahians, she informed me, share such burdens by each holding one handle and half the weight. I was being more American than polite, in her view. (Also, she had really wanted that chicken.) Over time, I would learn that all of these qualities—the welcoming demeanor, an obligation to be kind to strangers, the teasing, the prying, the passionate arguing, the acceptance of sexual diversity, the wry upbraiding by one's elders—were common not only among these pilgrims but among Bahians generally and especially among Bahian *povo de santo* (practitioners of candomblé) whom I met. I thoroughly empathized with tourists who wanted to spend more time among *povo de santo* and learn more about their faith and lives.

One such interviewee was Demond, an African American businessman in his early forties. He had also been to the sisterhood's festival but found it too heavily syncretized with Catholicism. He did not understand why the black women of the *irmandade* sat patiently in the church while white priests said Mass. He had expected it to be a traditional candomblé ceremony and complained that all the African

American tourists who went to it would mistake it for authentic Afro-Brazilian religion when it was anything but. Demond had hired an escort, whom he paid for his time and services as a companion, to take him to Cachoeira for the festival. Demond said that they considered the sex to be incidental and off the clock. The guide also took Demond to a terreiro, but not his own. There Demond stood for hours, feeling the pounding drumbeats and swaying with the music. He fought the urge to "roll," or surrender to possession by an orixá or other entity.

"So I was there, and I could feel it like it was pressing against my head . . . pulsing . . . and I thought, I am not gonna do this. I am not gonna fall out and make a fool of myself. This is *not* like church in Alabama," he said, laughing. He had a big smile and a warm personality that was buttressed by his self-deprecating sense of humor. "Later, I wished I had [rolled]. It was like, the old gods, African gods, asking to come into your life and you say no." He looked sad for a moment as he tried to find the words to explain the connection he had felt. "[It was] like he or she, this orixá, was . . . there all along, going along with you in life, but you had to come to Brazil, to that place, where they kept it alive better and whatever thing it is that is a barrier between people and those spirits is somehow less here, and so you have to come *here* to have a chance to meet this orixá, this part of your past, and connect to it. . . . It's like it was meant to be."

"So you regret not being more into it, then?" I asked him. He smiled again. "So, yeah, to answer your question *directly*, . . . I regret [not rolling]. It was a serious missed opportunity. But next time [I'll do it]. Because I will come back, and I will go back there again."

Key to Demond's understanding is that the existence of orixás in Brazil is not something random that he stumbled upon while traveling. It's something that he was *meant* to discover, something fated. His patron deity, or orixá, was always with him in the background, and he simply became aware of it because he traveled to a place in the diaspora that was "closer" to Africa metaphysically. The orixá and its effects on his life predated his trip to Brazil. In this way, Bahia is a metonym for Africa, and his experience of the space—including through sexual modes of understanding—is an imagining of a utopian system of relations.

While I don't think Demond considered the garoto accompanying him to be a spiritual guide in any usual sense of the phrase, the fact that the garoto was the one who introduced him to this spiritual practice and its attendant possibilities for connection with Africa and the diaspora is not incidental. In the romantic ethos of the tourist's Bahia, it makes sense to be swept up in a series of sexual and spiritual awakenings as a result of a torrid romance. But here, the spiritual awakening is racialized. The tourist yearns for an idealized past that might have been. His experience, while no less real or significant, is a subjunctive form of nostalgia, a past that could have happened, but didn't.

Nostalgia marks the key difference between the sex tourism I described in the *saunas* of Rio de Janeiro and the "romance tourism" so prevalent in Bahia. In fact, the very notion that tropical tourist destinations are static, unchanging, less "developed," and therefore more "authentic" is part of the same system of economic oppressions and colonial frameworks that help keep these locations impoverished and unstable. Large, foreign-owned, all-inclusive resort complexes that sap up scarce water for golf courses and electricity for central air-conditioning and that funnel profits away from local establishments and into corporate accounts in the United States and Europe also help to keep tropical tourist destinations feeling as if they are lost in a simpler time.[23] But their business practices do help ensure that there is a steady supply of low-paying jobs available as prostitutes so that tourists who are willing to venture out of the resort complex can have a vacation romance.

To better understand romance tourism and its complexities, it is less important to critique "romance" in the sexual sense of torrid love affairs (even across economic disparity). Rather, what is vital to the analysis is "romance" in the classical literary sense of romanticism: a way of apprehending the world that is marked by the privileging of emotion and aesthetics over rationalism and material reality, honoring the sublimeness of untrammeled nature and the picturesque over the realities of pollution and social degradation, and the framing of tourists as intrepid travelers on journeys of spiritual and emotional import rather than as wealthy interlopers whose privilege allows them to carry certain ideologies in tow for evangelism and export.

However, in my case study, the men I am describing are African American gay men who are finding lovers who are often Afro-Brazilian and are often heterosexually identified. The cross-cultural sexual interactions require an additional interpellation of these identities in the romantic narrative. That is, in order to understand this particular sexual economy, it's necessary to understand how the garotos and their clients make sense of each other's racial and sexual subjectivity, and what role this subjectivity plays in the creation of subjunctive nostalgia.

Finding Africa, Finding Love

Tourists fail to understand the complexities of Afro-Brazilian life. They develop a subjunctive nostalgia for how that life functions in relation to other forms of blackness in the diaspora. Their understanding of black Bahian culture may be enough to spark nostalgia, but their knowledge is limited. This is, of course, the nature of being a tourist. The tourist is necessarily an amateur, not a scholar. Yet for Afro-Brazilian anthropologists like Pinho and da Silva as well as for some garotos, tourists are also exporters of racial identity models. Ronaldo, an Afro-Brazilian hustler and vendor who worked the tourist beaches looking for men and women, explained. "I like white skin, but the gringos prefer black skin like mine. It's good this way. The gay guys especially like my skin," he says, pulling his shirt up to show me his bare torso. "See? No hair. Smooth. Gay guys like this." Then in English: "Just black skin, strong body, no fat." When I asked him if white and black gringos had different preferences, he remarked, "Oh, this thing was so confusing to me. The other gringos. One time I explained I was *negro*," he said, pointing to his own skin. "But you," he pointed to me as if I were the tourist in question, "are *moreno* [brown] but the guy did not like that. . . . So now I do not talk about this."

Much like African American tourists who make an ancestral pilgrimage to the slave castles of the Gold Coast only to be dismayed or hurt by the competing constructions of race when they are called *obruni* or *abruni* (white foreigner) by Ghanaians, Bahians reject the frameworks of kinship that tourists seem ready to foist upon them.[24] Brazilians are, in fact, notorious for the sheer number and complexity of racial categories that operate in society (at both regional and national levels). For example, when given the choice of either filling in a blank describing their "race" on a census form or choosing between four government-mandated options, Brazilians self-selected 135 different categories for "race," including creole, whitish, pinkish white, burnt yellow, navy blue, black Indian, white Indian, cinnamon, tinted copper, waxy, jambo, part brown, purple brown, beach-burnt, burnt rose, redheaded, redbone, green, and regular.[25]

It should come as no surprise, therefore, that not all African American tourists read as "black" in Bahia. When the Harvard University professor Henry Louis Gates Jr. filmed the second part of his 2011 documentary *Black in Latin America* about being black in Brazil, he visited

Bahia and promptly began reveling in subjunctive nostalgia for can-domblé, carnival, and capoeira, noting that no amount of his "fanta-sizing about Bahia" had prepared him for "how very close to Africa this all is, . . . [this] sense of immediacy and intimacy with the African continent." But as the film continues, he begins unpacking a bit of Bra-zilian history and Bahian culture and it becomes clear that he's not necessarily seen as sharing the same racial identity as the people to whom he speaks.

"In Brazil, racial categories are on steroids," he explains in a voice-over. To demonstrate this, Gates does an impromptu survey. "Hey, my brother, how you doing?" he says to a working-class man in the market-place. "Come here. I want to ask you something. So if I lived in Brazil, what color would I be?" The man looks mildly uncomfortable, perhaps because of the camera, perhaps because of the impromptu interview and having to speak through a translator, perhaps because this is actu-ally an impolite question by most Brazilians' standards. *"Caboclo?"* the man says, hesitantly. Subsequent Bahians speculate that he's *moreno*, *mulato*, *cafuso*, or *moreno claro*. The people draw from different kinds of racial categories, some based on color. *Moreno* simply means "brown" but can be used for almost anyone, including very light-skinned people who have brown hair. It's so broad that some people add *claro* (light) to *moreno* to separate the subject from the very dark-skinned people who also claim *moreno* status. But Gates's interviewees also draw on somewhat-underused formal categories. A *caboclo* is someone of mixed indigenous and African heritage, a *cafuzo* is of mixed indigenous and European heritage, but both are flexible terms with somewhat-different meanings in different regions. A dark-skinned woman says to Gates's translator, "He's *negro*, but I'm not racist!"

Gates passes up the chance to investigate the response, but it's ac-tually quite revealing. Saying someone is *negro*, which literally means "black," can be seen as an insult, especially if said to one's face. It's con-sidered polite to "lighten" someone up, usually by calling them *moreno*. Even dark-skinned people can "lighten" themselves in this way. A col-lege student in Brazil once explained to me that categorization has less to do with skin color and more to do with facial features and hair. This white Brazilian said with no trace of irony, "Even black people are *moreno* here. But you cannot have the nose," he continued, flatten-ing his nose with a finger quite matter-of-factly, "the lips, or the bad hair and be *moreno*. Unless you have money. Then you're whatever you say you are!" Despite the possible racism in the student's sentiment, he was correct that "money whitens," which is also part of the reason the Afro-Brazilian garotos were reluctant to accept their clients as their black "brothers," to use Gates's term.

Gates concludes his conversation in the marketplace by asking the group of Brazilian men around him their own racial identifications. After hearing them claim a diverse array of self-descriptors, he concludes the scene by pronouncing, "But the good news is—we're all black."

While tourists can be forgiven for not being cultural experts, Gates's television series represents precisely the kind of foreign appropriation of Afro-Brazilian culture that da Silva derides as "a myth-making attempt" to render Afro-Brazilian history "collective property." Gates's popular documentary carries with it his full weight as a Harvard professor (to say nothing of his fame as a public intellectual and prominent friend of President Obama), which is why he and his film editors would have done well to have heeded da Silva's admonition that it is precisely because Bahian blackness "makes no useful sense on its own terms and holds little interest for Black foreign tourists" that it becomes a matter of tourists'—and Gates's own—"personal mythologies of identity."

As performance studies scholar E. Patrick Johnson has observed, "The fact of blackness is not always self-constituting. Indeed, blackness, like performance, often defies categorization." Johnson compares "blackness" to the term "queer" in that its theoretical usefulness lies in its ineffable and ephemeral qualities. However, he also warns against precisely the kind of totalizing appropriation demonstrated in Gates's encounter with the Bahians. "By founding blackness on a socially constructed monolithic black community, the rhetoric of black authenticity discourse . . . confounds ideological allegiance and skin color such that radical political coalitions are forestalled."[26] That is, by appropriating Bahian blackness through the ethnocentrism of US racial identity politics rather than apprehending its usefulness on its own terms, Gates actually forecloses a more radical political and performative exchange.

What Gates himself stumbles upon in his documentary, but does not unpack for his viewers, is that the fact that Brazilians have many more racial categories with which to talk about race is less interesting than *how* they navigate the very discourse of race itself, dancing and dodging racial issues, deftly avoiding definitions instead of immediately leaping to them as in the United States, quickly falling back upon the national refrain that Brazil is a "racial democracy" where there is no racism. And this discomfort with the discourse of race is precisely why the popularity of Bahia among African American visitors who want to engage in ethnic, cultural, and spiritual tourism is so confounding to many Bahians whom I know. That these strangers—all viewed as wealthy and many viewed as something other than black—would travel so far to celebrate their blackness can be perplexing, amusing, or even irritating to Bahians.

"Africa is here, man," Lennard, a lithe and chipper, middle-aged African American tourist, explained to me, indicating the Bahian street with a sweep of his hand. "It's in the samba they dance, or even the way they dance when it's not samba, when it's just at the club or whatever. The way they can move their hips and bodies like that. That's all from Angola. It's in their bodies, and the dancing, oh and the food. I ate at Mama Bahia [an expensive restaurant in the Pelourinho area] and they serve the shrimps with the heads still on. Very African. . . . And it's in the spicy gravy. They're using African chilies and other African spices. It runs through everything about this place." When I ask if he thinks Mama Bahia is authentically African, he laughs. "They might not have places like that with the tablecloths and the expensive wine and whatever in Africa, but the spirit is authentic African, for sure. . . . It's not like soul food, which is African but American. . . . It's purer than that here."

Lennard had gone to the restaurant with Alex, a garoto he met on the gay section of the beach in Porto da Barra. They had spent the week together up to that point, but Lennard was beginning to lose interest, expressing irritation that the garoto was always asking him for more money and to buy him things. "It's kind of unfortunate . . . because I was really hoping he would introduce me to some more of his . . . friends. . . . That maybe one of them would join up with us. . . . Or maybe I'd spend a couple days with one or two of them when him and me were done, but right now I just want him to go away. . . . I'm sitting here nervous with you because I'm afraid he'll walk up on us, and I'll be stuck with him trailing after me all day like a lost dog." He rolls his eyes.

Although it's only been four days, the "romance" had faded fast. Unlike tourists in the *saunas* whose time with garotos is tightly regulated, romance tourism has the potential to get messy. Stephen, an African American gay tourist who had retired in Bahia, explained, "I fell in love with a boy as soon as I arrived. I bought him a car, which he sold. I bought him gifts, which he sold. And my friends . . . tried to tell me he was a whore, he was a porn actor. I refused to believe them. . . . Because I was in love." He clapped his hands together in a mock ingenue pose before shrugging it off. "And then one day I was at a party, and you know, they had videotapes playing on some of the TVs and all these people were standing around laughing. And I came and pushed, shouldered through to the front, and there was Alberto on his stomach, biting the pillow in some *Boys from Brazil*–type porno." He laughed mirthlessly.

Although some tourists, as I described in previous chapters, considered being a porn star to be a turn-on, for Stephen, it was anything but. He had dated garotos when he'd visited on vacation, and when he fell in love, he thought it would be different precisely because Alberto was not a sex worker.

Barton, an African American tourist who was in the process of retiring to Bahia, had a similar disillusionment the first time he came to Bahia for an extended period of time. "I got downsized from my company where I used to do computers. Well, who the hell is going to hire a fifty-two-year-old man—yes, I know I look younger, but I'm fifty-two and ain't gonna tell no lies—at a hundred thousand dollars when some twenty-two-year-old kid fresh out of college will do it for forty?" He gave a devilish wink and smoothed his brow with both hands. "I had been planning on moving down here eventually, but I'll end up [here] sooner than I thought. I could either work another fifteen or twenty years in San Francisco and retire . . . there and still have to live like . . . a bum, or I could come down here now and live like a king. So I bought this . . . condo overlooking the ocean and got myself a little boyfriend."

As he went on detailing his past relationship with his "little boyfriend," he seemed alternately perplexed that he had been "taken in" and nostalgic for the good days in the beginning. "He was straight . . . and I knew it, I guess, but I didn't care because he seemed into me and it was nice so I thought maybe [we had] a little wiggle room with *that*," he said, wagging his finger at some unseen object and wrinkling his nose as if the specter of bisexuality was lurking in the corner and being especially smelly.

"Wiggle room?" I asked. "Like straight men actually falling for boyfriends?"

"You see that here [in Bahia]. I was stupid and in love. I bought him presents. . . . Nice clothes. Furniture. . . . Just nice things, you know. All the time his other friends—straight guys all of them—they came to me and told me how much better they would treat me and how he was no good. They wanted to be my boyfriend. Can you imagine?" He clutched invisible pearls. "All these hot boys—you've seen them, seen the type anyway, so you know what they're like—but I didn't listen. . . . I was like, do you think my black ass was born yesterday? . . . I *know* what he's doing. But once I helped him get his own place, then his girlfriend's family said she could marry him . . . since he had a place for her to live now. And that was the end of it."

"So you being generous caused it to end?" I asked.

"Mmmm . . . I think I knew he would do it when I got him the place, but I couldn't help myself. And I wanted him to be happy. How fucked up is that?"

Barton waited as if he actually expected an answer. "I don't know. *Is* it fucked up?" I said finally, feeling unsure what he wanted to hear. But he was moving on.

"We fucked a few times after that. . . . [W]hen he needed money he would come to me and tell me he missed me and he missed being with men and needed my cock and, well, whatever. You know how they do. But it was just that he wanted new shoes or . . . whatever. He could have just told me that. But I wasn't gonna kick him out of bed, either!"

In these examples, it is not race that must be interpellated across cultures but sexuality and desire. And while the men don't directly cite racial interpellation as a source of stress in the relationship, garotos I knew who had African American boyfriends (or had had them in the past) tended to be exasperated about discussions of race. Yet garotos had their own interesting discussions with one another about their understandings of race and masculinity in their performances with these clients.

Under Pressure

I'm sitting in the abandoned upstairs of a restaurant in Bahia with João, whom I've been seeing a lot of lately. João is a sweet-natured and somewhat-shy twenty-five-year-old with a pretty face and lean body. He has moderately dark skin. He would read as black if he were from the United States, but he can call himself moreno in Bahia—if he talked about race much, but he doesn't. In fact, he usually goes to great lengths to avoid it. He is smart but didn't finish school, and so he found his career options limited. His brains have earned him the respect of the other garotos on the street even though he is not as physically imposing as they are. With us is Edi, a hulking, thirty-six-year-old with enormous muscles, a booming voice, very dark skin, and a large gap in his front teeth. He tells me early on that he is "of Ogum with Oxum," meaning that his patron orixá is the warrior god Ogum, who uses his strong arms to forge iron weapons. Looking at Edi's biceps, which are larger than my head, this seems completely appropriate. His secondary orixá is Ogum's beloved, Oxum, a beautiful river goddess whose children are said to have a strong streak of narcissism. I later realize that, when it comes to Edi, Oxum is giving Ogum a run for his money.

The manager of the restaurant is an effeminate gay man named Nando who knows Edi from their candomblé terreiro. Nando is a portly moreno who wears a white turban-like wrap around his head and earrings and plucks his eyebrows down to nearly nothing. When I first met Nando, he looked me straight in the eye and told me there was no male prostitution in the area and I might as well go away. Later, I walked down the street in front of Nando's restaurant alongside a garoto interlocutor who greeted Nando by name as he stood in his front door exchanging *fofocos* (little bits of gossip) with neighbors, prompting a flash of embarrassment across Nando's face but no apology. Now Nando sneaks me upstairs to do interviews with garotos in private, winking conspiratorially. He knows every garoto in the neighborhood and he's excited by the idea that there's the beginning of a book taking shape in the sweltering attic space of his business. Hosting an academic is far more exciting than putting up with just another sex tourist.

Edi describes the peculiarity of tourists who want romance instead of just sex, but who also want that romance with heterosexual men like himself. "Tourists prefer *heteros* . . . so we [garotos] think of it as a way of having fun while also making some money, . . . another 1,000 reais [USD (2010) 550] a month, maybe, which isn't much to you, but it's more than you would earn working somewhere honest. And it's enough to save if you're careful." Edi has had a string of boyfriends whom he's lived with, but at the moment he's single. Sometimes he stays with friends or girlfriends, but mostly he lives with his mother. He doesn't like to do individual programas and prefers being a kept man. Because of this fact, he says he isn't really a garoto although he talks often of being in "the life," which is how prostitutes refer to their work.

"In my case, I'm more open, more direct. . . . I'll ask the tourist what he likes, if he wants that, if he likes this. I'm not going to make a *rodeio* [play games or go in circles] with him. He's a tourist, but he isn't stupid. Because he's been to several countries, see?" Edi strongly associated travel with education and culture, reasoning that tourists were cosmopolitan by definition. "Some garotos de programa don't want to walk with a tourist or to go to restaurants, drink, eat, go out, because others may see them and know what they are. They just want to do the programa and take the money."

Edi leaned in, his hands flat on the table, his biceps bulging. "But me, I want to be his friend. Because if he wants to be my friend, then when we sit in a restaurant, I can get what he likes, too. I have nicer things, a nicer quality of life when I am with him. I can have more than the other type of garoto de programa, . . . which is why I say I am a guide and not a GP [pronounced "jeh-peh," slang for garoto de programa]." He leans back with a shrug, brushing off the very idea. "I don't want to be in this life [of prostitution], but my mother needs to pay the water, the light, the food; the children ask, 'What's to eat?' and there isn't anything, you know? That's the truth of this line of work. So it's good to be with a tourist."

Edi has had many boyfriends: some local Brazilian men, some tourists, some expats. He is affectionate with them and engages in kissing and cuddling. Most garotos I know—especially the ones in Bahia who work the streets—don't like engaging in this kind of affection. Some would rather be passive in anal sex than kiss and cuddle, which they say makes them feel disgusting and ashamed, whereas "giving your ass" is unpleasant but ends soon enough and requires little effort beyond lying there. Perhaps because his masculine comportment is unassailable and there are very few of his peers who could threaten him physically, however, Edi speaks about kissing gringos quite openly.

João nods sympathetically. He's also affectionate, but he's of a different "type" than Edi. João is something of a "twink" in gay parlance, or a smooth and boyish young man who is cute or perhaps even handsome, but who doesn't traffic in rugged masculinity. Edi, as a somewhat older body builder with a rough face, is far from being a twink. Most garotos I know who are his type have successful careers as "rough trade," heterosexual men who are exclusively *ativo* and who will penetrate gay men or allow themselves to be orally "serviced" by them, but who do not reciprocate and who do not kiss. They may have rough or dispassionate sex with clients, preferring to touch and see the men as little as possible. Such men can make a lot of money filling this niche, but they don't transition well into boyfriends. Nonetheless, by working against his type, Edi seems to have had some good successes.

"I'm *hetero*, I'm *normal*, . . . ativo, but when I'm going to have sex with an *entendido* [polite term for a homosexual], I'm going to have a good time, you understand? Which is why I am not a garoto. I'm not going to have a problem with it, you see? Because I am a guide and I only do this with someone who is my friend, who I am spending time with." Edi is unwilling to strategically identify as bisexual like some men despite admitting freely to feeling pleasure with other men.

Nando appears with a free round of *cachaça* shots. Edi throws him a smile and Nando's eyes linger a little too long, his looks washing over

Edi's shoulders as he tells him about the various flavors he has brought for us. I wonder if there's already a sexual history between them but decide not to pry where our host is concerned just yet.

"Edi, I wonder about something," I say once Nando is gone. "Do the tourists talk about your race much? About color?"

Edi smiles, nodding. "Oh yes, the gringo comes in search of blacks. . . . Gringos want the black guy; they want the *pressão* of the black. Because the black guy has a real pressão." *Pressão* means "pressure," but it can also mean something like a "drive." I must look confused because Edi sighs, and his tone of voice reminds me of someone explaining something basic to a small child.

"The blood of the black guy when it's hot—whether he's with a man or a woman—[is] pure madness [*loucura pura*]. The black man in bed, he doesn't need to be drinking this here," Edi says, tapping his cachaça glass, "in order to have sex. No. I myself am a sex machine [*sou uma máquina pra transar*]. I am a machine. And I get very mischievous when I'm in bed. When the pressure rises in my veins, I go crazy. Pure madness! So if I was fucking you, you would have to beg me to stop or I just wouldn't stop!" He's miming pounding pelvic thrusts, and he laughs loudly at his own antics. "Because it's in the blood! Mmmm, I am practically a specialist in this area."

He explains, somewhat haltingly, that pressão is a racial thing. Black men, he tells me, simply have more pressão—so much, in fact, that they have a need to fuck that is barely controllable. And that's why he can have sex with men almost easily as with women. He, as a black man, is so hypersexual that he penetrates without regard for the object of his sexual urges. He blames this pressure on his blood, which he says is literally hotter than the blood of white people. When he gets excited, the blood flows faster and heats up, literally creating pressure. Although I doubt Edi is aware of it, his views on black male sexuality may be rooted in nineteenth-century Brazilian medical and legal discourse. Following slavery, white society feared black freedmen, whom they saw as sexually voracious predators who could barely control their impulses and who might sodomize a young white boy as easily as rape a white woman. His views are also reminiscent of colonial anthropological theories about Sotadic Zones, or tropical climates that caused the people to be hypersexual and prone to sodomy.[27]

I decide not to be pedantic with Edi, though. Instead, I want to understand how Edi's vision of race and sexuality matches with that of the tourists and how they navigate the transmission of this sexual energy in light of that.

"But tourists don't know all this about pressão," I protest. "Yet they all seem to be here looking for Afro-Brazilians."

"It's true," João says, entering the dialogue. "Tourists want *negros*. I'm still too white for them." He laughs and holds his lean, dark-brown arm next to Edi's muscular, black one. "They only want *negros*," he repeats. "So much that when I go out with friends who are blacker than me [*mais negão*], I have to say [to the tourist], 'No, stay with me!' Because they prefer guys who are even blacker still [*mais negro melhor*]. I can lose a client if he meets too many of my friends!"

"But why do they want that? What do you think is the reason?"

"Because they think black is the culture of Bahia, right?" João says, sounding somewhat agitated. "They come to have sex with a black person of really dark color, the blacker the better. The majority are like this. The [white] Italians and Germans, too, but especially Americans. . . . It's the image of Brazil for them. But the worst thing about the foreigners is they think that all the black Brazilians have a very big penis, that the blacker you are, the bigger your penis is, see? But this is just a fantasy." The garotos talk about their penis sizes a lot, and not all of it is exaggeration. João's penis is of average size, he's explained to me on more than one occasion, but is smaller than those of most of his friends in the industry. He doesn't seem bothered by this and it rarely costs him a client because, he reasons, he's got the nicer face.

I try to turn the conversation back to Edi's understanding of blood and pressão. João gets a bit bored and wanders off to look out the window. But there's something that doesn't make sense to me about Edi. If Edi simply has so much pressão that he needs to release it, I ask, and this is the reason he can easily have sex with men, then what is the role of attraction?

"Sure," he says, once he understands my question. "I have felt attracted to men. I'm not going to say that I haven't. . . . You can ask me and I will tell everything, no lies." He goes on at length explaining that even though he is heterosexual, it is easier to have sex with young men than with old ones. He still has a surplus of pressão, but older men aren't as good at exciting him, at making his blood run hot. "The problem isn't [just] that you open the wallet and get the money to pay. You have to have chemistry, you know?" he concludes.

João drifts back over, suddenly rejoining the conversation. "I agree with this. It's like I myself have told you before: . . . with an old man we go for the money, but if it's a young guy, then we get into it [*tem pessoa jovem que a gente faz mesmo*]." João sits back down, focused again on our conversation. He has a short attention span. Edi, however, has started talking over João, apparently reminded of a story that he wants to tell. As he does so, he grows increasingly loud and, to my surprise, angry.

"You see, I've lived with a [Brazilian] man for two years, even though I was with my girlfriend, too. But I always hid that I had a girlfriend because he wouldn't like it. If I told him, he would want to kill me! He always said he wanted me just for him. . . . He discovered us one day, and it was over. . . . So I am not a garoto because of this: because I liked to live with that gay guy not only for his money but because of his friendship. But you know what? I have these arms here and I can always take up an *enchada* [a farming tool] and work! I never want to depend on anyone. There will always be these guys, these Americans, who come here only to use us, João! They use me. 'How much do you want?' [they ask] and they open their wallets. 'Here! Here you go!' [*Tá aqui!*]." Edi is angry as he imitates a tourist, miming throwing money. He tips his cachaça back. "And then there are those who come in search of love, harmony, affection. And *that's* better for me."

João interrupts this thundering monologue with a laugh: "You talk so seriously! He talks seriously, doesn't he?" I'm actually a bit surprised that anybody would have the nerve to laugh at Edi when he's so visibly upset, but João is an old friend and laughs as though this were pure bravado on Edi's part.

Edi scowls. "I'm not talking seriously for you. If I had all the press here in front of me," he says, gesturing to an imaginary press conference audience, "everything I'm saying here I would say in front of the press. . . . There are a lot of garotos in Salvador, and they only want the good life but they don't want to do anything [to earn it]. If you're gay and have a good quality of life, you know what I'm going to want? That you take me from the bottom of society to the top. I don't want to stay dependent on your money. I'm going to want you to get me a good job because I know if I depend on you and your money for shit [*depender da merda do seu dinheiro*]—well, tomorrow or the day after you could just kick me out. This just happened to a friend of mine here in Barra. That's why I don't like American women tourists. They never want to help you. They just want sex. A gay man understands my mind and wants to improve my quality of life."

João nods in agreement and looks at me. "That's true. Women just want to use people, that's all. Women want you to give them money and things."

Edi concurs. "That's why I say I prefer to live with a gay guy. *Women use you, but gays help you.* They improve your quality of life. I'm a man [*homem*]. But I can do anything with a gay, . . . well, except I will never let him penetrate me [even though] there are others who do [allow that]."

"They just don't talk about it, right?" João says, giving a half eye roll.

"Right. They go inside the room and then whatever happens once you're inside will stay there. The homem is suddenly a *passivo*! But there are some garotos who you can't even put your hand near his ass or he'll get pissed off. I can do anything with a gay, but do you know why I do not let him penetrate me? I'm no more of a man than he is, but for me when you get to loosen up a tight asshole, that's the best."

João laughs, but he's blushing. He covers his face, embarrassed about this new level of frankness but also surprised by Edi's matter-of-fact tone describing something vulgar. He shakes his head, laughing so hard I fear he's going to fall off his chair.

Edi continues undaunted. "I like it when it's really elastic, when it's tight and you open it up. I like to fuck assholes like that. I'm never going to get fucked by a queer [*dar pra passivo*] because I don't have the head to be passivo. I like to tear it up instead . . . because it's in my blood. It's like I told you. The blood of the *negro* is hotter; it makes more pressão when you are excited. That's why we are like animals in bed. And giving your ass doesn't do anything; . . . the pressão is about the dick, and tearing up an ass is the best for that."

Later that night in my apartment, as I wrote up my notes from the interviews, I thought about how many times I had heard tourists talk about the hypersexuality of people of color, not only in Brazil but throughout the tropics. And yet here was the same discourse internalized in a heterosexual black male as a point of pride. "*Sou uma máquina pra transar,*" Edi had said. "I am a sex machine." And for Edi, this was linked to his own race and his superior status as ativo. Thus, being passivo, for Edi, was seen as inappropriate for a big black man such as himself. Being passivo was not only a weaker position but—in some sense—a whiter one.

The African American tourists I knew were educated and thought deeply about race and processes of racialization. And yet the fantasy of the hypersexual, overendowed black male persisted and was, in fact, heightened by the difference in class and nationality. Stephen, who previously described his failed relationship with a garoto, was one such person. As a black expat fluent in Portuguese, he knew a great deal about Bahian culture and its racial politics. Yet in describing the guys in the *saunas* in Bahia he was quick to revert to stereotypes. "The dicks on these guys are huge! Once you go black, [you never go back], right?" he said. "Well, once you go Bahian, I say!"

Racial essentialism is potent not only for tourists who project fantasies onto Bahia regardless of how the Bahians see themselves. Racial essentialism is so embedded within the garotos' own understandings of their sexual experiences with clients that it is part of what fuels Bahia's sexual economy. Race and sexuality are tightly linked in essentialist renderings of Bahia, and this mode of conceptualization leaves little room for deconstructing and analyzing the complexities of this interstitial part of identity.

Performing Circum-Atlantic Masculinity

Heterosexual African American men may *also* experience subjunctive nostalgia in Bahia, and they also have sexual relationships of varying commercial degrees with sex workers in the beachfront neighborhoods and historic center. While these heterosexual liaisons were not my primary area of research, there are some noticeable differences that are worth exploring to better illuminate how performativity functions differently in same-sex contexts.

The most striking difference is that heterosexual African American sex tourists showed a strong preference for Bahian *mulatas*, or mixed-race women of both white and black ancestry. This interest is something the anthropologist Williams also found in her research. "The processes of exoticization of Brazilian women of African descent are not the exclusive domains of white European and North American men," she writes. "Despite claims of diasporic solidarity with black people in other parts of the world, heterosexual African American men also exoticize Brazilian women of African descent . . . [and seemed] particularly interested in an aesthetic that privileges race mixture, light skin tones, and curly/wavy hair."[28] Beyond simply being a woman of mixed race, the *mulata* is an archetypal figure in Brazilian literature, cinema, art, and popular culture who is closely associated with sensuality. She is young, curvaceous, spontaneous, and sexually available. She is a highly romantic figure, known for her joie-de-vivre, but she often meets a tragic end. Williams quotes Ahmad, a thirty-five-year-old African American tourist, who described Brazilian women as "loose women ready for sex. . . . That's what we think of when we think of Brazilian women: tan lines, cocoa brown skin, big asses, and ready to fuck."[29]

For those sex tourists showing a marked preference for light-skinned Brazilian women of mixed race, subjunctive nostalgia functions differently. This same preference was also widely observed by Woods and Hunter's African American interlocutors who frequent Rio and not Bahia, which indicates that their sex tourism is less bound to roots tourism. The sociologist Margaret Hunter has also observed the social and sexual preference for light-skinned African American women in the United States, a phenomenon in dating that extends into the African American community itself.[30] Thus, the body of the *mulata* in Brazil's sexual economy does not stand in metonymically for Africa in quite the same way as that of the masculine, dark-skinned Bahian man does for the gay African American men I knew who explored Afro-Brazilian cultural events and sites. Some of this preference is undoubtedly related to the stereotype of the "black buck," which sees black masculinity as brutish, rough, and virile. Imagery of this type dominates in US culture through hip-hop videos, TV shows, and popular movies. It's also been internalized in Brazil, as Edi expressed eloquently with his theory of pressão. But the interlocutors I am describing who were most focused on *packaging* roots tourism and sex tourism together show how the black male body was eroticized for the inherent masculinity and blackness that accrued to it by virtue of its putative Africanness. For these men, the body of the garoto was asked to perform metonymically in order to create a heightened experience of community.

Performance studies scholars have invested significant attention to questions of cultural memory. Joseph Roach focuses specifically on "Circum-Atlantic" cultural performances (building off of Paul Gilroy's "Black Atlantic") to show how they rely on a "three-sided relationship of memory, performance, and substitution."[31] He calls this process surrogation, the substitution that happens as people constantly substitute one thing for another in the search for an original. The metonymic process I've just described in which the sex tourist imagines diasporic community is one possible example of surrogation. For performance theorist Diana Taylor, culture is materialized in the body over time through repertoires. Performance is unrepeatable—strictly speaking—and can never be wholly reproduced, yet it congeals in cultural forms.[32] For Roach, this manifests through *kinesthetic imagination*, or the "expressive movements as mnemonic reserves, including patterned movements made and remembered by bodies. . . . [Such movements are] a psychic rehearsal for physical actions drawn from a repertoire culture provides."[33] That is, memories in a community may be retained and transformed over generations in the body. Such a conceptualization of memory has been important for scholars invested in understanding feelings and (often-traumatic) memory across diasporic communities. Thus, although Demond (and tourists like him) may have no prior actual knowledge of candomblé, he nonetheless felt in his body the mnemonic reserve—the associations that exist after an experience and that may be called upon again to reignite the experience—calling his body to move, to "roll" with an orixá. In this way, Demond sought access to that cultural repertoire for himself.

Although rather mystical, the idea of cultural repertoires is important for understanding a phenomenon like roots tourism in the black diaspora. And Roach's theory of surrogation and Taylor's related views on cultural repertoires provide a useful basis for understanding subjunctive nostalgia, particularly for thinking about tourist connections to ritualized patterns found in candomblé and capoeira. However, there are elements of candomblé and capoeira that function in the lives of garotos who must deploy them as part of a performance of racialized masculinity in such a way as to appeal to and connect with African American tourists. Taylor's notion of repertoire shows how capoeira can be passed down from slaves to present-day Bahian men and why such men now "play" it for crowds of tourists in the historic Pelourinho neighborhood. However, it's harder to extend the cultural repertoire of capoeira and all this attention to embodied memories to all permutations, especially those like the transformation of capoeira into a subgenre of gay porn. How to account for the sex workers' performance of racialized cultural repertoires in such a context wherein the intention of the performers has shifted from memorializing and embodying resistance to selling sex?

For Taylor and Roach, performance is unstable. The garotos shift their performances, altering approaches and tactics, as Heitor, the "medical student," did as he rapidly tried on different roles first for me and then for the African American female exchange student. He drew on a repertoire of narratives that he used with different types of tourists, experimenting to see which one might yield the best result.

Race and sexuality are also unstable, at least in Brazil. In previous chapters, I've shown how garotos move fluidly through different sexual identifications depending on the nature of their interactions with clients and each other. Making these moves is at the heart of what I'm describing as the performative labor of masculinity. However, race in Brazil is equally as complicated as sexuality. As the sociologist Edward Telles explains, "Although social meanings based on race are omnipresent, memberships in particular categories are often not fixed. This is particularly true for the Brazilian case where racial classification is especially ambiguous or fluid. The way[s] persons classify each other and identify themselves are sometimes contradictory and also vary depending on the social situation."[34] Essential to the Brazilian performance of race, then, is a continuous process of redefinition and refinement. Navigating this within the matrix of masculinity in such a way as to capitalize on one's virtuosity is an important performative skill and can be essential to one's success as a garoto.

But in the United States, race is expected by rigid societal structures to be totally stable. As Telles explains, "Racial self-identity is not a core component of identity for many Brazilians as it is in the United States, and there is little sense of solidarity with or *belonging* to a racial group. Brazilians often prefer the notion of color rather than race because it captures such fluidity."[35] Thus, when the tourist arrives with very fixed notions about the constancy of race and its centrality to identity, there is a disjuncture. It is not merely the case that the gringo and the Brazilian have different racial identification systems but that their views on the very nature of race itself as a concept are incompatible. The garoto must not only perform race across difference but produce a sense of constancy even as he is rewarded financially for the inconstancy of race and his performative flexibility. Such is the queer paradox produced by subjunctive nostalgia.

Passive Longing, Active Nostalgia

Brazilians have their own concept of nostalgia. *Saudades* is one of Portuguese's famously "untranslatable" words, invoking the sense not only of missing someone or something but also of a kind of melancholic longing for something or someone one has known. It's a term frequently encountered in music, poetry, and everyday conversation. Could this culturally specific affect—saudades—explain subjunctive nostalgia? Perhaps in part. The tourists I met did not usually arrive knowing this concept, and saudades doesn't account for the feelings and affects that diasporic communities may have for a "home" they never knew. It is this confluence of affects that can propel diasporic subjects into the subjunctive mode, inspiring them to imagine new connections to a lost and unknown home and new metonymic ways of connecting to others. Such an active approach to nostalgia that focuses on forging new connections and meanings moves beyond saudades. And African American gay men making their sexual pilgrimages in Bahia bring new forms of erotic investments into their relationship to home, queering their connections to home via their affects and attachments to local Bahian men.

These men whose tourist practices incentivize performances of racialized masculinity on the part of garotos are, in effect, queering Africa itself through their black diasporic pilgrimage and their attempts to uncover the queerness of the Bahian cultural repertoire—unearthing the complicated queerness of candomblé houses, reveling in the homo-erotics of capoeira—and they do so through participation in communities like Bahian Heat, which some may find problematic, but which also did build an affirming black gay community for men of all ages, as the sixty-something Wilson poignantly described. In this sense, the black gay tourism industry in Bahia reveals not only how discourses of racial essentialism undergird the sexual economy of Bahia but also how people can and do use the power of the erotic in their efforts to construct racial identities and relate to Africa and the diaspora.

Many of the men in my study described experiencing homophobia in the black community and racism in the white gay community in the United States. They complained of popular discourses conflating blackness, masculinity, and heterosexuality and bristled at notions espoused by West African political leaders and black evangelicals alike that homosexuality is fundamentally a white thing, a product of colonialism and borne out of desire to destroy black masculinity. So unlike heterosexual black tourists in Bahia, these men were invested in uncovering the queerness of Africa, which they see as being alive and evident in Afro-Brazilian culture. In their own way, they're reading an archive and theorizing it for themselves. Although the bodies and performances most rewarded in this economy are hypermasculine and black, this case illustrates that sexuality runs through multiple facets of black subjectivity and that sexuality remains an important and under-theorized site for understanding travel and movement and circulation in the diaspora.

Yet there remains an important performative disjuncture between the clients and the garotos. The tourists place a premium on the garotos' ability to make them feel part of a community. They want a moment of authentic belonging within Bahian culture through its various forms and idioms, but they also want an affective bridge to a broader black diasporic community that spans beyond the present and the present-day geography of Bahia. What they value in their relationship with garotos is the shared embodiment of culture, which is made manifest through sexual practice and literally shared bodies.

Even as the tourist values these cultural memories through the kind of surrogation Roach describes, the hustler experiences the value of performance differently. For the garoto—whose identity is always in a state of becoming, of coming ontologically unmoored—the value of the performance is entirely in the social capital he can acquire. Garotos access cosmopolitanness through their interactions with their gringo clients as they stroll through town, reperforming themselves for their Bahian community, and they expect the gringos to take them, as Edi said, "from the bottom of society to the top." Responding to the tourists' subjunctive nostalgia, they become ever more mercurial, their performances increasingly volatile, even as the tourists feel more fixed and static in their identities by virtue of their newly expanded sense of community.

EPILOGUE

Suppress prostitution, and capricious lusts will overthrow society.
SAINT AUGUSTINE

The big difference between sex for money and sex for free is that sex for money usually costs a lot less. **BRENDAN BEHAN**

Beto longed to go to Europe. He worked the tourist beaches in Bahia selling jewelry to tourists but made most of his money from selling sex to men he met this way. "This tourist is sending me a plane ticket!" he would say, causing eye rolls and snickers from the other, more jaded *garotos*. Beto was young and energetic, deeply curious about the world and perpetually upbeat. He fantasized about going to parties with a rich *gringo* where there would be "lots rich people and they're all going to be nice . . . because they have to be because I will have money." While Beto recounted this fairy tale one evening, Evandro—a big, macho guy full of personality and bravado—joined in, imagining that if *he* ever went to Europe on the arm of a gay gringo, he would abandon the man and seduce a string of rich, young heiresses (minor royalty perhaps) or maybe marry an elderly woman who would promptly die of a heart attack from the tremendous orgasm he would give her on their wedding night, leaving him with money, a house, and a visa.

I found it rather telling that these men who work the beaches didn't fantasize about seducing some American heiress, given the prevalence of popular culture from the United States in Brazil. Evandro explained that I was being naive. "Everyone knows you can't even get a US visa without pay stubs and a house," he explained, "so even if the guy is American, you can only go to Europe." Beto nodded in agreement and looked pityingly at me for my cluelessness. How could I not know that it's more feasible to seduce British royalty than get a US tourist visa? Even the daydreams of garotos are subject to the Department of Homeland Security, it seems.

Despite having a lot of ambitions to do so, very few of the dozens of garotos I know have made good on plans to go to school or start a business, let alone buy a car or a house. And while several have gone abroad with their gringos, this is rare. Beto's plane ticket never came. He decided he wanted to become a fruit vendor and planned to work up from a fruit cart to a store. But the last time I saw him (it had been three years since his tourist had disappointed), he was working in a low-end venue, quickly aging out and unable to compete. He briefly dabbled in petty crime before fleeing to São Paulo. When he did get money, he spent it on CDs, clothes, and booze. Despite his hardships, he continued rigorous condom use and reported getting health screenings. He still talked of Europe from time to time. In his more somber moments, Beto knows he will—in all likelihood—die without seeing Europe, but still he believes that his dream is realizable and it keeps him going.

Throughout this book, I've described how changes in political economy affect masculinity and sexuality, influencing the lives of people like Beto in unexpected ways. The gay tourist industry in Brazil, and the sexual marketplace of desire with it, fluctuate alongside peaks and troughs in the currency exchange. As the Great Recession hit the economies of the United States and Europe in 2008, Brazil's economy remained strong. The US Federal Reserve bought US treasury bonds by creating new money, artificially propping up banks by overpaying on bonds in an economic policy called quantitative easing. Investors looked around for opportunities and saw huge potential in emerging markets like Brazil, which had experienced massive growth in the preceding years due to profits from high commodity prices for its exports and discoveries of large offshore oil reserves, allowing it to overtake the United Kingdom as the world's eighth-largest economy. Further bolstered by the foreign cash flooding the country, Brazil saw the continued rise of a consumer class crescendo alongside a decrease in poverty and a drop in unemployment. This is the era of my research and explains why so many men from poor backgrounds were intent on joining their peers in the rush toward consumerism. As Adilson remarked, "Every day more *boys* are knocking on the *sauna* door . . . but these ones don't know how to behave. They still need to learn the *postura* and how to show they are *homens* and how to follow the rules and not to be lazy all the time." And the garotos fetched high prices, causing many tourists to bemoan that they could no longer afford to travel to Brazil as often or buy unlimited *programas.*

However, Brazil did not invest in reforms or infrastructure and suffered under the weight of crony capitalist projects. Moreover, all this foreign direct investment caused inflation and price spikes, and so Brazilian central bankers raised interest rates in response. Ultimately, though, they were powerless against the US government. When the Fed decided to moderate quantitative easing in 2013 as my research was ending, investors pulled their money out of Brazil simultaneously in order to bring their money home to the United States, strengthening the dollar. At the same time, Brazil saw the commodity prices on its exports drop precipitously. Middle-class Brazilians suddenly found themselves with wallets full of devalued currency and surrounded by astronomically high prices. Meanwhile, the government continued spending billions of dollars on new constructions for stadiums, revitalized ports, and other major projects for the World Cup and Olympic Games, to which Brazil had committed itself during boom times.

Hundreds of thousands of Brazilians, many of them young, middle-class people, took to the streets during the Confederations Cup (essentially a dry run in 2013 for the next year's World Cup) in major cities across the country in what became known rather winkingly as the "Vinegar Revolution"—so named for the makeshift vinegar-laced gas masks protestors wore—voicing their economic discontent and protesting transportation cost increases, wasteful government spending, and poor social services. Millions watched as protestors overtook numerous cities, including the capital, literally dancing atop the congressional chambers, their shadows flickering in the glow of burning tires and detritus. Police retribution across the country was fierce and brutal.

The effects of the financial shockwaves were felt almost immediately in the sexual economy as programas in Brazil suddenly got cheap again for gringo visitors. During the Great Recession, gringos had complained that the Brazilian real was too strong and they could afford only a few programas over the course of their vacations. Some gringos in the United States also had lost their jobs in the recession, and many could no longer afford to stay as long as they could back in the "good old days" when the dollar went farther. But, with gringo purchasing power now on the rise again, *saunas* will likely teem with gringos once more. The sexual economy will reconstitute itself, and the quotidian performances of garotos will adjust as gringos again become highly sought after. Changes in the sexual economy are further complicated by the emergence of apps for gay hookups such as Grindr and Scruff, which surged in popularity near the end of my fieldwork too late for me to properly study. These apps allowed foreigners easier access to sex with local men (including some low-income "gringo chasers" and garotos, who began to appear on the apps alongside potential noncommercial sex partners).

There is no shortage of young men in Brazil who want opportunity and access to a middle-class consumer lifestyle. Although unemployment was generally low during the years I studied the sexual economies of Brazil, the garotos complained then as they do now that what was missing was access: truly viable routes leading to good jobs that offer career paths. As Carlos, the garoto from Manaus who had been so enamored of his military life before he ended up in a *sauna*, explained angrily, "In Rio, it's all about who you know. Even a shitty job like being a waiter in this restaurant, you have to know somebody. So me, I speak okay English. I'm smart, I studied, I was in the military. I know how to work. But if I go to that hotel over there, they want a résumé. And what do I put on it? Ah, here I did *sacanagem*?" As he invoked *sacanagem*, or "dirty/sexual things," Carlos punched his finger on the table, hitting an unseen bullet point on the imaginary résumé angrily.

"For these three years right here I was a *sauna boy*? Here, I fucked gringos in the ass these three years, and I would like a job now, please?"

Carlos's anger and frustration are understandable. He worked in the sexual economy as a legitimate way to lift himself and his family out of poverty, but when it came time to exit, he found he could not overcome the institutionalized stigma of his profession. Even if he lied about his work history in the *sauna*, he had an employment gap on his résumé.

Carlos explained that he had acquired skills such as speaking English, and he learned to chat with foreigners and feign interest about a wide array of favorite tourist topics, including US geography and its regional specialties, music, and popular culture, and he had also learned how to be self-directed and responsible about time and money management, but he could not easily talk about these skills—all of which would come in handy in the tourist sector—without revealing to potential employers his involvement in commercial sex. Thus, the stigmatization of sex workers becomes institutionalized and continues to affect them even if they move into what society regards as "honorable work." The social punishment for men selling sex to men, especially heterosexually identified men, is severe and long-lasting.

But the sexual marketplace provided what the government and the conventional private sector could not: a path out of poverty that provided money to support themselves and their families, social access to patrons who might pay for education or provide travel opportunities, and even emotional connections. Shortly after this conversation, the lean and boyish Carlos gave up on his idea of leaving the industry and reinvented himself as a *bofe* (muscular butch guy), becoming wildly successful financially after embracing his fate as a garoto. Oftentimes, as with Beto, such successes do not come to pass, but sometimes they really do.

But as Adilson warned earlier: there are skills the *boys* need to learn if they are to succeed in their ambitions. One needs to learn to master the art of self-presentation, including the postura, the walk, the bodily comportment, the habitus, and all the affects—*tesão, pegada, carinho*—that go into shaping masculinity. Some of the men I've introduced in this book have become accomplished arbiters of these elusive qualities. At least as of my last interactions with them, Wesley and Robert had returned from their cruise and were enjoying their queer transnational family together. Wesley's career in pornography has launched him to minor celebrity status in the global adult film industry. On the other hand, Adilson eventually did lose "his gringo." He remained upbeat, but he lost most of the economic gains he had made and currently lives in a favela in Rio's South Zone.

A few of the men have transitioned out of the industry; some, buttressed by the English they've acquired while selling sex, work as servers in touristy areas, others sell drugs, and some have managed to complete job skills classes. One became a sushi chef. A few, unlike Beto, managed to travel abroad. Most, however, are continuing to sell sex. Some whom I met when they were new to the scene have now become high earners in their *saunas* and sought after as "kept boys" by tourists and locals alike. Many, though, still sell sex but gradually do so less and less frequently as the years go by, dissolving into the ranks of temporary, part-time, and seasonal sex workers who sell sex only when an expense arises or during especially lucrative times like *carnaval*.

In their daily lives, as they go to work, plan new business ventures, date women or men, start families, go out with friends, or go back to school, few people whom sex workers meet know or suspect that they are part of Brazil's sexual economy. Yet these men have been forever shaped by their participation in it, experiencing Brazil's global economic flows at the most visceral levels, embodying and reflecting through their complex performances of racialized masculinity and sexuality at the individual level so much of the larger political economy that shapes the nation.

The relationships I have described are fundamentally about translating idioms of desire across cultural difference. Key to this enterprise is the manipulation of affects and performances of racialized masculinity. And so clients will always come from afar to marvel at these embodiments, attracted by what they believe is exotic difference. Yet from Bahia to Rio to the Amazon, their sexual exchanges also reveal the paradoxes of desire in that the garotos and the clients are seldom as different as they imagine. Indeed, it is often through the pursuit of authentically performed masculinity within a racial imaginary that disappointment arises.

The expectation is that the garoto must not only be a virtuoso performer but also symbolically stand in for national fantasies. The garoto must embody the masculinity of Brazil and personify Brazilianness, itself a nearly impossible task. Yet in another sense, the garoto really does share a corporeal connection with the nation. The changes and fluctuations in its economy shape his lived reality, and his embodiment shifts along with it. And so there will always be more *boys*—*boys* with mothers to support and *boys* with dreams of travel, curious *boys* and hungry *boys*—who will come knocking on Adilson's *sauna* door, ready to walk into the steamy environs, slip on that blue towel, and go hunting for their first time.

Acknowledgments

It's been nearly a decade since this project began to emerge during some long discussions about anthropology of the Afro-Atlantic world at the University of Chicago in 2005. The book required the support of many friends, colleagues, interlocutors, and mentors. It therefore seems worth tracing a bit of the project's path and thanking those who showed kindness along the way or even accompanied me for a bit of the journey.

I left behind a short but successful career in public policy at the Chicago Board of Education to return to graduate school, feeling disillusioned with politics and education reform, yet also newly and intimately aware of the interconnected issues of poverty, urban development, race, and gender. Having gone to school only by virtue of a Pell Grant and having come in hopeful refugee fashion (like so many queers before) from a poor background in a rural midwestern town to the nearest major city, I was soon disillusioned by the mainstream gay community's emphasis on consumerism, assimilation, normativity, and apparent disinterest in progressive and coalitional politics. Eventually, all these interests would come together as I began to study the topic of gay travel and international marketing aimed at capturing pink dollars, choosing Brazil for an exploratory summer of research primarily because it topped the travel lists of gay travel writers and was enjoying a tremendous economic boom that had generated intense interest from private, public, and academic sectors.

Almost immediately upon arrival in São Paulo, male sex workers took me for a potential client and approached me on the street. I hadn't planned on writing about sex tourism per se, but the men—confused and intrigued by me—eventually began an extended conversation about tourism, money, economics, sexual identity, and cultural difference that would send my project and my life off in an unexpected direction.

In Brazil, I am especially grateful to Thaddeus Blanchette, Ana Paula da Silva, Adriana Piscitelli, Freddy Stracke, Flavio Lenz, Alex Castro, Hélion Póvoa-Neto, Fernando Bingre, Sonia Corrêa, Gláucia de Oliveira Assis, Kerstin Tiefenbacher, Guilherme Pierantoni, Tiago Tamborino, Rodrigo Azevedo, Felipe Moreira Gil, Laura Murray, Soraya Simões, Keila Simpson, Robson Cruz, and Dartanha Silva. They shared their work with me, welcomed me to Brazil, opened up access to a community of scholars, and introduced me to new ways of conceptualizing my work. Thad and Ana Paula were especially influential in my Brazilianization. I also owe a debt of gratitude to Gabriela Leite, the longtime leader of the sex worker rights movement in Brazil. She once made a gift to me of an inscribed copy of her own book, encouraging me to promise that one day I would return the favor with a signed copy of this one. Although our collaboration continued, I regret that she did not live long enough for me to keep my promise.

I also thank Stephan Palmié and Anwen Tormey at the University of Chicago for shaping and overseeing my early thinking about this project and supporting me during my initial and sometimes awkward forays into the field. At Northwestern University, I am forever indebted to my mentor, E. Patrick Johnson, who recognized the implications and potential of this project even before I did, and who carefully shaped the development of my work and my person over the years. I often struggle to explain to undergraduate students intent on continuing their studies the importance of selecting one's mentor and to articulate to them what that relationship is like. My best pop culture analogy for them comes from vampire lore: an adviser is your "maker," and it behooves you to have a strong and benevolent one because you are bound to each other forever. I'm grateful and honored to find myself in EPJ's lineage.

I owe a similar debt of gratitude to Mary Weismantel, who proved a generous teacher, meticulous editor, and friend. She also demanded that I not lose my anthropological core and helped me to find a way to wed my performance studies and gender studies background with my ongoing training in ethnography. And I would have been utterly adrift without the additional support of D. Soyini Madison, who taught me that ethnography is art as well as social science, and Ramón Rivera-Servera, who served as a model for the kind of scholar I aspire to be.

After I graduated, the good people at Williams College welcomed me into the profession, honoring me with the distinction of being the first to enter a tenure track line devoted to the Program in Women's, Gender, and Sexuality Studies. At Williams College, I owe many thanks to Roger Kittleson, Amy Holzapfel, Margaux Cowden, Olga Shevchenko, Carol Ockman, Annelle Curulla, Rashida Braggs, Ondine Chavoya, Julie Cassiday, and Anjuli Raza Kolb for reading drafts of this book and providing me with their invaluable insights. I also thank Katie Kent, Lucie Schmidt, Mérida Rúa, and Sara Dubow for their support during these vital early years. My students in my sexual economies and global sex seminars provided valuable insights, especially Madeline Vuong, Erica Lansburg, and Chienfa Wong. I also thank Leyla Rouhi and the Oakley Center for the Humanities and Social Sciences for providing financial and institutional support in the form of their manuscript review program for junior faculty. João Sodré's notes on the manuscript also helped tremendously, and he contributed a great deal to strengthening my understanding of Brazilian law, culture, and history. I owe a special debt to Pavithra Prasad and Jennifer Tyburczy for countless hours spent in the trenches. Audiences at lectures I gave at Cambridge University, Rice University, Oberlin College, and Amherst College also provided feedback and discussion that helped shape my thinking on various aspects of the book.

And I thank Richard Parker for sharing the expertise he accumulated over decades in this field. He is that rare scholar whose own successes make him ever more gracious—not less so—and his passion for the field is infectious. Serving as a reader for multiple drafts of the manuscript, Don Kulick provided wit, candor, and rigorous critique. Don's work profoundly shaped my project even before I met him, and I am thrilled to have gotten over my initial and irrational fear of meeting him, because he has proven to be a most giving scholar.

I must also praise Doug Mitchell (no relation), Kyle Wagner, Ashley Pierce, and the whole team at the University of Chicago Press for their guidance in the publication process. Pam Bruton has likewise shown enormous personal patience and excellent editorial skill. I also thank the anonymous reviewers from the press for their detailed insights, recommendations, and support. Peer review remains the backbone of the academy, but it is profoundly unfair how rarely we get a chance to thank the anonymous colleagues who counsel us on our work.

Research also requires money. At Williams College, I wish to thank the Office of the Dean of Faculty and the Hellman Family Foundation for financial support. Likewise, I thank the following programs and funding sources at Northwestern: the Society of Fellows and its Presidential Fellowship, the Mellon Cluster Fellowship, the Lila Heston Fellowship, the Roberta Buffett Center for International and Comparative Studies, the Sexualities Project, the Graduate School, the School of Communications, the Northwestern Summer Language Grant Committee, the Program in Gender and Sexuality Studies, the Department of Performance Studies, and the Center for Interdisciplinary Research in the Arts. The National Science Foundation's program in cultural anthropology provided funding for a related project that nonetheless shaped the conclusion of this one as well.

Many other people also helped along the way. Soraia Oliveira and Ana Lima taught me much about not only language but also the culture of my adopted home. I must also thank Susan Dewey, Carole Vance, Carol Leigh, Denise Brennan, Lauren Berlant, Jack Halberstam, Bill Leap, Martin F. Manalansan IV, Ellen Lewin, Peter Aggleton, Erica Lorraine Williams, Tiantian Zheng, Héctor Carrillo, Steven Epstein, Patrick Larvie, Patty Kelly, Jeffrey Masten, John Collins, Brodwyn Fischer, Ann Haugo, Elizabeth Reitz Mullenix, John Poole, Katie Zien, Jay Sosa, Kareem Khubchandani, Andrew Brown, Elias Krell, Melissa Minor, Mbongeni N. Mtshali, Nikki Yeboah, Ashley Black, Lauren Markofsky, Megan Geigner, Faith Kares, Paul Amar, Bianca D'Souza, Bill Earner, Venetia Clarke, Pippa Grenfell, Lisa Biggs, Victoria Fortuna, Brandon Fischer, Michelle Liu Carriger, Kalle Westerling, Nicolette Manglos, Phoebe Cohen, Ashley Barnes, Jesús Hernández, Kimberly Kay Hoang, Anna Fishzon, David Francis, Emilie Ringe, Mark Butler, Anirudh Khandadai, Georgina Perry, Jane Ayres, Kristen DeHahn, Evren Savci, Yaa Sarpong, Amanda de Lisio, Keeanga-Yamahtta Taylor, Jake Silver, Vivian Huang, Kiaran Honderich, Enmanuel Martinez, Nic Mai, Marlon Bailey, Jason Stichter, C. Riley Snorton, Juan Pablo Rivera, Danny Gough, LaShandra Sullivan, Marcia Ochoa, Jessica Fisher, J. T. Way, Ebony Coletu, and Luis-Manuel Garcia. I also thank my family for their support, especially my mother, Darlene Halm, and my sister, Julie Mitchell. Thank you also to Dinesh Kalwani, who was there through it all.

Finally, I thank all my interlocutors—both *gringos* and *garotos*—who shared their stories with me and who spoke with such candor, humor, and emotion. I especially thank those garotos who became invested, involved their friends, and tried to make sure I "got it right." And perhaps most importantly of all, I thank my primary research assistant,

Gustavo, who worked tirelessly with me in the field in the last few years of the project, who taught me much about living in Brazil, who brokered introductions and removed barriers, who kept me safe amid everything from muggers to illness to vampire bat attacks, and who quite probably saved my life in a back alley in Bahia. He asked for anonymity and no credit, but without him this work quite simply would not exist.

Notes

INTRODUCTION

1. I am breaking with the existing preference for *michê* in
    social science research because it has a connotation of low-
    class and sometimes-violent street hustling that some men
    found offensive. Following my interlocutors, I generally use
    garoto, as shorthand for *garoto de programa*.
2. Sérgio Carrara and Júlio Assis Simões, "Sexualidade, cultura
    e política: A trajetória da identidade homossexual mascu-
    lina na antropologia brasileira," *Cadernos Pagu* 28 (2007):
    65–99.
3. I have chosen not to capitalize "black" when referring to
    the racial and ethnic category because—as I document in
    subsequent chapters—my Brazilian participants did not
    necessarily feel that they were part of the same larger Black
    diasporic community that is rooted in a common sense of
    Blackness that some of my African American interviewees
    expressed.
4. Alan Bryman, *The Disneyization of Society* (New York: Sage,
    2004), 2.
5. Ibid., 3.
6. Bruce Pietrykowski, *The Political Economy of Consumer Behav-
    ior: Contesting Consumption* (New York: Routledge, 2011), 95.
7. Erving Goffman, *The Presentation of Self in Everyday Life*
    (Garden City, NY: Doubleday, 1959).
8. Diário de Noticias Global, "Turismo gay assegura 30% das
    receitas do Rio de Janeiro durante o Carnaval," February 14,
    2015, accessed February 25, 2015, http://www.dn.pt/inicio/
    globo/interior.aspx?content_id=4401789&page=1.
9. Nicole Froio, "Rio de Janeiro: The Most Gay Friendly Desti-
    nation in the World?," *Independent*, July 26, 2011, accessed

October 5, 2013, http://blogs.independent.co.uk/2011/07/27/rio-de-janeiro
-the-most-gay-friendly-destination-in-the-world/.

10. Ibid.

11. Diana Renee, "Rio de Janeiro in the Running for Most Gay-Friendly
Award," *Jakarta Globe*, October 22, 2009, accessed October 10, 2010, http://
tinyurl.com/26p5vr6.

12. For more on this topic and the range of complicated issues it raises, see
Arnaldo Cruz-Malavé and Martin Manalansan, *Queer Globalizations:
Citizenship and the Afterlife of Colonialism* (New York: New York University
Press, 2002).

13. Mark Padilla, *Caribbean Pleasure Industry: Tourism, Sexuality, and AIDS in
the Dominican Republic* (Chicago: University of Chicago Press, 2007), 24.

14. "Brothel-style" refers to the common setup of a commercial sexual venue
in which sex workers wait and socialize with one another and clients in a
common area and then make use of available rooms on the premises for
turning a trick.

15. See, e.g., Lisa Keen, "Caribbean Gay Bashing Could Harm Tourism," *Pride-
Source: Between the Lines*, May 4, 2006, accessed October 5, 2013, http://
www.pridesource.com/article.html?article=18564.

16. Howard L. Hughes, *Pink Tourism: Holidays of Gay Men and Lesbians* (Wallingford, UK: CABI, 2006), 84.

17. Ibid., 5.

18. Ibid., 75–77.

19. As a rule, I have changed names to protect the identities of participants. I
have also altered and/or redacted some nonessential identifying information. In a few, very rare instances, a participant appears under a second
pseudonym to de-link potentially identifying information.

20. Júlio Assis Simões, Isadora Lins França, and Marcio Macedo, "Jeitos de
corpo: Cor/raça, gênero, sexualidade e sociabilidade juvenil no centro de
São Paulo," *Cadernos Pagu* 35 (2010): 37–78.

21. On the question of whether to capitalize "Latino" (a move that risks reify-
ing the idea of a monolithic Latin American culture and ethnicity), I have
deferred to the *Chicago Manual of Style*. As a descriptor rooted in geography, "Latino" did not present quite the same set of issues and questions
for my interviewees as the term "Black" did.

22. My thanks to Thaddeus Gregory Blanchette for pointing this out.

23. Lauren Berlant, "Cruel Optimism," *Differences* 17, no. 3 (2006): 20 (italics
in original).

24. Ibid. (italics in original).

25. Don Kulick, *Travesti: Sex, Gender, and Culture among Brazilian Transgendered
Prostitutes* (Chicago: University of Chicago Press, 1998).

26. Laura Moutinho, *Razão, "cor" e desejo: Uma análise comparativa sobre relacionamentos afetivos-sexuais "inter-raciais" no Brasil e na Áfricado Sul* (São
Paulo: Editora da UNESP, 2004).

27. Marie-Eve Carrier-Moisan, "Gringo Love: Affect, Power, and Mobility in Sex Tourism, Northeast Brazil" (PhD diss., University of British Columbia, 2012).

28. I am mindful of the critique many Latin American studies scholars have made regarding the use of the term "American" to refer to people from the United States when, in reality, anyone from the Americas might have an equal claim to this demonym; however, I am reluctantly following popular usage in large part because it is also how my Brazilian interlocutors actually use the term.

29. For more on the "accidental sex tourist," see Thaddeus Gregory Blanchette and Ana Paula da Silva, "'Nossa Senhora da Help': Sexo, turismo e deslocamento transnacional em Copacabana," *Cadernos Pagu* 25 (2005): 249–80.

CHAPTER ONE

1. Small sections of this chapter appeared previously in my "Fare Tales and Fairy Tails: How Gay Sex Tourism Is Shaping the Brazilian Dream," *Wagadu: A Journal of Transnational Feminist Studies* 9 (Spring 2011): 93–114.

2. My special thanks to João Sodre for pressing this point.

3. Judith Butler, *Gender Trouble: Feminism and the Subversion of Identity* (New York: Routledge, 1999), 45, 179.

4. Travestis often do not identify as "transgendered" (*transgêneros*), which many see as a bourgeois foreign import. Travestis, however, do not typically identify as women or men per se or as trans women, but rather as travestis (i.e., as a distinct category). For much more, see Kulick's *Travesti*.

5. Deborah Cameron and Don Kulick, *Language and Sexuality* (Cambridge: Cambridge University Press, 2003), 139.

6. Diana Taylor, *The Archive and the Repertoire: Performing Cultural Memory in the Americas* (Durham, NC: Duke University Press, 2003), 22.

7. Kerwin Kaye, "Sex and the Unspoken in Male Street Prostitution," *Journal of Homosexuality* 53, nos. 1–2 (2007): 37–73.

8. Rubens de Camargo Ferreira Adorno and Geraldo Pereira da Silva Junior, "Visibilidade e invisibilidade do trabalho de garotos de programa," in *Juventudes contemporâneas: Um mosaico de possibilidades*, ed. Juarez Dayrell, Maria Ignez Costa Moreira, and Márcia Stengel (Belo Horizonte: Editora PUCMINAS, 2011), 172.

9. Margareth Rago, *Os prazeres da noite: Prostituição e códigos da sexualidade feminina em São Paulo, 1890–1930* (Rio de Janeiro: Paz e Terra, 1991), 38 (my translation).

10. Lucia Rabello de Castro, "What Is New in the 'South'? Consumer Culture and the Vicissitudes of Poor Youth's Identity Construction in Urban Brazil," *Young: Nordic Journal of Youth Research* 14, no. 3 (2006): 179, 182, 184.

11. James N. Green, *Beyond Carnival: Male Homosexuality in Twentieth-Century Brazil* (Chicago: University of Chicago Press, 1999). For some interesting

historical parallels in New York, see George Chauncey, *Gay New York: Gender, Urban Culture, and the Makings of the Gay Male World, 1890–1940* (New York: Basic Books, 1994), 27.

12. Green, *Beyond Carnival*, 33–34.

13. BRIC stands for Brazil, Russia, India, and China, countries seen as having achieved the same stage of economic development.

14. Ibid., 246, 255. See also Richard Parker, *Beneath the Equator: Cultures of Desire, Male Homosexuality, and Emerging Gay Communities in Brazil* (New York: Routledge, 1999).

15. Néstor Osvaldo Perlongher, *O negócio do michê: Prostituição viril em São Paulo* (São Paulo: Brasiliense, 1987).

16. Ben Bollig, "Exiles and Nomads: Perlongher in Brazil," *Hispanic Research Journal* 7, no. 4 (2006): 337–51.

17. Perlongher, *O negócio do michê*, 26.

18. Paulo H. Longo, "The Pegação Program: Information, Prevention, and Empowerment of Young Male Sex Workers in Rio de Janeiro," in *Global Sex Workers: Rights, Resistance, and Redefinition*, ed. Kamala Kempadoo and Jo Doezema (New York: Routledge, 1998), 231–39; Paulo H. Longo, *Michê* (Rio de Janeiro: Planeta Gay Books, 1998).

19. In Longo's time, michês worked in several main areas of male prostitution: Galeria Alaska (a shopping complex in Copacabana), Quinta da Boa Vista (a large public park area), Central do Brasil (the train station), Bar Maxim's (a beachfront bar), and Via Ápia/Cinelândia (in the downtown business district). Projeto Pegação suffered funding difficulties and internal management issues and disbanded before Longo's sudden death at the age of forty-two from heart failure.

20. "Credit in Brazil: Maxing Out," *Economist*, July 14, 2012.

21. Harris Meyer, "Safe Sex a Tough Sell in Sensuous Brazil," *American Medical News*, November 17, 1989, 9.

22. Parker, *Beneath the Equator*, 86–87; Trevisan, *Perverts in Paradise* (London: GMP, 1986), 134–54.

23. Leandro de Oliveira, "Sexual Diversity in the Erotic Market: Gender, Interaction and Subjectivities in a Suburban Nightclub in Rio de Janeiro," in *Sexuality, Culture and Politics—a South American Reader*, ed. Centro Latino-Americano em Sexualidade e Direitos Humanos (CLAM) (Rio de Janeiro: CLAM, 2013), 508–28.

24. Carrara and Simões, "Sexualidade, cultura e política."

25. Don Kulick, "Soccer, Sex and Scandal in Brazil," *Anthropology Now* 1, no. 3 (2009): 32–42.

26. Jon McKenzie, *Perform or Else: From Discipline to Performance* (New York: Routledge, 2001).

27. Maurya Wickstrom, *Performing Consumers: Global Capital and Its Theatrical Seductions* (New York: Routledge, 2006).

28. John F. Collins, "Public Health, Patronage and National Culture: The Resuscitation and Commodification of Community Origins in Neoliberal Brazil," *Critique of Anthropology* 28, no. 2 (2008): 237–55. For more on race in the historical center, see Lívio Sansone, "O Pelourinho dos jovens negro-mestiços de classe baixa da grande Salvador," in *Pelo Pelô: História, cultura e cidade*, ed. Editora da Universidade Federal da Bahia (Salvador, BA: Editora da Universidade Federal da Bahia, 1995), 59–70.

29. Polly Pattullo, *Last Resorts: The Cost of Tourism in the Caribbean*, 2nd ed. (New York: Monthly Review Press, 2005), 76–77.

30. Elizabeth Bernstein, *Temporarily Yours: Intimacy, Authenticity, and the Commerce of Sex* (Chicago: University of Chicago Press, 2007), 103.

31. Dean MacCannell, *The Tourist: A New Theory of the Leisure Class* (New York: Schocken Books, 1976).

32. Katherine Frank, *G-Strings and Sympathy: Strip Club Regulars and Male Desire* (Durham, NC: Duke University Press, 2002).

33. Bernstein, *Temporarily Yours*, 103–4.

34. Richard Parker, *Bodies, Pleasures, Passions: Sexual Culture in Contemporary Brazil* (Boston: Beacon Press, 1991), 122.

35. Ibid., xiv.

36. Vera Paiva, *Fazendo arte com a camisinha: Sexualidades jovens em tempos de AIDS* (São Paulo: Summus Editorial, 2000), 42.

37. Parker, *Bodies*, xiv–xv.

38. Butler, *Gender Trouble*, 45.

39. Sara Ahmed, *Queer Phenomenology: Orientations, Objects, Others* (Durham, NC: Duke University Press, 2006).

40. Patricia Ticineto Clough and Jean O'Malley Halley, eds., *The Affective Turn: Theorizing the Social* (Durham, NC: Duke University Press, 2007), 316.

41. Deborah B. Gould, *Moving Politics: Emotion and ACT UP's Fight against AIDS* (Chicago: University of Chicago Press, 2009), 19.

42. Ibid., 20.

43. Melissa Ditmore, "In Calcutta, Sex Workers Organize," in *The Affective Turn: Theorizing the Social*, ed. Patricia Ticineto Clough and Jean O'Malley Halley (Durham, NC: Duke University Press, 2007), 171. See also Arlie Russel Hochschild, *The Managed Heart: Commercialization of Human Feeling* (Berkeley: University of California Press, 1983); Wendy Chapkis, *Live Sex Acts: Women Performing Erotic Labor* (New York: Routledge, 1997).

44. Ditmore, "In Calcutta, Sex Workers Organize," 170.

45. Elizabeth Wissinger, "Always on Display: Affective Production in the Modeling Industry," in *The Affective Turn: Theorizing the Social*, ed. Patricia Ticineto Clough and Jean O'Malley Halley (Durham, NC: Duke University Press, 2007), 231–60.

46. Nigel Thrift, "Intensities of Feeling: Towards a Spatial Politics of Affect," *Geografiska Annaler* 85 (2004): 60.

CHAPTER TWO

1. Julia Kristeva, *Powers of Horror: An Essay on Abjection* (New York: Columbia University Press, 1982).
2. Mary Douglas, *Purity and Danger: An Analysis of Concepts of Purity and Taboo* (New York: Routledge, 2003), 124.
3. Leo Bersani, *Is the Rectum a Grave? And Other Essays* (Chicago: University of Chicago Press, 2010), 29–30.
4. Trevisan, *Perverts in Paradise*, 38.
5. For much more detail on how carnival structures Brazilian society, see Roberto da Matta, *Carnivals, Rogues, and Heroes: An Interpretation of the Brazilian Dilemma* (Notre Dame, IN: University of Notre Dame Press, 1991).
6. Lin Chew, "Reflections by an Anti-trafficking Activist," in *Trafficking and Prostitution Reconsidered: New Perspectives on Migration, Sex Work and Human Rights*, ed. Kamala Kempadoo, Jyoti Sanghera, and Bandana Pattanaik (London: Paradigm Publishers, 2005), 65–66.
7. José Muñoz, "Feeling Brown: Ethnicity and Affect in Ricardo Bracho's *The Sweetest Hangover (and Other STDs)*," *Theater Journal* 52, no. 1 (2000): 67.
8. Ibid., 69.
9. bell hooks, *Black Looks: Race and Representation* (Boston: South End Press, 1992), 23.
10. Ibid., 25.
11. Patricia Hill Collins, *Black Sexual Politics: African Americans, Gender, and the New Racism* (New York: Routledge, 2004), 263.
12. Cited in ibid., 264.
13. Donna Goldstein, *Laughter Out of Place: Race, Class, Violence, and Sexuality in a Rio Shantytown* (Berkeley: University of California Press, 2003); Linda-Anne Rebhun, *The Heart Is Unknown Country: Love in the Changing Economy of Northeast Brazil* (Stanford, CA: Stanford University Press, 2002).
14. Bernstein, *Temporarily Yours*.
15. Kulick, *Travesti*, 46.
16. James C. Scott, *Domination and the Arts of Resistance: Hidden Transcripts* (New Haven, CT: Yale University Press, 1990), 191.
17. Michel de Certeau, *The Practice of Everyday Life* (Berkeley: University of California Press, 1984).
18. James C. Scott, *Weapons of the Weak: Everyday Forms of Peasant Resistance* (New Haven, CT: Yale University Press, 1985), 292.
19. Don Kulick, "Causing a Commotion: Public Scandal as Resistance among Brazilian Transgendered Prostitutes," *Anthropology Today* 12, no. 6 (1996): 3.
20. Nancy Scheper-Hughes, *Death without Weeping: The Violence of Everyday Life in Brazil* (Berkeley: University of California Press, 1992), 505.
21. Lila Abu-Lughod, "The Romance of Resistance: Tracing Transformations of Power through Bedouin Women," *American Ethnologist* 17, no. 1 (1990): 41, 42.

1. Significant portions of this chapter were published previously as "Turbo-Consumers™ in Paradise: Tourism, Civil Rights and Brazil's Gay Sex Industry," *American Ethnologist* 38, no. 4 (November 2011): 666–83.

2. There is a clear parallel here to gay porn, especially the "gay-for-pay" genre in which ostensibly straight men engage in sex with men. Some of this type of porn emphasizes the financial aspect so that negotiations are included on film or highlight the men's amateur status, especially prizing all the "firsts" for the man as he explores giving and receiving oral sex and sometimes building up to his "first time" bottoming. Eventually, the men graduate into inducting other straight men into *their* first-time "gay-for-pay" experiences, even as they apparently become more comfortable with their own desires and experience of pleasure. Often, this seems to expend their usefulness to a given site, and many men disappear from such sites, move on to others, work in escorting, or leave the industry.

3. See also Dennis Altman, foreword to *Men Who Sell Sex: International Perspectives on Male Prostitution and HIV/AIDS*, ed. Peter Aggleton (Philadelphia: Temple University Press, 1999), xiii–xix.

4. Hughes, *Pink Tourism*.

5. Joseph Andoni Massad, *Desiring Arabs* (Chicago: University of Chicago Press, 2007).

6. Alana Semuels, "Gay Marriage a Gift to California's Economy," *Los Angeles Times*, June 2, 2009.

7. Gabriel Giorgi, "Madrid en transito," *GLQ* 8, no. 1/2 (2002): 57–79.

8. Eve Kosofsky Sedgwick, *Between Men: English Literature and Male Homosocial Desire* (New York: Columbia University Press, 1985).

9. See Blanchette and da Silva, "'Nossa Senhora.'"

10. "A Better Today: Brazil's Growing Middle Class Wants the Good Life, Right Now," *Economist*, November 14, 2009.

11. Mitchell, "Fare Tales and Fairy Tails."

12. De Castro, "What Is New in the 'South'?," 185.

13. It is difficult to say whether tourists in other locations make use of this knowledge in the same way. Brazil is an expensive destination to reach and to stay in, meaning that the tourists necessarily have more income (and income correlates strongly with education). Because discourses of Latin homosexuality also circulate so commonly in porn (albeit without formal sociological terms), it does seem likely that gay men from a variety of classes would have knowledge of these patterns.

14. Bernstein, *Temporarily Yours*.

15. See Adriana Piscitelli, "On 'Gringos' and 'Natives,'" *Vibrant* 1 (2004): 87–114.

16. Alyssa Cymene Howe, "Queer Pilgrimage: The San Francisco Homeland and Identity Tourism," *Cultural Anthropology* 16, no. 1 (2001): 35–61.

17. Giorgi, "Madrid en transito," 77n26.
18. Gordon Waitt and Kevin Markwell, *Gay Tourism: Culture and Context* (New York: Haworth Hospitality Press, 2006), 79.
19. Julia O'Connell Davidson and Jacqueline Sanchez-Taylor, "Fantasy Islands: Exploring the Demand for Sex Tourism," in *Sun, Sex, and Gold: Tourism and Sex Work in the Caribbean*, ed. Kamala Kempadoo (Lanham, MD: Rowman and Littlefield, 1999), 37–54; Jeremy Seabrook, *Travels in the Skin Trade: Tourism and the Sex Industry* (Chicago: Pluto Press, 1996), 38–39.
20. In 2009 Regent Entertainment Media bought a majority in PlanetOut Inc. There is a long and quite complicated series of business dealings between LPI, PlanetOut, Regent, and Here Media Inc. regarding various media holdings and buyouts, and there are now investigations into crimes having to do with hiding the company's poor financial shape. What is relevant to my point here is that the demographic targeted in the marketing materials (and also visible in the magazine's ads) has remained more or less consistent regardless of who happens to control the holdings or the state of the company's finances at any given moment.
21. LPI Media, *PNO Publishing Media Kit*, ed. LPI Media (2006), accessed March 23, 2009, http://out.com/pubmediakit/adv/pdf/pno_publishing _mediakit.pdf.
22. "Unfriendly Border," *Economist*, August 25, 2005.
23. M. V. Lee Badgett, Holning Lau, Brad Sears, and Deborah Ho, "Bias in the Workplace: Consistent Evidence of Sexual Orientation and Gender Identity Discrimination," June 2007, Williams Institute, University of California–Los Angeles, http://web.stanford.edu/group/scspi/_media/pdf/ key_issues/sexual_policy.pdf.
24. Community Marketing Inc., *Gay and Lesbian Travel Profiles*, 2008, accessed March 23, 2009, http://www.communitymarketinginc.com/mkt_mts _tdp.php.
25. The statistics are probably inflated, and the sample likely does not represent *Out* magazine's actual readership. I am less interested in the "fact" of the TurboConsumer™ than I am in the TurboConsumer™ as a marketing construct. Moreover, gay magazines in general are a poor barometer of the consumer interests of the "mainstream" gay community because they have been plagued with flagging readership and circulation as readers turn to the Internet for content. I do not believe they represent a majority of gay men (and they certainly don't speak for or to lesbians, bisexuals, transgender, or queer people), but they do reflect a very powerful subset of affluent gay consumers for whom gay tourism is an important undertaking.
26. Parker, *Beneath the Equator*, 197.
27. Stephen O. Murray, "Male Homosexuality in Guatemala: Possible Insights and Certain Confusions from Sleeping with the Natives," in *Out in the Field: Reflections of Lesbian and Gay Anthropologists*, ed. Ellen Lewin and William L. Leap (Chicago: University of Illinois Press, 1996), 244.

28. E.g., see Ara Wilson, *The Intimate Economies of Bangkok: Tomboys, Tycoons, and Avon Ladies in the Global City* (Berkeley: University of California Press, 2004).

29. E.g., see Stephen Donaldson and Wayne Dynes, *History of Homosexuality in Europe and America* (New York: Routledge, 1992), 5; Rictor Norton, *Mother Clap's Molly House: The Gay Subculture in England, 1700–1830* (London: Heretic Books, 1992); George E. Haggerty, *Men in Love: Masculinity and Sexuality in the Eighteenth Century* (New York: Columbia University Press, 1999).

30. John D'Emilio, "Capitalism and Gay Identity," in *The Lesbian and Gay Studies Reader*, ed. Henry Abelove, Michele Aina Barale, and David M. Halperin (London: Routledge, 1993), 467–76.

31. Jon Binnie, *The Globalization of Sexuality* (London: Sage, 2004), 142.

32. Heidi J. Nast, "Queer Patriarchies, Queer Racisms, International," *Antipode* 34, no. 5 (2002): 874–909.

33. Padilla, *Caribbean Pleasure Industry*, 212. Both the clients and the male sex workers in Padilla's study are strikingly similar to my own, but Padilla does not describe the clients making the leap between believing that the straight-identified male sex workers are gay and actually inducing them to "come out" as a matter of civil rights. While we are both concerned with sexual political economy and gay consumerism, Padilla's study is much more expert in issues of public health than my own, and he rounds out his ethnographic data with substantial quantitative evidence. In contrast, I devoted a great deal of my time with tourists to explicitly asking them to be reflexive about their own motivations for travel, which is not an overt focus of Padilla's work.

34. Human Rights Campaign, *Buying for Equality 2009*, ed. Human Rights Campaign Foundation, last modified 2009, accessed March 23, 2009, http://www.hrc.org/buyersguide2009/.

35. Ann Pellegrini, "Consuming Lifestyle: Commodity Capitalism and Transformations in Gay Identity," in *Queer Globalizations: Citizenship and the Afterlife of Colonialism*, ed. Arnaldo Cruz-Malave and Martin F. Manalansan IV (New York: New York University Press, 2002), 138–39.

36. Michael Warner, *Fear of a Queer Planet: Queer Politics and Social Theory* (Minneapolis: University of Minnesota Press, 1993), xxxi.

37. Jeff Maskovsky, "Do We All 'Reek of Commodity'? Consumption and the Erasure of Poverty in Lesbian and Gay Studies," in *Out in Theory: The Emergence of Lesbian and Gay Anthropology*, ed. Ellen Lewin and William L. Leap (Chicago: University of Illinois Press, 2002), 269.

38. Martin F. Manalansan IV, *Global Divas: Filipino Gay Men in the Diaspora* (Durham, NC: Duke University Press, 2003), 68.

39. Maskovsky, "Do We All 'Reek of Commodity'?," 268.

40. Padilla, *Caribbean Pleasure Industry*, 141–67.

41. See also Jasbir Kuar Puar, *Terrorist Assemblages: Homonationalism in Queer Times* (Durham, NC: Duke University Press, 2007).

42. Massad, *Desiring Arabs*, 188.

43. Joseph Carrier, *De los otros: Intimacy and Homosexuality among Mexican Men* (New York: Columbia University Press, 1995), 241; Roger N. Lancaster, *Life Is Hard: Machismo, Danger, and the Intimacy of Power in Nicaragua* (Berkeley: University of California Press, 1994).

44. Hanns Ebensten, *Volleyball with the Cuna Indians and Other Gay Travel Adventures* (New York: Viking, 1993); Chris Girman, *Mucho Macho: Seduction, Desire, and the Homoerotic Lives of Latin Men*, Haworth Gay and Lesbian Studies (New York: Harrington Park Press, 2004).

45. Annick Prieur, *Mema's House, Mexico City: On Transvestites, Queens, and Machos* (Chicago: University of Chicago Press, 1998), 192–94.

46. Parker, *Bodies*, 127–31; Trevisan, *Perverts in Paradise.*

47. Lancaster, *Life Is Hard*, 249.

48. James Wafer, *The Taste of Blood: Spirit Possession in Brazilian Candomblé* (Philadelphia: University of Pennsylvania Press, 1991).

49. For an extended discussion of this notion, see Green, *Beyond Carnival.*

50. Héctor Carrillo, *The Night Is Young: Sexuality in Mexico in the Time of AIDS* (Chicago: University of Chicago Press, 2002); Matthew C. Gutmann, *Changing Men and Masculinities in Latin America* (Durham, NC: Duke University Press, 2003); Stephen O. Murray, ed., *Latin American Male Homosexualities* (Albuquerque: University of New Mexico Press, 1995).

51. Kulick, *Travesti.*

52. Carrier, *De los otros*; Lancaster, *Life Is Hard*, 239.

53. For the most emphatic defense, see James Lorand Matory, *Black Atlantic Religion: Tradition, Transnationalism, and Matriarchy in the Afro-Brazilian Candomblé* (Princeton, NJ: Princeton University Press, 2005).

54. Prieur, *Mema's House*; Carrier, *De los otros.*

55. Dennis Altman, "Global Gaze / Global Gays," *GLQ* 3, no. 4 (1997): 437–65; Joseph Andoni Massad, "Re-orienting Desire: The Gay International and the Arab World," *Public Culture* 14 (2002): 361–85.

56. Parker, *Bodies*, 86–87; Richard Parker, "Changing Brazilian Constructions of Homosexuality," in *Latin American Male Homosexualities*, ed. Stephen O. Murray (Albuquerque: University of New Mexico Press, 1995), 241–55; Trevisan, *Perverts*, 134–54.

57. Kulick, *Travesti*, 86–89.

58. See also Altman, foreword to Aggleton, *Men Who Sell Sex.*

59. Patrick Larvie, "Natural Born Targets: Male Hustlers and AIDS Prevention in Urban Brazil," in *Men Who Sell Sex: International Perspectives on Male Prostitution and HIV/AIDS*, ed. Peter Aggleton (Philadelphia: Temple University Press, 1999), 171.

60. Patrick Larvie, "Homophobia and the Ethnoscape of Sex Work in Rio de Janeiro," in *Sexual Cultures and Migration in the Era of AIDS: Anthropological and Demographic Perspectives*, ed. Gilbert Herdt (New York: Oxford University Press, 1997), 152.

61. Longo, "Pegação Program," 235.

62. Francesca Elizabeth Richards, "La vida loca (the Crazy Life): An Exploration of Street Kids' Agency in Relation to the Risk of HIV/AIDS and Governmental and Non-governmental Interventions in Latin America" (master's thesis, University of Sussex, 2005).

63. Parker, *Beneath the Equator*, 68–69.

64. Padilla, *Caribbean Pleasure Industry*, 33.

65. Ana Luisa Liguori and Peter Aggleton, "Aspects of Male Sex Work in Mexico City," in *Men Who Sell Sex: International Perspectives on Male Prostitution and HIV/AIDS*, ed. Peter Aggleton (Philadelphia: Temple University Press, 1999), 103–25; Jacobo Schifter and Peter Aggleton, "*Cacherismo* in a San Jose Brothel—Aspects of Male Sex Work in Costa Rica," in Aggleton, *Men Who Sell Sex*, 141–58.

66. Jacobo Schifter, *Lila's House: Male Prostitution in Latin America* (New York: Haworth Press, 1998), 63–64.

67. Trevisan, *Perverts in Paradise*, 37–38; Longo, *Michê*; Perlongher, *O negócio do michê*.

68. Jasbir Kuar Puar, "Circuits of Queer Mobility: Tourism, Travel and Globalization," *GLQ* 8, nos. 1–2 (2002): 124.

69. Carrara and Simões, "Sexualidade, cultura e política."

70. MacCannell, *Tourist*.

CHAPTER FOUR

1. A modified version of this chapter was previously published as "Padrinhos gringos: Turismo sexual, parentesco queer e famílias do future," in *Gênero, sexo, amor e dinheiro: Mobilidades transnacionais envolvendo o Brasil*, ed. Adriana Piscitelli, Glaucia de Oliveira Assis, and José Miguel Nieto Olivar, Coleção Encontros (Campinas, SP: Pagu / Núcleo de Estudos de Gênero, University of Campinas, 2012), 31–56.

2. Kaye, "Sex and the Unspoken."

3. Jim O'Neill, Roopa Purushothaman, and Dominic Wilson, "Dreaming with BRICs: The Path to 2050," in *Goldman Sachs Annual Report* (2003).

4. Gustavo Palencia, "Honduras' Zelaya to Stay in Brazil Embassy," *Reuters Canada*, December 6, 2009.

5. Denise Chrispim Mari, "Hillary discute questão nuclear do Irã com Amorim em Brasília," *O Estado de S. Paulo*, March 3, 2010.

6. Folha Online, "Classe média já é mais da metade da população economicamente ativa, diz FGV," August 5, 2008, accessed October 5, 2013, http://www1.folha.uol.com.br/folha/dinheiro/ult91u429888.shtml; Fábio Veras Soares, Rafael Perez Ribas, and Rafael Guerreiro Osório, "Evaluating the Impact of Brazil's Bolsa Família: Cash Transfer Programs in Comparative Perspective," *Latin American Research Review* 45, no. 2 (2010): 173–90.

7. Paul Amar, "Operation Princess in Rio de Janeiro: Policing 'Sex Trafficking,' Strengthening Worker Citizenship, and the Urban Geopolitics of Se-

curity in Brazil," *Security Dialogue* 40, nos. 4–5 (2009): 513–41; Luiz Inácio Lula da Silva, "Mensagem oficial do Presidente Luiz Inácio Lula da Silva por ocasião do III Congresso da ABLGT," paper presented at III Congresso da ABLGT, April 21, 2009, Brasília, http://acapa.virgula.uol.com.br/mobile/noticia.asp?codigo=7904.

8. See Blanchette and da Silva, "'Nossa Senhora.'"

9. Paul Amar, *The Security Archipelago: Human-Security States, Sexuality Politics, and the End of Neoliberalism* (Durham, NC: Duke University Press, 2013).

10. Puar, *Terrorist Assemblages*.

11. Lisa Duggan, *The Twilight of Equality? Neoliberalism, Cultural Politics, and the Attack on Democracy* (Boston: Beacon Press, 2003).

12. Carla de Meis, "House and Street: Narratives of Identity in a Liminal Space among Prostitutes in Brazil," *Ethnos* 30, nos. 1–2 (2002): 3–24.

13. Susan Dewey, editorial, in "Demystifying Sex Work and Sex Workers," *Wagadu: A Journal of Transnational Feminist Studies* 8 (2010): 1–13; Jeferson Bacelar, *A família da prostituta* (São Paulo: Atica, 1982).

14. For a prime example of this, see the Oscar-winning documentary *Born into Brothels: Calcutta's Red Light Kids*, directed by Zana Briski and Ross Kauffman, 2004 (available on DVD from Image/ThinkFilm, 2006).

15. Patty Kelly, *Lydia's Open Door: Inside Mexico's Most Modern Brothel* (Berkeley: University of California Press, 2008).

16. Kulick, *Travesti*.

17. Ellen Lewin, *Gay Fatherhood: Narratives of Family and Citizenship in America* (Chicago: University of Chicago Press, 2009).

18. Kath Weston, *Families We Choose: Lesbians, Gays, Kinship* (New York: Columbia University Press, 1997), 116.

19. D'Emilio, "Capitalism and Gay Identity."

20. Charles I. Nero, "Why Are Gay Ghettoes White?," in *Black Queer Studies: A Critical Anthology*, ed. E. P. Johnson and Mae Henderson (Durham, NC: Duke University Press, 2005), 228–45; Marlon Ross, "Beyond the Closet as Raceless Paradigm," in Johnson and Henderson, *Black Queer Studies*, 161–89.

21. Weston, *Families We Choose*, 37.

22. Mary L. Gray, *Out in the Country: Youth, Media, and Queer Visibility in Rural America* (New York: New York University Press, 2009).

23. Ruth Landes, *The City of Women* (New York: Macmillan, 1947); Peter Fry, "Male Homosexuality and Afro-Brazilian Possession Cults," in *Latin American Male Homosexualities*, ed. Stephen O. Murray (Albuquerque: University of New Mexico Press, 1995), 193–220.

24. It's also worth noting that international adoption laws in Brazil do not necessarily serve Brazilian parents well. See Claudia Fonseca, "Family Belonging and Class Hierarchy: Secrecy, Rupture and Inequality as Seen through the Narratives of Brazilian Adoptees," *Journal of Latin American and Caribbean Anthropology* 14, no. 1 (2009): 92–114; Andrea Cardarello, "The Movement of the Mothers of the Courthouse Square: 'Legal Child

Trafficking,' Adoption and Poverty," *Journal of Latin American and Caribbean Anthropology* 14, no. 1 (2009): 140–61.

25. Although I generally prefer using the terms of self-identification that the men themselves in the industry employ, for clarity's sake I tend to still refer to them as "heterosexually identified" when they identify as "*bi*" only to their gringo boyfriends.

26. Gregory Mitchell, "Organizational Challenges among Male Sex Workers in Brazil's Tourist Zones," in *Policing Pleasure: Sex Work, Policy, and the State in Global Perspective*, ed. Susan Dewey and Patty Kelly (New York: New York University Press, 2011), 159–71.

27. Marshall Eakin, *Brazil: The Once and Future Country* (New York: St. Martin's Press, 1997).

28. Alida Metcalf, *Family and Frontier in Colonial Brazil: Santana de Parnaíba, 1580–1822* (Berkeley: University of California Press, 1992), 189.

29. Ana Maria Lugão Rios, "The Politics of Kinship: Compadrio among Slaves in Nineteenth-Century Brazil," *History of the Family* 5, no. 3 (2010): 287–98.

30. Marcos Lanna, "God-Parenthood and Sacrifice in Northeast Brazil," *Vibrant* 4, no. 2 (2007): 125.

31. Scheper-Hughes, *Death without Weeping*, 158.

32. Ibid., 98.

33. Lanna, "God-Parenthood," 125.

34. Goldstein, *Laughter Out of Place*, 109.

35. Ibid., 124.

36. Ibid., 134.

37. Rebhun, *Heart Is Unknown Country*, 117.

38. Luiz Mott and Marcelo Ferreira de Cerqueira, *Matei porque odeio gay* (Salvador, BA: Editora Grupo Gay da Bahia, 2003).

39. See Padilla, *Caribbean Pleasure Industry*.

CHAPTER FIVE

1. John Urry, *The Tourist Gaze* (London: Sage, 1990).

2. Edward M. Bruner, "The Maasai and the Lion King: Authenticity, Nationalism, and Globalization in African Tourism," *American Ethnologist* 28 (2008): 883.

3. For more on the role of the FTZ in shaping society in Manaus, see Leo A. Despres, *Manaus: Social Life and Work in Brazil's Free Trade Zone* (Albany: State University of New York Press, 1991).

4. For full coverage and court documents, see Sandy Frost, "Brazilian Judge Rejects Schair's Request for Habeas Corpus," *Newsvine*, 2009, accessed October 5, 2013, http://tinyurl.com/pyhwvb3.

5. Marcelo Cerqueira, "Manaus aposta firme em turismo GLS," Groupo Gay de Bahia, accessed August 22, 2014, http://www.ggb.org.br/turismo-manaus.html.

6. Barry Thomson, "Beyond Ecotourism: Going Native," *Earth Island Journal,* Autumn 2000, 27.
7. Patrick Tierney, "The Jungle Booking," *Forbes,* 1997, accessed October 5, 2013, http://anthroniche.com/darkness_documents/0063.htm. Originally available at http://www.forbes.com/fyi/1997/0310/092.html.
8. Ibid.
9. Ibid.
10. Ibid. I have not heard of this plan moving forward.
11. Mark Aitchison, "Ecotourism and the Brazilian Amazon," *Américas,* July/ August 2010, 56.
12. Ibid., 57.
13. Ibid.
14. Luciana Coelho Marques, "An Evaluation of Ecolodges in the Brazilian Amazon," paper presented at Cuarta Feria Ecoturistica y de Produccion, Santo Domingo, July 15–23, 2000, http://kiskeya-alternative.org/publica/ diversos/ecolodge-brasil.html.
15. See Martha Honey, "Protecting Eden: Setting Green Standards for the Tourism Industry," *Environment* 45, no. 6 (2003): 8–22.
16. Marques, "Evaluation of Ecolodges."
17. Matthew Clark, "Kurt Holle's Ecolodge Employs Locals while Slowing the Devastation of the Amazon," *Christian Science Monitor,* February 1, 2010.
18. Tierney, "Jungle Booking." There are no people known as the "Satura Mawé," even as an alternate spelling. However, the Satere-Mawe (or Satere-Maue) are a well-documented indigenous group who number around seven thousand people and are known for their initiation rituals and cultivation of the plant used to make *guaraná,* a stimulant.
19. Ernie Alderete, "Manaus: Sensual Capital of the Amazon," accessed May 1, 2006, www.navigayytion.com.
20. Gay men also do this but tend to make friends in this way only in gay social spaces such as gay bars, so their opportunities for this kind of socializing are much more limited than straight men's.
21. Keen, "Caribbean Gay Bashing."
22. For a thorough and nuanced study of the territorialization of male prostitution in Manaus, see Jean Moreira Alcântara, *Territórios invisíveis: Territorialidades dos garotos de programa na area central de Manaus* (Manaus: UFAM, 2009). See also Rita Suely Bacuri de Queiroz, *Territórios do prazer: Ambiente e prostituição na area central de Manaus* (Manaus: UFAM, 1999); and, for comparison, Andresa Martina Vicentini, *Um olhar sobre a prostituição masculine* (São Paulo: Scortecci, 2008).
23. Alcântara, *Territórios invisíveis,* 65.
24. Ibid., 69.
25. The data are not published or publicly available. My thanks to Dartanha Silva for giving me permission to disseminate information from this internal study.

26. Padilla, *Caribbean Pleasure Industry*, 99.
27. See statistics on GDP and per capita income at the Instituto Brasileiro de Geografia e Estatística website, http://www.ibge.gov.br/home/presidencia/noticias/noticia_impressao.php?id_noticia=1288.
28. Bacchus, post (05:56 p.m.) to "Manaus Datasheet 2012," *Roosh V Forum*, September 2, 2012, accessed March 7, 2014, http://www.rooshvforum .com/thread-15568.html?highlight=Manaus.
29. Jane Desmond, *Staging Tourism: Bodies on Display from Waikiki to Sea World* (Chicago: University of Chicago Press, 1999).
30. John Comaroff and Jean Comaroff, *Ethnicity, Inc.* (Chicago: University of Chicago Press, 2009), 27.
31. Pierre Bourdieu, "Gender and Symbolic Violence," in *Violence in War and Peace*, ed. Nancy Scheper-Hughes and Phillippe I. Bourgois (Malden, MA: Blackwell, 2004), 339–42.
32. Trinh T. Minh-Ha, director, *Naked Spaces: Living Is Round* (Berkeley, CA: Moongift Films, 1983), video.
33. Catherine A. Lutz and Jane L. Collins, *Reading "National Geographic"* (Chicago: University of Chicago Press, 1993).
34. Amar Singh, "TV Crew Accused of Killing Lost-Tribe Children with Flu," *London Evening Standard*, March 27, 2008, accessed February 21, 2015, http://www.standard.co.uk/news/tv-crew-accused-of-killing-losttribe -children-with-flu-6676501.html.
35. Rudi C. Bleys, *The Geography of Perversion: Male-to-Male Sexual Behavior outside the West and the Ethnographic Imagination, 1750–1918* (New York: New York University Press, 1995). For the classic Brazilian example of colonial views of indigenous sexuality, see Charles C. Mann, *1491: New Revelations of the Americas before Columbus* (New York: Knopf, 2005). For more on queerness and ecology, see Catriona Sandilands, "Unnatural Passions? Notes toward a Queer Ecology," *Invisible Culture* 1, no. 9 (2005): 1–31.
36. Johannes Fabian, *Time and the Other: How Anthropology Makes Its Object* (New York: Columbia University Press, 1983), xi.

CHAPTER SIX

1. Residents of Salvador da Bahia, called *soteropolitanos*, refer to the city as either Salvador or Bahia, using the names interchangeably and referring to themselves as *baianos* (Bahians). For many years, the city was known primarily as Bahia, but this is also the name of the state. My preferred shorthand is Bahia because it better captures the language of my interlocutors and also the language circulated through the names and wares of stores, restaurants, and cultural venues frequented by tourists (e.g., Mama Bahia).
2. Erica Lorraine Williams, *Sex Tourism in Bahia: Ambiguous Entanglements* (Champaign: University of Illinois Press, 2013), 32.

3. See Seabrook, *Travels in the Skin Trade*; Chew, "Reflections."

4. See Jewel Woods and Karen Hunter, *Don't Blame It on Rio: The Real Deal behind Why Men Go to Brazil for Sex* (New York: Grand Central Publishing, 2008); T. Denean Sharpley-Whiting, *Pimps Up, Ho's Down: Hip Hop's Hold on Young Black Women* (New York: New York University Press, 2007), 40.

5. Williams, *Sex Tourism in Bahia*, 21.

6. Anadelia Romo, *Brazil's Living Museum: Race, Reform, and Tradition in Bahia* (Chapel Hill: University of North Carolina Press, 2010).

7. Renato Rosaldo, "Imperialist Nostalgia," *Representations* 26 (1989): 108.

8. Ibid.

9. See Benedict Anderson, *Imagined Communities: Reflections on the Origin and Spread of Nationalism* (London: Verso, 1983).

10. Ana Paula da Silva, "Black Tourism in Brazil," *O Mangue: Race, Sex, Gringos and Life in Rio de Janeiro* (blog), January 7, 2010, accessed October 5, 2013, http://omangueblog.blogspot.com/2010/01/black-tourism-in-brazil.html.

11. MacCannell, *Tourist*.

12. Patricia de Santana Pinho, *Mama Africa: Reinventing Blackness in Bahia* (Durham, NC: Duke University Press, 2010), 50.

13. Williams, *Sex Tourism in Bahia*, 43.

14. Ibid., 15.

15. Sharpley-Whiting, *Pimps Up*, 40.

16. Woods and Hunter, *Don't Blame It on Rio*.

17. J. L. King and Karen Hunter, *On the Down Low: A Journey into the Lives of "Straight" Black Men Who Sleep with Men* (New York: Harlem Moon, 2005). For a critical assessment of the discourse of the "down low," see C. Riley Snorton, *Nobody Is Supposed to Know: Black Sexuality on the Down Low* (Minneapolis: University of Minnesota Press, 2014); Jeffrey Q. McCune Jr., *Sexual Discretion: Black Masculinity and the Politics of Passing* (Chicago: University of Chicago Press, 2014).

18. Williams, *Sex Tourism in Bahia*, 95.

19. For a performance studies perspective on the slave castles and roots tourism in West Africa, see Sandra L. Richards, "Who Is This Ancestor? Performing Memory in Ghana's Slave Castle-Dungeons," in *Sage Handbook of Performance Studies*, ed. D. Soyini Madison and Judith Hamera (Thousand Oaks, CA: Sage, 2006), 489–508; Sandra L. Richards, "What Is to Be Remembered? Tourism to Ghana's Slave Castle-Dungeons," *Theatre Journal* 24, no. 4 (2005): 617–37.

20. Pinho, *Mama Africa*, 50, 168.

21. Collins, "Public Health, Patronage and National Culture."

22. E. Patrick Johnson, "Feeling the Spirit in the Dark: Expanding Notions of the Sacred in the African American Gay Community," *Callaloo* 21, no. 1 (1998): 399–416.

23. Pattullo, *Last Resorts*.

24. For a compelling account, see D. Soyini Madison, *Acts of Activism: Human Rights as Radical Performance* (Cambridge: Cambridge University Press, 2010).

25. Sales Augusto dos Santos, "Who Is Black in Brazil? A Timely or a False Question in Brazilian Race Relations in the Era of Affirmative Action?," *Latin American Perspectives* 33, no. 149 (2006): 30–48.

26. E. Patrick Johnson, *Appropriating Blackness: Performance and the Politics of Authenticity* (Durham, NC: Duke University Press, 2003), 2, 25.

27. Richard Francis Burton, "Terminal Essay: Pederasty," in *A Plain and Literal Translation of the Arabian Nights' Entertainments, Now Entitled the Book of the Thousand Nights and a Night: With Introduction, Explanatory Notes on the Manners and Customs of Moslem Men, and a Terminal Essay Upon the History of the Nights* (Denver: Burton Society, 1899), 10.

28. Williams, *Sex Tourism in Bahia*, 93.

29. Ibid., 92–93.

30. Margaret L. Hunter, "Colorstruck: Skin Color Stratification in the Lives of African American Women," *Sociological Inquiry* 68 (1998): 517–35.

31. Joseph Roach, *Cities of the Dead: Circum-Atlantic Performance* (New York: Columbia University Press, 1996), 2.

32. Taylor, *The Archive and the Repertoire*, 19.

33. Roach, *Cities of the Dead*, 26.

34. Edward E. Telles, *Race in Another America: The Significance of Skin Color in Brazil* (Princeton, NJ: Princeton University Press, 2004), 217.

35. Ibid., 218.

Glossary

ativo. Active; a top, penetrative in intercourse

ativo liberal. "Liberal top"; meaning that a man will perform oral sex but not be *passivo*

barbie. A gay man obsessed with working out, synonymous with the gentrified gay neighborhood of Ipanema

bicha. A gay man, a queer, a fag (pejorative, but can be affectionate and/or ironic within the community; less pejorative than *viado*)

bofe. A butch, or masculine, guy (somewhat-antiquated term)

bofedade. Butchness

boy. An English import into Portuguese, slang for rent boy or male sex worker

bunda. Ass, specifically the Brazilian ass, which takes its ideal form as round, perky, and somewhat heart-shaped for women and bubble-butted for men

cabine. A room for rent in a *sauna*

caçador. A hunter; slang and somewhat-derogatory term for a male hustler who looks for *gringo* clients on the streets

candomblé. A syncretic, possession-based faith focused on West African *orixás* and known stereotypically for its veneration of women and gay male priests

capoeira. A popular martial-art form disguised as a dance; a form of resistance that descended through slaves in Brazil

carinho. Affection, caring, tenderness

carioca. Of Rio de Janeiro; a resident of Rio de Janeiro

carnaval. Six-day festival before Lent begins that is characterized by themed street parties in individual neighborhoods (*blocos*), large samba parades, inversions of high and low, and sexual license; tourism (including sex tourism) increases around this time

compadrio. The system of godparenthood

completo. Sexually versatile, both a top and a bottom in anal sex

Copacabana. A beachfront neighborhood associated with tourism, known for having a middle-class red-light district with indoor and outdoor venues

coroa. An older, wealthier man with the potential for being a sugar daddy

cu. Ass; asshole

dono. One's boss, benefactor

favela. Shantytown, slum; *favelas* have varying degrees of infrastructure

favelados. Residents of a *favela*

fortão (pl. *fortões*). A beefy, muscular guy

garoto. Short for *garoto de programa*; a male sex worker

gayzinho. Diminutive form of the noun "gay"; a little gay guy

golpe do baú. Treasure chest coup; landing a *coroa* as a sugar daddy

gringo. A foreigner; not necessarily an ethnic category or slur

homem (pl. *homens*). A straight guy; literally, "man"

Ipanema. The upper-middle-class neighborhood next to Copacabana, associated with wealthier gays and beaches with barbies

jeitinho. A work-around, a clever solution to a situation, telling stories of *jeitinhos* is something of a national pastime and point of pride in Brazil

michê. A hustler, typically a street-based male sex worker; can be slightly pejorative

moreno. A vague ethnic category; mixed race, or light-skinned but with brown hair; can be specified as *moreno claro* (light *moreno*) to "lighten" someone

negro. An Afro-Brazilian person; a black person

nordestinos. Northeasterners; people from states in the Northeast, including Bahia

normal. Heterosexual; literally, "normal"

orixás. The West African divine spirits honored in *candomblé*

padrinhos. Godparents

pais-de-santo. Fathers-of-saint; priests or religious leaders in *candomblé*; often associated with homosexuality though this is a stereotype (female leaders are known as *mães-de-santo* and are both more common and more venerated)

Papai Noel. Father Christmas; Santa Claus; a sugar daddy

parentesco. Kinship

passivo. A bottom; passive in anal sex

patrão (pl. *patrões*). A patron; a boss

pau. Slang for "penis"; literally, "wooden stick"

pegada. Swagger, a forcefully masculine demeanor

pegar. To pick up or hook up with a person (e.g., a client, a woman); literally, "to catch"

postura. Posture, manner

programa. A session with a client; literally, "program"

sauna. A gay bathhouse with or without brothel-style male prostitution

termas. A heterosexual bathhouse; always has brothel-style female prostitution

terreiro. *Candomblé* place of worship

tesão. Horniness; sexual excitement; "tension"

tias. Aunties; effeminate older gay men

transgênero. A transgendered person

travesti. An emic category (predating the importation of the category of *transgênero*) describing a person who does not identify with the (male) sex assigned to her at birth but does not identify as a woman per se; *travestis* generally wish to retain their penises; they are commonly associated with prostitution and sometimes hairdressing

viado. Faggot, fag (pejorative)

Zona Norte. The North Zone of Rio de Janeiro; a poor and working-class area north of the city center

Bibliography

Abu-Lughod, Lila. "The Romance of Resistance: Tracing Transformations of Power through Bedouin Women." *American
Ethnologist* 17, no. 1 (1990): 41–55.

Adorno, Rubens de Camargo Ferreira, and Geraldo Pereira da
Silva Junior. "Visibilidade e invisibilidade do trabalho de
garotos de programa." In *Juventudes contemporâneas: Ummo-
saico de possibilidades*, edited by Juarez Dayrell, Maria Ignez
Costa Moreira, and Márcia Stengel, 163–80. Belo Horizonte:
Editora PUCMINAS, 2011.

Ahmed, Sara. *Queer Phenomenology: Orientations, Objects, Others.*
Durham, NC: Duke University Press, 2006.

Aitchison, Mark. "Ecotourism and the Brazilian Amazon." *Américas*, July/August 2010, 56–57.

Alcântara, Jean Moreira. *Territórios invisíveis: Territorialidades
dos garotos de programa na area central de Manaus.* Manaus:
UFAM, 2009.

Alderete, Ernie. "Manaus: Sensual Capital of the Amazon." Accessed May 1, 2006. www.navigaytion.com.

Altman, Dennis. Foreword to *Men Who Sell Sex: International
Perspectives on Male Prostitution and HIV/AIDS*, edited by
Peter Aggleton, xiii–xix. Philadelphia: Temple University
Press, 1999.

———. "Global Gaze / Global Gays." *GLQ* 3, no. 4 (1997): 437–65.

Amar, Paul. "Operation Princess in Rio de Janeiro: Policing 'Sex
Trafficking,' Strengthening Worker Citizenship, and the
Urban Geopolitics of Security in Brazil." Security Dialogue
40, nos. 4–5 (2009): 513–41.

———. The Security Archipelago: Human-Security States, Sexuality Politics, and the End of Neoliberalism. Durham, NC:
Duke University Press, 2013.

Anderson, Benedict. *Imagined Communities: Reflections on the Origin and Spread of Nationalism*. London: Verso, 1983.

Bacchus. Post (05:56 p.m.) to "Manus Datasheet 2012." *Roosh V Forum*, September 2, 2012. Accessed March 7, 2014. http://www.rooshvforum.com/thread -15568.html?highlight=Manaus.

Bacelar, Jeferson. *A família da prostituta*. São Paulo: Atica, 1982.

Badgett, M. V. Lee, Holning Lau, Brad Sears, and Deborah Ho. "Bias in the Workplace: Consistent Evidence of Sexual Orientation and Gender Identity Discrimination." June 2007. Williams Institute, University of California–Los Angeles. http://web.stanford.edu/group/scspi/_media/pdf/ key_issues/sexual_policy.pdf.

Berlant, Lauren. "Cruel Optimism." *Differences* 17, no. 3 (2006): 20–36.

Bernstein, Elizabeth. *Temporarily Yours: Intimacy, Authenticity, and the Commerce of Sex*. Chicago: University of Chicago Press, 2007.

Bersani, Leo. *Is the Rectum a Grave? And Other Essays*. Chicago: University of Chicago Press, 2010.

"A Better Today: Brazil's Growing Middle Class Wants the Good Life, Right Now." *Economist*, November 14, 2009.

Binnie, Jon. *The Globalization of Sexuality*. London: Sage, 2004.

Blanchette, Thaddeus Gregory, and Ana Paula da Silva. "'Nossa Senhora da Help': Sexo, turismo e deslocamento transnacional em Copacabana." *Cadernos Pagu* 25 (2005): 249–80.

Bleys, Rudi C. *The Geography of Perversion: Male-to-Male Sexual Behavior outside the West and the Ethnographic Imagination, 1750–1918*. New York: New York University Press, 1995.

Bollig, Ben. "Exiles and Nomads: Perlongher in Brazil." *Hispanic Research Journal* 7, no. 4 (2006): 337–51.

Bourdieu, Pierre. "Gender and Symbolic Violence." In *Violence in War and Peace*, edited by Nancy Scheper-Hughes and Phillippe I. Bourgois, 339–42. Malden, MA: Blackwell, 2004.

Briski, Zana, and Ross Kauffman, directors. *Born into Brothels: Calcutta's Red Light Kids*. 2004. DVD, Image/ThinkFilm, 2006.

Bruner, Edward M. "The Maasai and the Lion King: Authenticity, Nationalism, and Globalization in African Tourism." *American Ethnologist* 28 (2008): 881–908.

Bryman, Alan. *The Disneyization of Society*. New York: Sage, 2004.

Burton, Richard Francis. "Terminal Essay: Pederasty." In *A Plain and Literal Translation of the Arabian Nights' Entertainments, Now Entitled the Book of the Thousand Nights and a Night: With Introduction, Explanatory Notes on the Manners and Customs of Moslem Men, and a Terminal Essay Upon the History of the Nights*. Denver: Burton Society, 1899.

Butler, Judith. *Gender Trouble: Feminism and the Subversion of Identity*. New York: Routledge, 1999.

Cameron, Deborah, and Don Kulick. *Language and Sexuality*. Cambridge: Cambridge University Press, 2003.

Cardarello, Andrea. "The Movement of the Mothers of the Courthouse Square: 'Legal Child Trafficking,' Adoption and Poverty." *Journal of Latin American and Caribbean Anthropology* 14, no. 1 (2009): 140–61.

Carrara, Sérgio, and Júlio Assis Simões. "Sexualidade, cultura e política: A trajetória da identidade homossexual masculina na antropologia brasileira." *Cadernos Pagu* 28 (2007): 65–99.

Carrier, Joseph. *De los otros: Intimacy and Homosexuality among Mexican Men*. New York: Columbia University Press, 1995.

Carrier-Moisan, Marie-Eve. "Gringo Love: Affect, Power, and Mobility in Sex Tourism, Northeast Brazil." PhD diss., University of British Columbia, 2012.

Carrillo, Héctor. *The Night Is Young: Sexuality in Mexico in the Time of AIDS*. Chicago: University of Chicago Press, 2002.

Cerqueira, Marcelo. "Manaus aposta firme em turismo GLS." Groupo Gay de Bahia. Accessed August 22, 2014. http://www.ggb.org.br/turismo-manaus .html.

Chauncey, George. *Gay New York: Gender, Urban Culture, and the Makings of the Gay Male World, 1890–1940*. New York: Basic Books, 1994.

Chew, Lin. "Reflections by an Anti-trafficking Activist." In *Trafficking and Prostitution Reconsidered: New Perspectives on Migration, Sex Work and Human Rights*, edited by Kamala Kempadoo, Jyoti Sanghera, and Bandana Pattanaik, 65–82. London: Paradigm Publishers, 2005.

Chrispim Mari, Denise. "Hillary discute questão nuclear do Irã com Amorim em Brasília." *O Estado de S. Paulo*, March 3, 2010.

Clark, Matthew. "Kurt Holle's Ecolodge Employs Locals while Slowing the Devastation of the Amazon." *Christian Science Monitor*, February 1, 2010.

Clough, Patricia Ticineto, and Jean O'Malley Halley, eds. *The Affective Turn: Theorizing the Social*. Durham, NC: Duke University Press, 2007.

Collins, John F. "Public Health, Patronage and National Culture: The Resuscitation and Commodification of Community Origins in Neoliberal Brazil." *Critique of Anthropology* 28, no. 2 (2008): 237–55.

Collins, Patricia Hill. *Black Sexual Politics: African Americans, Gender, and the New Racism*. New York: Routledge, 2004.

Comaroff, John, and Jean Comaroff. *Ethnicity, Inc*. Chicago: University of Chicago Press, 2009.

Community Marketing Inc. "Gay and Lesbian Travel Profiles." 2008. Accessed March 23, 2009. http://www.communitymarketinginc.com/mkt_mts _tdp.php.

"Credit in Brazil: Maxing Out." *Economist*, July 14, 2012.

Cruz-Malavé, Arnaldo, and Martin Manalansan. *Queer Globalizations: Citizenship and the Afterlife of Colonialism*. New York: New York University Press, 2002.

Da Matta, Roberto. *Carnivals, Rogues, and Heroes: An Interpretation of the Brazilian Dilemma*. Notre Dame, IN: University of Notre Dame Press, 1991.

Da Silva, Ana Paula. "Black Tourism in Brazil." *O Mangue: Race, Sex, Gringos and Life in Rio de Janeiro* (blog), January 7, 2010. Accessed October 5, 2013. http://omangueblog.blogspot.com/2010/01/black-tourism-in-brazil.html.

Da Silva, Ana Paula, and Thaddeus Gregory Blanchette. "'Nossa Senhora da Help': Sexo, turismo e deslocamento transnacional em Copacabana." *Cadernos Pagu* 25 (2005): 249–80.

Davidson, Julia O'Connell, and Jacqueline Sanchez-Taylor. "Fantasy Islands: Exploring the Demand for Sex Tourism." In *Sun, Sex, and Gold: Tourism and Sex Work in the Caribbean*, edited by Kamala Kempadoo, 37–54. Lanham, MD: Rowman and Littlefield, 1999.

Dean, Tim. *Unlimited Intimacy: Reflections on the Subculture of Barebacking*. Chicago: University of Chicago Press, 2009.

De Castro, Lucia Rabello. "What Is New in the 'South'? Consumer Culture and the Vicissitudes of Poor Youth's Identity Construction in Urban Brazil." *Young: Nordic Journal of Youth Research* 14, no. 3 (2006): 179–202.

De Certeau, Michel. *The Practice of Everyday Life*. Berkeley: University of California Press, 1984.

De Meis, Carla. "House and Street: Narratives of Identity in a Liminal Space among Prostitutes in Brazil." *Ethnos* 30, nos. 1–2 (2002): 3–24.

D'Emilio, John. "Capitalism and Gay Identity." In *The Lesbian and Gay Studies Reader*, edited by Henry Abelove, Michele Aina Barale, and David M. Halperin, 467–76. London: Routledge, 1993.

De Oliveira, Leandro. "Sexual Diversity in the Erotic Market: Gender, Interaction and Subjectivities in a Suburban Nightclub in Rio de Janeiro." In *Sexuality, Culture and Politics—a South American Reader*, ed. Centro Latino-Americano em Sexualidade e Direitos Humanos (CLAM), 508–28. Rio de Janeiro: CLAM, 2013.

Desmond, Jane. *Staging Tourism: Bodies on Display from Waikiki to Sea World*. Chicago: University of Chicago Press, 1999.

Despres, Leo A. *Manaus: Social Life and Work in Brazil's Free Trade Zone*. Albany: State University of New York Press, 1991.

Dewey, Susan. Editorial. In "Demystifying Sex Work and Sex Workers." Special issue, *Wagadu: A Journal of Transnational Feminist Studies* 8 (2010): 1–13.

Diário de Notícias. "Turismo gay assegura 30% das receitas do Rio de Janeiro durante o Carnaval." February 14, 2015. Accessed February 25, 2015. http://www.dn.pt/inicio/globo/interior.aspx?content_id=4401789&page=1.

Ditmore, Melissa. "In Calcutta, Sex Workers Organize." In *The Affective Turn: Theorizing the Social*, edited by Patricia Ticineto Clough and Jean O'Malley Halley, 170–86. Durham, NC: Duke University Press, 2007.

Donaldson, Stephen, and Wayne Dynes. *History of Homosexuality in Europe and America*. New York: Routledge, 1992.

Douglas, Mary. *Purity and Danger: An Analysis of Concepts of Purity and Taboo.* New York: Routledge, 2003.

Duggan, Lisa. *The Twilight of Equality? Neoliberalism, Cultural Politics, and the Attack on Democracy.* Boston: Beacon Press, 2003.

Eakin, Marshall. *Brazil: The Once and Future Country.* New York: St. Martin's Press, 1997.

Ebensten, Hanns. *Volleyball with the Cuna Indians and Other Gay Travel Adventures.* New York: Viking, 1993.

Fabian, Johannes. *Time and the Other: How Anthropology Makes Its Object.* New York: Columbia University Press, 1983.

Folha Online. "Classe média já é mais da metade da população economicamente ativa, diz FGV." August 5, 2008. Accessed October 5, 2013. http:// www1.folha.uol.com.br/folha/dinheiro/ult91u429888.shtml.

Fonseca, Claudia. "Family Belonging and Class Hierarchy: Secrecy, Rupture and Inequality as Seen through the Narratives of Brazilian Adoptees." *Journal of Latin American and Caribbean Anthropology* 14, no. 1 (2009): 92–114.

Frank, Katherine. *G-Strings and Sympathy: Strip Club Regulars and Male Desire.* Durham, NC: Duke University Press, 2002.

Froio, Nicole. "Rio de Janeiro: The Most Gay Friendly Destination in the World?" *Independent*, July 26, 2011. Accessed October 5, 2013. http:// blogs.independent.co.uk/2011/07/27/rio-de-janeiro-the-most-gay-friendly -destination-in-the-world/.

Frost, Sandy. "Brazilian Judge Rejects Schair's Request for Habeas Corpus." *Newsvine*, 2009. Accessed October 5, 2013. http://tinyurl.com/pyhwvb3.

Fry, Peter. "Male Homosexuality and Afro-Brazilian Possession Cults." In *Latin American Male Homosexualities*, edited by Stephen O. Murray, 193–220. Albuquerque: University of New Mexico Press, 1995.

Giorgi, Gabriel. "Madrid en transito." *GLQ* 8, no. 1/2 (2002): 57–79.

Girman, Chris. *Mucho Macho: Seduction, Desire, and the Homoerotic Lives of Latin Men.* Haworth Gay and Lesbian Studies. New York: Harrington Park Press, 2004.

Goffman, Erving. *The Presentation of Self in Everyday Life.* Garden City, NY: Doubleday, 1959.

Goldstein, Donna. *Laughter Out of Place: Race, Class, Violence, and Sexuality in a Rio Shantytown.* Berkeley: University of California Press, 2003.

Gould, Deborah B. *Moving Politics: Emotion and ACT UP's Fight against AIDS.* Chicago: University of Chicago Press, 2009.

Grandin, Greg. *Fordlandia: The Rise and Fall of Henry Ford's Forgotten Jungle City.* 1st ed. New York: Metropolitan Books, 2009.

Gray, Mary L. *Out in the Country: Youth, Media, and Queer Visibility in Rural America.* New York: New York University Press, 2009.

Green, James N. *Beyond Carnival: Male Homosexuality in Twentieth-Century Brazil.* Chicago: University of Chicago Press, 1999.

Gutmann, Matthew C. *Changing Men and Masculinities in Latin America*. Durham, NC: Duke University Press, 2003.

Haggerty, George E. *Men in Love: Masculinity and Sexuality in the Eighteenth Century*. New York: Columbia University Press, 1999.

Honey, Martha. "Protecting Eden: Setting Green Standards for the Tourism Industry." *Environment* 45, no. 6 (2003): 8–22.

hooks, bell. *Black Looks: Race and Representation*. Boston: South End Press, 1992.

Howe, Alyssa Cymene. "Queer Pilgrimage: The San Francisco Homeland and Identity Tourism." *Cultural Anthropology* 16, no. 1 (2001): 35–61.

Hughes, Howard L. *Pink Tourism: Holidays of Gay Men and Lesbians*. Wallingford, UK: CABI, 2006.

Human Rights Campaign. *Buying for Equality 2009*. Edited by Human Rights Campaign Foundation. Last modified 2009. Accessed March 23, 2009. http://www.hrc.org/buyersguide2009/.

Hunter, Margaret L. "Colorstruck: Skin Color Stratification in the Lives of African American Women." *Sociological Inquiry* 68 (1998): 517–35.

Johnson, E. Patrick. *Appropriating Blackness: Performance and the Politics of Authenticity*. Durham, NC: Duke University Press, 2003.

———. "Feeling the Spirit in the Dark: Expanding Notions of the Sacred in the African American Gay Community." *Callaloo* 21, no. 1 (1998): 399–416.

Kaye, Kerwin. "Sex and the Unspoken in Male Street Prostitution." *Journal of Homosexuality* 53, nos. 1–2 (2007): 37–73.

Keen, Lisa. "Caribbean Gay Bashing Could Harm Tourism." *PrideSource: Between the Lines*, May 4, 2006. Accessed October 5, 2013. http://www.pridesource.com/article.html?article=18564.

Kelly, Patty. *Lydia's Open Door: Inside Mexico's Most Modern Brothel*. Berkeley: University of California Press, 2008.

King, J. L., and Karen Hunter. *On the Down Low: A Journey into the Lives of "Straight" Black Men Who Sleep with Men*. New York: Harlem Moon, 2005.

Kristeva, Julia. *Powers of Horror: An Essay on Abjection*. New York: Columbia University Press, 1982.

Kulick, Don. "Causing a Commotion: Public Scandal as Resistance among Brazilian Transgendered Prostitutes." *Anthropology Today* 12, no. 6 (1996): 3–7.

———. "Soccer, Sex and Scandal in Brazil." *Anthropology Now* 1, no. 3 (2009): 32–42.

———. *Travesti: Sex, Gender, and Culture among Brazilian Transgendered Prostitutes*. Chicago: University of Chicago Press, 1998.

Lancaster, Roger N. *Life Is Hard: Machismo, Danger, and the Intimacy of Power in Nicaragua*. Berkeley: University of California Press, 1994.

Landes, Ruth. *The City of Women*. New York: Macmillan, 1947.

Lanna, Marcos. "God-Parenthood and Sacrifice in Northeast Brazil." *Vibrant* 4, no. 2 (2007): 121–52.

Larvie, Patrick. "Homophobia and the Ethnoscape of Sex Work in Rio de Janeiro." In *Sexual Cultures and Migration in the Era of AIDS: Anthropological and Demographic Perspectives,* edited by Gilbert Herdt, 143–64. New York: Oxford University Press, 1997.

———. "Natural Born Targets: Male Hustlers and AIDS Prevention in Urban Brazil." In *Men Who Sell Sex: International Perspectives on Male Prostitution and HIV/AIDS,* edited by Peter Aggleton, 159–78. Philadelphia: Temple University Press, 1999.

Lewin, Ellen. *Gay Fatherhood: Narratives of Family and Citizenship in America.* Chicago: University of Chicago Press, 2009.

Liguori, Ana Luisa, and Peter Aggleton. "Aspects of Male Sex Work in Mexico City." In *Men Who Sell Sex: International Perspectives on Male Prostitution and HIV/AIDS,* edited by Peter Aggleton, 103–25. Philadelphia: Temple University Press, 1999.

Longo, Paulo H. *Michê.* Rio de Janeiro: Planeta Gay Books, 1998.

———. "The Pegação Program: Information, Prevention, and Empowerment of Young Male Sex Workers in Rio de Janeiro." In *Global Sex Workers: Rights, Resistance, and Redefinition,* edited by Kamala Kempadoo and Jo Doezema, 231–39. New York: Routledge, 1998.

Lutz, Catherine A., and Jane L. Collins. *Reading "National Geographic."* Chicago: University of Chicago Press, 1993.

LPI Media. *PNO Publishing Media Kit.* Edited by LPI Media. 2006. Accessed March 23, 2009. http://out.com/pubmediakit/adv/pdf/pno_publishing _mediakit.pdf.

Lula da Silva, Luiz Inácio. "Mensagem oficial do Presidente Luiz Inácio Lula da Silva por ocasião do III Congresso da ABLGT." Paper presented at III Congresso da Associação Brasileira de Lésbicas, Gays, Bissexuais, Travestis e Transexuais (ABLGT), Brasília, April 21, 2009.

MacCannell, Dean. *The Tourist: A New Theory of the Leisure Class.* New York: Schocken Books, 1976.

Madison, D. Soyini. *Acts of Activism: Human Rights as Radical Performance.* Cambridge: Cambridge University Press, 2010.

Manalansan, Martin F., IV. *Global Divas: Filipino Gay Men in the Diaspora.* Durham, NC: Duke University Press, 2003.

Mann, Charles C. *1491: New Revelations of the Americas before Columbus.* New York: Knopf, 2005.

Marques, Luciana Coelho. "An Evaluation of Ecolodges in the Brazilian Amazon." Paper presented at Cuarta Feria Ecoturistica y de Produccion, Santo Domingo, July 15–23, 2000. http://kiskeya-alternative.org/publica/ diversos/ecolodge-brasil.html.

Maskovsky, Jeff. "Do We All 'Reek of Commodity'? Consumption and the Erasure of Poverty in Lesbian and Gay Studies." In *Out in Theory: The Emergence of Lesbian and Gay Anthropology,* edited by Ellen Lewin and William L. Leap, 264–86. Chicago: University of Illinois Press, 2002.

Massad, Joseph Andoni. *Desiring Arabs.* Chicago: University of Chicago Press, 2007.

————. "Re-orienting Desire: The Gay International and the Arab World." *Public Culture* 14 (2002): 361–85.

Matory, James Lorand. *Black Atlantic Religion: Tradition, Transnationalism, and Matriarchy in the Afro-Brazilian Candomblé*. Princeton, NJ: Princeton University Press, 2005.

McCune, Jeffrey Q., Jr. *Sexual Discretion: Black Masculinity and the Politics of Passing*. Chicago: University of Chicago Press, 2014.

McKenzie, Jon. *Perform or Else: From Discipline to Performance*. New York: Routledge, 2001.

Metcalf, Alida. *Family and Frontier in Colonial Brazil: Santana de Parnaíba, 1580–1822*. Berkeley: University of California Press, 1992.

Meyer, Harris. "Safe Sex a Tough Sell in Sensuous Brazil." *American Medical News*, November 17, 1989, 9–12.

Minh-ha, Trinh T., director. *Naked Spaces: Living Is Round*. Video. Berkeley, CA: Moongift Films, 1983.

Mitchell, Gregory. "Fare Tales and Fairy Tails: How Gay Sex Tourism Is Shaping the Brazilian Dream." *Wagadu: A Journal of Transnational Feminist Studies* 9 (Spring 2011): 93–114.

————. "Organizational Challenges among Male Sex Workers in Brazil's Tourist Zones." In *Policing Pleasure: Sex Work, Policy, and the State in Global Perspective*, edited by Susan Dewey and Patty Kelly, 159–71. New York: New York University Press, 2011.

————. "Padrinhos gringos: Turismo sexual, parentesco queer e famílias do futuro." In *Gênero, sexo, amor e dinheiro: Mobilidades transnacionais envolvendo o Brasil*, edited by Adriana Piscitelli, Glaucia de Oliveira Assis, and José Miguel Nieto Olivar, 31–56. Coleção Encontros. Campinas, SP: Pagu / Núcleo de Estudos de Gênero, University of Campinas, 2012.

————. "TurboConsumers™ in Paradise: Tourism, Civil Rights and Brazil's Gay Sex Industry." *American Ethnologist* 38, no. 4 (November 2011): 666–83.

Mott, Luiz, and Marcelo Ferreira de Cerqueira. *Matei porque odeio gay*. Salvador, BA: Editora Grupo Gay da Bahia, 2003.

Moutinho, Laura. *Razão, "cor" e desejo: Uma análise comparativa sobre relacionamentos afetivos-sexuais "inter-raciais" no Brasil e na Áfricado Sul*. São Paulo: Editora da UNESP, 2004.

Muñoz, José. "Feeling Brown: Ethnicity and Affect in Ricardo Bracho's *The Sweetest Hangover (and Other STDs)*." *Theater Journal* 52, no. 1 (2000): 67–79.

Murray, Stephen O., ed. *Latin American Male Homosexualities*. Albuquerque: University of New Mexico Press, 1995.

————. "Male Homosexuality in Guatemala: Possible Insights and Certain Confusions from Sleeping with the Natives." In *Out in the Field: Reflections of Lesbian and Gay Anthropologists*, edited by Ellen Lewin and William L. Leap, 236–60. Chicago: University of Illinois Press, 1996.

Nast, Heidi J. "Queer Patriarchies, Queer Racisms, International." *Antipode* 34, no. 5 (2002): 874–909.

Nero, Charles I. "Why Are Gay Ghettoes White?" In *Black Queer Studies: A Critical Anthology*, edited by E. P. Johnson and Mae Henderson, 228–45. Durham, NC: Duke University Press, 2005.

Norton, Rictor. *Mother Clap's Molly House: The Gay Subculture in England, 1700–1830*. London: Heretic Books, 1992.

O'Neill, Jim, Roopa Purushothaman, and Dominic Wilson. "Dreaming with BRICs: The Path to 2050." *Goldman Sachs Annual Report*. 2003.

Padilla, Mark. *Caribbean Pleasure Industry: Tourism, Sexuality, and AIDS in the Dominican Republic*. Chicago: University of Chicago Press, 2007.

Paiva, Vera. *Fazendo arte com a camisinha: Sexualidades jovens em tempos de AIDS*. São Paulo: Summus Editorial, 2000.

Palencia, Gustavo. "Honduras' Zelaya to Stay in Brazil Embassy." *Reuters Canada*, December 6, 2009.

Parker, Richard. *Beneath the Equator: Cultures of Desire, Male Homosexuality, and Emerging Gay Communities in Brazil*. New York: Routledge, 1999.

———. *Bodies, Pleasures, Passions: Sexual Culture in Contemporary Brazil*. Boston: Beacon Press, 1991.

———. "Changing Brazilian Constructions of Homosexuality." In *Latin American Male Homosexualities*, edited by Stephen O. Murray, 241–55. Albuquerque: University of New Mexico Press, 1995.

Pattullo, Polly. *Last Resorts: The Cost of Tourism in the Caribbean*. 2nd ed. New York: Monthly Review Press, 2005.

Pellegrini, Ann. "Consuming Lifestyle: Commodity Capitalism and Transformations in Gay Identity." In *Queer Globalizations: Citizenship and the Afterlife of Colonialism*, edited by Arnaldo Cruz-Malave and Martin F. Manalansan IV, 134–45. New York: New York University Press, 2002.

Perlongher, Néstor Osvaldo. *O negócio do michê: prostituição viril em São Paulo*. São Paulo: Brasiliense, 1987.

Pietrykowski, Bruce. *The Political Economy of Consumer Behavior: Contesting Consumption*. New York: Routledge, 2011.

Pinho, Patricia de Santana. *Mama Africa: Reinventing Blackness in Bahia*. Durham, NC: Duke University Press, 2010.

Piscitelli, Adriana. "On 'Gringos' and 'Natives.'" *Vibrant* 1 (2004): 87–114.

Prieur, Annick. *Mema's House, Mexico City: On Transvestites, Queens, and Machos*. Chicago: University of Chicago Press, 1998.

Puar, Jasbir Kuar. "Circuits of Queer Mobility: Tourism, Travel and Globalization." *GLQ* 8, nos. 1–2 (2002): 101–37.

———. *Terrorist Assemblages: Homonationalism in Queer Times*. Durham, NC: Duke University Press, 2007.

Queiroz, Rita Suely Bacuri de. *Territóios do prazer: Ambiente e prostituição na area central de Manaus*. Manaus: UFAM, 1999.

Rago, Margareth. *Os prazeres da noite: Prostituição e códigos da sexualidade feminina em São Paulo, 1890–1930*. Rio de Janeiro: Paz e Terra, 1991.

Rebhun, Linda-Anne. *The Heart Is Unknown Country: Love in the Changing Economy of Northeast Brazil*. Stanford, CA: Stanford University Press, 2002.

Renee, Diana. "Rio de Janeiro in the Running for Most Gay-Friendly Award." *Jakarta Globe*, October 22, 2009. Accessed October 10, 2010. http://tinyurl.com/26p5vr6.

Richards, Francesca Elizabeth. "La vida loca (the Crazy Life): An Exploration of Street Kids' Agency in Relation to the Risk of HIV/AIDS and Governmental and Non-governmental Interventions in Latin America." Master's thesis, University of Sussex, 2005.

Richards, Sandra L. "What Is to Be Remembered? Tourism to Ghana's Slave Castle-Dungeons." *Theatre Journal* 24, no. 4 (2005): 617–37.

———. "Who Is This Ancestor? Performing Memory in Ghana's Slave Castle-Dungeons." In *Sage Handbook of Performance Studies*, edited by D. Soyini Madison and Judith Hamera, 489–508. Thousand Oaks, CA: Sage, 2006.

Rios, Ana Maria Lugão. "The Politics of Kinship: Compadrio among Slaves in Nineteenth-Century Brazil." *History of the Family* 5, no. 3 (2010): 287–98.

Roach, Joseph. *Cities of the Dead: Circum-Atlantic Performance*. New York: Columbia University Press, 1996.

Romo, Anadelia. *Brazil's Living Museum: Race, Reform, and Tradition in Bahia*. Chapel Hill: University of North Carolina Press, 2010.

Rosaldo, Renato. "Imperialist Nostalgia." *Representations* 26 (1989): 107–22.

Ross, Marlon. "Beyond the Closet as Raceless Paradigm." In *Black Queer Studies: A Critical Anthology*, edited by E. P. Johnson and Mae Henderson, 161–89. Durham, NC: Duke University Press, 2005.

Sandilands, Catriona. "Unnatural Passions? Notes toward a Queer Ecology." *Invisible Culture* 1, no. 9 (2005): 1–31.

Sansone, Lívio. "O Pelourinho dos jovens Negro-Mestiços de classe baixa da grande Salvador." In *Pelo Pelô: História, cultura e cidade*, edited by Editora da Universidade Federal da Bahia, 59–70. Salvador, BA: Editora da Universidade Federal da Bahia, 1995.

Santos, Sales Augusto dos. "Who Is Black in Brazil? A Timely or a False Question in Brazilian Race Relations in the Era of Affirmative Action?" *Latin American Perspectives* 33, no. 149 (2006): 30–48.

Scheper-Hughes, Nancy. *Death without Weeping: The Violence of Everyday Life in Brazil*. Berkeley: University of California Press, 1992.

Schifter, Jacobo. *Lila's House: Male Prostitution in Latin America*. New York: Haworth Press, 1998.

Schifter, Jacobo, and Peter Aggleton. "*Cacherismo* in a San Jose Brothel— Aspects of Male Sex Work in Costa Rica." In *Men Who Sell Sex: International Perspectives on Male Prostitution and HIV/AIDS*, edited by Peter Aggleton, 141–58. Philadelphia: Temple University Press, 1999.

Scott, James C. *Domination and the Arts of Resistance: Hidden Transcripts.* New Haven, CT: Yale University Press, 1990.

———. *Weapons of the Weak: Everyday Forms of Peasant Resistance.* New Haven, CT: Yale University Press, 1985.

Seabrook, Jeremy. *Travels in the Skin Trade: Tourism and the Sex Industry.* Chicago: Pluto Press, 1996.

Sedgwick, Eve Kosofsky. *Between Men: English Literature and Male Homosocial Desire.* New York: Columbia University Press, 1985.

Semuels, Alana. "Gay Marriage a Gift to California's Economy." *Los Angeles Times,* June 2, 2009.

Sharpley-Whiting, T. Denean. *Pimps Up, Ho's Down: Hip Hop's Hold on Young Black Women.* New York: New York University Press, 2007.

Singh, Amar. "TV Crew Accused of Killing Lost-Tribe Children with Flu." *London Evening Standard,* March 27, 2008. Accessed February 21, 2015. http://www.standard.co.uk/news/tv-crew-accused-of-killing-losttribe-children-with-flu-6676501.html.

Simões, Júlio Assis, Isadora Lins França, and Marcio Macedo. "Jeitos de corpo: Cor/raça, gênero, sexualidade e sociabilidade juvenil no centro de São Paulo." *Cadernos Pagu* 35 (2010): 37–78.

Snorton, C. Riley. *Nobody Is Supposed to Know: Black Sexuality on the Down Low.* Minneapolis: University of Minnesota Press, 2014.

Taylor, Diana. *The Archive and the Repertoire: Performing Cultural Memory in the Americas.* Durham, NC: Duke University Press, 2003.

Telles, Edward E. *Race in Another America: The Significance of Skin Color in Brazil.* Princeton, NJ: Princeton University Press, 2004.

Thomson, Barry. "Beyond Ecotourism: Going Native." *Earth Island Journal,* Autumn 2000, 27.

Thrift, Nigel. "Intensities of Feeling: Towards a Spatial Politics of Affect." *Geografiska Annaler* 85 (2004): 57–78.

Tierney, Patrick. "The Jungle Booking." *Forbes,* 1997. Accessed October 5, 2013. http://anthroniche.com/darkness_documents/0063.htm. Originally available at http://www.forbes.com/fyi/1997/0310/092.html.

Trevisan, João. *Perverts in Paradise.* London: GMP, 1986.

"Unfriendly Border." *Economist,* August 25, 2005.

Urry, John. *The Tourist Gaze.* London: Sage, 1990.

Veras Soares, Fábio, Rafael Perez Ribas, and Rafael Guerreiro Osório. "Evaluating the Impact of Brazil's Bolsa Família: Cash Transfer Programs in Comparative Perspective." *Latin American Research Review* 45, no. 2 (2010): 173–90.

Vicentini, Andresa Martina. *Um olhar sobre a prostituição masculina.* São Paulo: Scortecci, 2008.

Wafer, James. *The Taste of Blood: Spirit Possession in Brazilian Candomblé.* Philadelphia: University of Pennsylvania Press, 1991.

Waitt, Gordon, and Kevin Markwell. *Gay Tourism: Culture and Context.* New York: Haworth Hospitality Press, 2006.

Warner, Michael. *Fear of a Queer Planet: Queer Politics and Social Theory.* Minneapolis: University of Minnesota Press, 1993.

Weston, Kath. *Families We Choose: Lesbians, Gays, Kinship.* New York: Columbia University Press, 1997.

Wickstrom, Maurya. *Performing Consumers: Global Capital and Its Theatrical Seductions.* New York: Routledge, 2006.

Williams, Erica Lorraine. *Sex Tourism in Bahia: Ambiguous Entanglements.* Champaign: University of Illinois Press, 2013.

Wilson, Ara. *The Intimate Economies of Bangkok: Tomboys, Tycoons, and Avon Ladies in the Global City.* Berkeley: University of California Press, 2004.

Wissinger, Elizabeth. "Always on Display: Affective Production in the Modeling Industry." In *The Affective Turn: Theorizing the Social*, edited by Patricia Ticineto Clough and Jean O'Malley Halley, 231–60. Durham, NC: Duke University Press, 2007.

Woods, Jewel, and Karen Hunter. *Don't Blame It on Rio: The Real Deal behind Why Men Go to Brazil for Sex.* New York: Grand Central Publishing, 2008.

Index

Page numbers in italics refer to illustrations.

Lightning Source UK Ltd.
Milton Keynes UK
UKOW03f0446061216
289266UK00001B/3/P